Divided Over Hitler

Divided Over Hitler

The Rise and Ruin of the Aristocratic Schulenburg Family

EDWARD JARVIS

Foreword by Richard Corbett, CBE

McFarland & Company, Inc., Publishers
Jefferson, North Carolina

LIBRARY OF CONGRESS CATALOGUING-IN-PUBLICATION DATA

Names: Jarvis, Edward, 1975– author.
Title: Divided over Hitler : the rise and ruin of the aristocratic Schulenburg family / Edward Jarvis ; foreword by Richard Corbett, CBE .
Other titles: Rise and ruin of the aristocratic Schulenburg family
Description: Jefferson, North Carolina : McFarland & Company, Inc., Publishers, 2023 | Includes bibliographical references and index.
Identifiers: LCCN 2023002379 | ISBN 9781476691893 (paperback : acid free paper) ∞ ISBN 9781476649382 (ebook)
Subjects: LCSH: Schulenburg family. | Schulenburg, Friedrich, Graf von der, 1865–1939—Family. | Germany—History—1933–1945. | Social classes—Political activity—Germany—History—20th century. | Hitler, Adolf, 1889–1945—Influence. | Hitler, Adolf, 1889–1945—Assassination attempts. | Anti-Nazi movement—Germany. | Nobility—Germany—Biography. | Germany—Genealogy.
Classification: LCC DD243 .J37 2023 | DDC 943.086092/2—dc23/eng/20230118
LC record available at https://lccn.loc.gov/2023002379

BRITISH LIBRARY CATALOGUING DATA ARE AVAILABLE

ISBN (print) 978-1-4766-9189-3
ISBN (ebook) 978-1-4766-4938-2

© 2023 Edward Jarvis. All rights reserved

No part of this book may be reproduced or transmitted in any form or by any means, electronic or mechanical, including photocopying or recording, or by any information storage and retrieval system, without permission in writing from the publisher.

Front cover: The Mitte borough of Berlin, Germany, in 1937 (Thomas Neumann/ National Archive of Norway); (top) coat of arms for Duchess Melusine von der Schulenberg (British Museum)

Printed in the United States of America

McFarland & Company, Inc., Publishers
  Box 611, Jefferson, North Carolina 28640
    www.mcfarlandpub.com

"War is like love, it always finds a way."
—Bertolt Brecht, *Mother Courage and Her Children,* 1939

Table of Contents

Foreword by Richard Corbett, CBE — 1

Preface — 3

Introduction — 9

1. "Bewitched by English Ways": The House of Schulenburg, 1865–1933 — 19

2. "United by Pain, Divided by Politics": The Schulenburg Family and the Reich, 1933–1939 — 36

3. "A Statesman Bent Upon Action": Diplomacy and Dissent in the East, 1934–1941 — 54

4. "The Land That Is in Need of Heroes": War and Resistance, 1939–1943 — 71

5. "The Positions Will Be Held; If Necessary, to the Last Man!": War and War Crimes, 1943–1944 — 88

6. "We Want to Create Sacred, Inviolable Law Again": The July Plot, 1944 — 105

7. "Demanding a Better Future": Survivors and Surviving, 1945 and Beyond — 122

8. "A Grave Legacy": Recriminations, Restitution, and Reconciliation — 138

Table of Contents

Appendix I—Schulenburg Family Tree — 157

Appendix II—Biographical Notes — 159

Appendix III—Timeline — 179

Bibliography — 183

Index — 187

Foreword
by Richard Corbett, CBE

Many have wondered, speculated and made assumptions about the attitudes of German citizens to the rise and rule of Hitler and the Nazis.

This book illustrates in stark detail the motivations, pressures, assumptions and dramatically divergent choices made even by members of the same family—and a particularly interesting family, too, the Schulenburgs, with historical and personal ties to Britain. The focus is on the very different roads taken by three siblings, one an out-and-out Nazi ultimately involved in war crimes, another an early sympathizer who became disillusioned and was the principal organizer of the Valkyrie plan to assassinate Hitler, and one an early and active anti-fascist who married a Jew and fled for a while to Britain (where she somewhat improbably became a hero of the Durham miners) before returning to Germany and helping in the Resistance.

The twists and turns of the family are recounted in meticulously researched detail, starting with a look at its long aristocratic lineage that included the de facto Queen of King George I of Great Britain, Melusine von der Schulenburg, and the family's generations-long ties to Britain during the three centuries up to 1914, when the British and the Germans had exceptionally close economic, cultural and even affectionate ties, not least those ties between members of the respective Royal Families.

In the early 1900s, Friedrich Bernhard Karl Gustav Ulrich Erich Graf von der Schulenburg served as military attaché in the German embassy in London before returning to a high level military career in Germany, and it is his role and, especially, those of three of his children, that is the main focus of the book.

The book takes us through the rise of the Nazi party, its internal divisions, which are often overlooked by historians, how it tightened its grip not just on state institutions but also on educational, cultural and sporting organizations, and how it eliminated or sidelined those who opposed

Foreword by Richard Corbett, CBE

it. Recounting this through the lens of a particular family, whose members were centrally—if somewhat contrastingly—involved in many key moments, provides a fascinating narrative that any reader interested in this important period of European history will enjoy.

On a personal note, the book struck a special chord with me as someone whose father was parachuted in on D-Day and then captured, spending many months in successive German POW camps and experiencing the different attitudes of the various camp guards, and having myself lived with a German family for six months in 1973 in Kassel, where the legacy of German and European history was ever present.

Richard Corbett, CBE, is a former Member of the European Parliament and was the Labour Leader in the European Parliament from 2017 to 2020.

Preface

"And he shall judge among the nations, and shall rebuke many people; and they shall beat their swords into plowshares, and their spears into pruninghooks; nation shall not lift up sword against nation, neither shall they learn war any more."—Isaiah 2:4

"As I started to relax again, a familiar ghostly siren became louder and louder, and the mournful noise flooded the atmosphere."—Stella Hall, *No Way Back*, 2021

    The two main themes of this book are family and war. At the time of this writing, it feels as though war has been discussed more in the past few years than ever before and that this discussion has accelerated dramatically in the past few months. Most of us have grown up with the truism that war will always be with us, and now, for the first time in decades, western European military chiefs talk of preparedness for land war on the continent. However, while Santayana's chilling comment that "only the dead have seen the end of war" (*Soliloquies in England and Later Soliloquies*, 1922) has an enduring ring of truth, it says nothing of the human race's equally enduring capacity to survive and rebuild. At a particularly tense early point during the Cold War, my father commented to my grandfather that the superpowers' devastating new weapons surely meant the end of humanity, to which my grandfather replied, "They have been saying that since the invention of the bow and arrow." Encouragingly, much of the talk of war today focuses on the rejection of war as a method of resolving disputes; we praise the tireless efforts of individuals and organizations that are devoted to peace, and we condemn the would-be warlords. All of this is accompanied by constant and voracious study, both academic and general interest, of past wars, especially those of the twentieth century. We are also sadly aware that the current younger generation is the last to have the opportunity to learn about early twentieth century wars from the people who fought them. The youngest surviving veterans of the Second

Preface

World War are now in their mid-nineties, and those of the Korean War are in their late eighties. When firsthand testimony is no longer available, we are faced with the task of responsibly reconstructing nearly-lost stories from those past wars, piecing them together from many and varied scraps of evidence, so that every available lesson of those events may be learned. This work of historiography is an important part of honoring the sacrifices of those who forged peace against incredible odds, achievements that are not exclusive to any one nationality, creed, or gender.

With so much still being written about the Second World War and the Third Reich, it may strain credulity to talk about a case in this area being original, extraordinary, or unique; it is a daring claim and one that becomes harder to make with the passing of time, but the story of the aristocratic Schulenburg family unquestionably deserves these descriptors. No other family, in Germany or elsewhere, could boast such a remarkable cast of characters as the Schulenburgs; the head of the family was a Prussian Count and a senior cavalry officer who served on the Kaiser's staff and later became a Nazi party deputy, receiving the highest honors from Hitler. The Count had six almost impossibly different children; his daughter was a leftwing artist who married a Jew and courted the company of the most prominent radicals and dissidents of the age; one of those dissidents was her own brother, a disillusioned Nazi justice official who coordinated the Valkyrie plot to assassinate Hitler. Their older brother was a fanatical early follower of Hitler, a highly decorated paratroop officer later pursued by the Allies for the first documented war crimes of the Second World War. The Count's younger cousin, meanwhile, was the German ambassador to the Kremlin, no less; he subverted Hitler's orders, secretly sought to avert war, and finally joined his Schulenburg relatives in the plot to kill the Führer. Almost the only thing they all had in common, apart from a surname, was that they all paid a devastating price for their various personal convictions; only one of them would still be alive by May 1945.

These are merely the bare bones of the story; it is impossible to express in a few words just how extraordinary this story is, and as the details unfold the reader must simply delve in, discover, and digest the incredible. No other family in the Third Reich contained such extremes of commitment, such a range of personal contradictions, and such an all-consuming drive to act upon their convictions as the Schulenburgs. This book reconstructs the complex story of this aristocratic family and it documents, chapter by chapter, the lives of its key members, those who followed Hitler and those who plotted to kill him, those who served in the SS and those who served in the German Resistance. Outlining and then unpacking the

Preface

careers of the diverse Schulenburg siblings, this book explores their lives and loves, their motivations and influences, as each of them responded to the political extremes of the twentieth century in vastly and tragically different ways. The unlikely backstory of the Schulenburg dynasty is also unraveled, tracing their high noble origins with the Habsburgs and the Holy Roman Emperors, their close ancestral ties to the British Crown, and their intermarriages with elite families of Germany, England, and the United States. The ideological and psychological dynamics of this unusual case, such as the collapse of German nobility after the First World War, are detailed, in order to understand how—and, crucially, why—many aristocrats became enthralled by Hitler.

This book goes to the heart of the enduring enigma that is the German people's experience of the Third Reich, examining, through this underresearched case, invaluable perspectives on the decisions and dilemmas facing individual Germans. Expert and non-expert readers alike will discover previously little-known aspects of the social, political, military, and even sporting history of the Third Reich. Experts and scholars of the Third Reich may be surprised by the paradoxes contained in these pages: the four-star SS general with a socialist daughter and a Jewish son-in-law, whom he apparently liked; the dissident Nazi plotting to assassinate Hitler, whose own brother was implicated in horrific war crimes; and Hitler's diplomat at the Kremlin, his trusted expert on Russia, who was not even informed of the coming invasion of the USSR. Finally, the story would not be complete without a discussion of postwar reconciliation, a multilateral endeavor to which the sole surviving Schulenburg sibling became dedicated in exceptional and creative ways.

This is the first thorough historical treatment of the Schulenburg case. Drawing on a range of historical sources translated from five languages, including declassified wartime papers, personal recollections, and published documents spanning more than a century, these pages offer new insights on such diverse topics as the genesis of the Nazi party, the ideation of the SS, Partisan and anti–Partisan warfare, the Valkyrie plot, and the Third Reich's instrumentalization of sport, exercise, and health, all from the viewpoints of the people directly involved. Consulting previously top secret archival material from the National Archives in London, England, and official reports from the Army History Directorate in Athens, Greece, the book details dark and deplorable events from the German campaigns in Crete and Italy. In terms of literature, the field of Second World War and Third Reich studies is already densely populated, but original subjects still emerge. Many aspects of German history relative to the Schulenburg case

Preface

have been admirably dealt with in recent years, such as the "misalliance" between *Nazis and Nobles*—the title of Stephan Malinowski's outstanding 2020 book—while the depth and richness of historic Anglo-German relations were explored in Miranda Seymour's fascinating *Noble Endeavours* published in 2013. For broader subject matter and context, the works of Richard J. Evans and Ian Kershaw are incomparable guides, while it is still useful to revisit the earlier generation of Third Reich scholarship by the late William Shirer and Alan Bullock.

For material strictly pertaining to the Schulenburgs, this book draws upon a wide variety of texts and documents, published or printed in several languages; the author takes responsibility for nearly all of the translations into English of non–English phrases or terms, where translations have been necessary. The family's staunch Nazi members have been mentioned in numerous books in relation to their political and military activities, though in the case of at least one individual, the record is complicated by the imputation of war crimes, for which he did not live to be tried and was not convicted. In recent decades, prosecutors have reaffirmed these charges of war crimes, incidentally, while also reaffirming that there was no one left, by the war's end, to be prosecuted for them. They were, as mentioned above, the first Nazi war crimes to be investigated by the Allies while the war was still in progress, and as a result, they are quite well-documented; the National Archives in London preserve the Judge Advocate General's Office (War Office) papers, relating to the War Crimes Group (South East Europe) and predecessors (Case Files [SEE and other series]; [relating to] Matera, Italy; German reprisals against civilians). The Italian historians Paolo Paoletti (*The Limmari Massacre,* 1999) and Francesco Ambrico (*War Crimes at Matera,* 2003) have consolidated the historical record with excellent, well-documented accounts of those events.

Other key members of the Schulenburg family have drawn a significant amount of interest, including academic interest, for their particular areas of activity, mainly the German Resistance to Nazism, political art, and, especially postwar, promoting reconciliation and memory. Curiously, however, even with regard to these subjects that have spawned books and other tributes, there is a sense that the Schulenburgs' roles have been overlooked; several authors and commentators expressed surprise that no Schulenburg was even mentioned in the 2008 movie *Valkyrie* about the plot to assassinate Hitler. This is nothing new; key figures in the real-life Valkyrie or July plot have tended to be overshadowed by the daring and dashing protagonist, Colonel Claus von Stauffenberg, who was actually recruited by one of the Schulenburgs. Without the Schulenburgs there

Preface

would have been no July plot, as the late, great German historian Hans Mommsen demonstrated in his various works. These works, and some older German-language books, including those by some of the Schulenburgs' contemporaries—Johnnie von Herwarth, Albert Krebs, Kurt Student—are invaluable for completing the jigsaw puzzle of the Schulenburg timeline of events, facts, dates, and quotes. The role of sport and athletics in the Third Reich, in which one Schulenburg sibling played a nationally important part, is a fascinating subject covered by scholars Matthias Marschik and Julia Timpe and in older works by Guido von Mengden and Hans Joachim Teichler. This current work is the first book-length attempt to integrate and interpret these many and varied strands of this complex family's story, its dynamics, its dilemmas, its divisions, and its destinies, interwoven in a single comprehensive account.

My own interest in the Second World War, as for many people, is a lifelong affair. Like many lifelong pursuits, my interest has been revitalized and intensified at certain key moments, thanks to special individuals, most memorably my maternal grandparents, whose astonishing and closely-guarded wartime reminiscences provided my greatest education in this field. Years later, my friend Francesco "Franco" Ambrico enlisted my help with his research into the war crimes in Matera, Italy—resulting in the book mentioned above—and it is thanks to Franco that I first learned about the Schulenburg family. Franco went on to achieve great things in commemorating the Polish forces' sacrifices in the Second World War, for which he was decorated by the Polish government. Later still, it was my privilege to work with Second World War veterans in the final stages of their lives as a therapeutic care volunteer with the Red Cross. Their incredible memories of the war, ranging from Dunkirk to the opening of Hitler's bunker, remain as vivid in my mind today as the day they shared them with me, and I will never forget them.

It is, therefore, my great pleasure to be able to extend heartfelt thanks to many special people who have made this book project a reality. The realization of this extraordinary story in its current fine form is thanks to the expertise of Layla Milholen and the team at McFarland, presided over by Rhonda Herman; I am extremely grateful to you all. My enthusiasm for writing this book received a huge boost from the support and encouragement of Richard Corbett, CBE, former Member of the European Parliament (MEP), Leader of the Labour Group in Europe and a distinguished author, who kindly contributed the enthusiastic foreword; my sincere thanks. I was also honored and grateful to have the advice and comments of Seb Dance, former MEP and now Deputy Mayor of London, whose

Preface

insights, observations, and personal interest in this story were helpful and inspiring. Thanks also go to my friends and colleagues at the Royal Historical Society who tolerate me as a Fellow. To all of those mentioned here I express my deepest gratitude, as well as to my patient fiancée Rachanee.

For many and varied pieces of information, feedback, advice, and guidance, I also wish to thank, in alphabetical order, Fritz Backhaus at the German Historical Museum (DHM; Deutsches Historisches Museum) in Berlin, Lisa Caspari at the Topf & Söhne Place of Remembrance in Erfurt, Germany, Sergeant First Class Alfred "Clay" Chambers, U.S. Army (Ret.), Sabine Fischer-Strebinger at the Tisa von der Schulenburg Foundation in Dorsten, Germany, Paul Oechsner in Weimar, Germany, and Dr. Thomas Weissbrich at the DHM in Berlin. I am also indebted to the staffs of the British National Archives, the Greek Army History Directorate, the Schulenburg Foundation, and the Teehaus Trebbow Memorial. One of my most recent sources of encouragement has been my niece, Stella. A keen writer, she showed me her drafts of a fictional story set in the Second World War; I have borrowed one memorable line from the story to use as an epigraph for this Preface. Her thoughtful and sensitive writing not only reenergized my interest in the topic but also reassured me that young people do share our fascination with the hardest of times lived by the greatest of generations and that the quest for a time of peace on Earth, when "nation shall not lift up sword against nation," goes on.

Introduction

"I have often felt a bitter sorrow at the thought of the German people, which is so estimable in the individual and so wretched in the generality"—Johann Wolfgang von Goethe, *Goethes Gespraeche*, 1813

"We all live under the same sky, but we don't all have the same horizon."—attributed to Konrad Adenauer, *Readers Digest*, 1972

In 1929, readers in the English-speaking world were faced with an unexpected bestseller by a German author with a French name, Erich Maria Remarque. That year, which was so tense and uncertain in other spheres, was a rich and fruitful one in the world of literature, with the appearance of escapist first novels by Graham Greene (*The Man Within*) and John Steinbeck (*Cup of Gold*). Young authors just a few years older than Greene and Steinbeck were more focused on harsh reality, as they had witnessed it in the trenches; Ernest Hemingway's *A Farewell to Arms* and Richard Aldington's controversial (and now almost forgotten) *Death of a Hero* were both published in that year. At a distance of ten years from the Treaty of Versailles, critics felt that the public's appetite for stark, dark war novels had already been satiated, and they doubted the ability of another firsthand war story, from Germany, of all places, to make a positive impact. Remarque's *All Quiet on the Western Front* (in German *Im Westen nichts Neues*; literally "no news in the west" but meaning "nothing to report on the Western Front") did more than make a positive impact. It first appeared in unassuming fashion, serialized in a liberal German newspaper, at the end of 1928. It was picked up by a young Australian, Arthur W. Wheen—himself a wounded war veteran, like Remarque—who set about translating it. "Unexpected bestseller" soon became an understatement; inside of just eighteen months *All Quiet on the Western Front* had sold two and a half million copies, it had been translated into a staggering twenty-two languages, and it had already been made into an acclaimed double Oscar-winning Hollywood movie.

Introduction

Extolled as antiwar literature, Remarque's book was not the first novel to earn that label—it was at least the third so-called antiwar novel of 1929 alone—but it also struck a new and different chord; readers from the war-winning nations of Britain and the United States were now invited to set aside their tribal instincts and patriotic bias and glimpse the Great War from the German point of view. Approaching the book as an exercise in reconciliation confirmed what former soldiers already knew in their bones: that the experience of the trenches was chillingly similar for all armies, whether technically defeated or, in the somewhat pyrrhic sense of the 1918 Allies, victorious. The whole question of victory and defeat, however, was unresolved and highly contentious in Remarque's homeland; not even the devastating economic crash or the tense political standoff between Nazis and communists could divert attention from the burning controversy of Versailles. Remarque's book, predictably, appalled the Nazis. It seemed to refute every myth that they had spent the years since the war trying to build up; in his pages, Remarque exposed a German soldiery that was human rather than superhuman and a disillusioned Germany of realism and reflection rather than an idyllic "Heimat"—a spiritual German home—of legends and heroism. Internationally, however, *All Quiet on the Western Front* nourished a longing for peace between former foes, testified to the widely recognized commonality of the experience of war, and contributed to the growing rejection of war itself as ultimately having no winners. All of these tensions and dynamics conspired to make 1929 a pivotal year for the story told within these pages; it was the last year, in fact, that the Nazis could be dismissed as an insignificant minority force in politics. From 1930, those tensions and dynamics would gradually lead to catastrophe for the Schulenburg family and all of Germany.

Less than twenty years after *All Quiet on the Western Front*, victors and defeated would survey each other once again, with shock and incomprehension, across the divide of a newly destroyed Europe. This time, the unspoken transnational solidarity of the trenches, the tacit mutual respect of the 1918 veterans, and the sensation of a shared experience were gone. The world, instead, scrutinized the gaunt faces of ordinary Germans and asked "Why?" What was it about the Germans? How had Germany, the cradle of civilization, the nation of Beethoven, Goethe, Hegel, and Schiller, been so easily and so completely seduced by that whining, gesticulating mountebank with the ludicrous hairstyle? Recalling Goethe's ambivalent appraisal of the Germans as "so estimable in the individual and so wretched in the generality" only seemed to deepen the mystery. A series of pseudo-psychological explanations began to be trotted out; the

Introduction

German people had been placed in a trance-like state, perhaps, subjected to advanced brainwashing techniques, or drugged via the water supply; some even posited that the Führer's manic arm-waving had induced a form of mass hypnosis. All of these theories ultimately proved unsatisfactory, as did sweeping characterizations of Germans "following blindly as if possessed" (Shirer 1960: 6). While sensationalist attempts to explain away the Nazi following have failed, the temptation to lay blanket blame on the German people has also been resisted. Some sought to make crucial distinctions at an early stage; future German chancellor and Nobel laureate Willy Brandt (1913–1992), in his 1946 book *Criminals and Other Germans* (*Verbrecher und andere Deutsche*), wrote that "Germans must bear responsibility, but responsibility is not the same as guilt." Then began the vast debate over how that responsibility should be discharged. Undeniably, the distinctions, definitions, and possible solutions are complex, and, like war itself, the problem of reconciliation shows no signs of going away.

Nearly eight decades have now passed since the end of the Second World War, and with each passing year it becomes clearer than ever that falling under the spell of a contemptuous, belligerent demagogue is not the exclusive weakness of any one nation; it could even be said that no nation is immune to hysterical rhetoric and fearmongering. Today, as ever, strategies can be developed to disable empathic responses, neutralize compassion, put common sense on pause, and derail any positive instinct, especially when presented with some new and terrible foe. As for the motivations of individual Germans in the Third Reich to do what they did, there were clearly countless different courses of action to take, according to countless and vastly different individual situations and circumstances. Germans' responses to Nazism ranged from commitment to condemnation, from devotion to disgust, from toleration to terror, and everything in between, including incomprehension, indifference, and simple self-preservation. Generalizations are ultimately useless. No two German stories are identical, and historians are united in warning against simplistic interpretations and lazy good-versus-evil readings. This book tells the story of one family in which no two individual responses to Nazism were quite the same, and all of the viewpoints mentioned above were represented, usually in extreme form. They, as much as anyone, are the people who characterize the twentieth century; this was their era, and these were the contrasting feelings that circulated. Like the German people in general, nothing was simple or predictable about the Schulenburg family. This may be illustrated by a comparatively insignificant event in Dorsten, in the Ruhr region, which takes us back to the bleak postwar years.

Introduction

Today, in the small former mining town of Dorsten, near Recklinghausen in the Ruhr, stands the convent of St. Ursula, in the care of the Ursuline sisters, officially called the Order of St. Ursula. The convent dates back to 1699, while the order originated in sixteenth-century Italy. In 1948, an evidently refined, cultured, and extremely charming lady in her middle to late forties arrived at the Dorsten convent with the intention of testing her vocation as a nun. She was a former Protestant who had only recently converted to Roman Catholicism. She was the only daughter from a family of six children and she herself was childless. She had studied drawing and sculpture and had practiced both professionally, with considerable success. She had spent time living in England, in two distinct periods, each time in the run-up to a world war. This lady was much, much older than the typical novice, but she was admitted, and she would eventually take the religious name of Sister Paula. These basic details, however, do not even begin to illustrate her incredible story. There was, in fact, nothing typical about Sister Paula, whose secular name was Elisabeth Karoline Mary Margarete Veronika Gräfin (Countess) von der Schulenburg—"Tisa" for short—and one possible description for her would be "consummate survivor." Besides the two world wars mentioned, she had "survived"—so to speak—two marriages and two divorces, which, along with her age, made her an even more atypical novice in the Roman Catholic Church of 1948. Raised as a Lutheran, she had first married a Jew and later converted to Catholicism. By all accounts, everyone who met Tisa—including the author Remarque, as well as Bertolt Brecht, Thomas Mann, Stefan Zweig, Albert Einstein, and a succession of German premiers—realized that they were in the presence of an exceptional, extraordinary individual.

No less extraordinary was the family that Tisa was born into in December 1903. With regard to her immediate family, too, Tisa was the sole survivor by 1948, but the family unit was once lively, colorful, and numerous. The Schulenburg family of Tressow Castle consisted of parents who were both pureblood aristocrats—on each side of their own families they were scions of Germany's oldest and best-known noble families—and their six children, born within that critical period from 1898 to 1914. After that fateful year of 1914, the family's destinies would become inseparable from the extreme and polarizing forces that slowly dissected and dismembered German society. The aristocracy was crushed and demoralized by the 1918 defeat and the abolition of the monarchy, and many of them were prepared to grasp at any available lifeline to survive, especially if it promised to thwart the advance of Soviet-inspired communism. Opposition to communism was often a unifying factor amidst the social breakdown of

Introduction

postwar Germany, while the more divisive and polarizing question was what to do about it; increasingly extreme nationalist forces promised to "save" Germany from ruin, but they somehow had to convince powerful sectors of society such as the army, big business, and the aristocracy. To say that Tisa's family was profoundly divided over what should fill the void left by the abolished monarchy is an understatement.

Members of the Schulenburg family who became sympathetic to the new right wing saw themselves as maintaining, defending, and perpetuating the values and traditions of the nobility and the homeland—the sacred "Heimat"—through accepting or espousing the interesting ideas of this maverick called Hitler, who was, admittedly, a newcomer and an upstart. The Schulenburgs were landowners, cavalry officers, and diplomats; they were proud nobles and staunch royalists, winners of countless orders and decorations with extraordinary names such as the Order of the White Elephant and the Order of Henry the Lion. Where their main priority converged with the young rightwing upstarts was in defense of the "Heimat" and the "Volk." These are challenging and peculiarly German concepts that have no direct translation in English; they are bound up with German Romanticism and Idealism, alluding to an ethereal, spiritual, and ideological "homeland" and its destined "race" or "folk." These would prove to be useful concepts for the Nazis to latch onto, but they were not the only strong influences on the Schulenburgs.

The Schulenburgs, especially Tisa's parents, Friedrich and Freda, were also great fans of all things English; they were "Anglophiles," to be precise. Their affection for England was deep-rooted, able to be traced back quite directly to the English Royal throne, and it is worth taking a moment to consider this unusual backstory. The most famous individual in the Schulenburg family tree, in fact, is Ehrengard Melusine von der Schulenburg (1667–1743), later Duchess of Kendal and Duchess of Munster, among many other titles, and generally known as Princess Melusine. She is remembered for her "dalliance" with King George I of Great Britain and Ireland (1660–1727), to whom she bore no fewer than three illegitimate but duly ennobled and titled children. This romantic relationship was in reality no dalliance, of course, but a committed and stable marriage to all effects, except, as far as is known, legal and ecclesiastical effects. Among the titles bestowed upon Melusine (who, incidentally, was said to be no great beauty) was that of Princess of Eberstein, a title that was created especially for her in 1723 by Charles VI of Vienna (1685–1740), Holy Roman Emperor, of the House of Habsburg. Although Princess Melusine never publicly wed King George, it was widely believed that this new title,

Introduction

raising the erstwhile duchess to a princess, was intended to serve as tacit recognition that the pair had in fact married in secret. Sir Robert Walpole, British prime minister at the time and privy to innumerable secrets of state, said Princess Melusine was "as much the Queen of England as anyone was" (Day 2018).

Princess—or Queen—Melusine, de facto co-ruler with England's King George I, was to be thanked for establishing the Schulenburg family's ancestral English connections and also for their being granted noble status of their own. Christian Günther von der Schulenburg (1684–1765), son of Friedrich Achaz von der Schulenburg (1647–1701), was a descendent of the first, centuries-old, titled house of Schulenburg, on both sides of his family, but he had not inherited any noble title himself. His mother was Margaretha Gertrud von der Schulenburg (1659–1697), beloved older sister of Princess Melusine. Christian Günther was made a Count (Graf) on December 7, 1728, by the same Habsburg Charles VI, Holy Roman Emperor, who had made Christian Günther's aunt a princess only five years previously; it is not clear exactly how or why this influenced Charles VI's decision to ennoble this branch of the Schulenburgs. By the late nineteenth century there were nine titled branches of the Schulenburg family in total, each additional branch being created when a descendent of an existing branch became ennobled in their own right; the most common motivation for this was to reward distinguished military service to a reigning royal. The family nucleus at the center of our story, the Schulenburgs of Tressow Castle, descends from the third and fourth branches of the Schulenburgs, and, through Christian Günther, from the very first branch.

Encouraged by their familial connection to the Hanover monarchs, the Schulenburgs' love of England would blossom during an enjoyable extended stay in London early in the twentieth century; this experience nourished the family's self-identification as staunch Anglophiles and fostered an open, internationalist outlook in the younger family members. These would prove to be unusual attributes in the higher ranks of German society in the coming decades, and this was also a cruel omen for a family set to be deeply divided in its loyalties, sympathies, and ideologies. Once the options for Germany's future became clear, some of the Schulenburgs, like many German nobles, became convinced that their interests were best served by an alliance—or misalliance, according to some interpretations—with the Nazis, setting aside huge differences in aspiration and morality (Malinowski 2020: 2–3). The Schulenburg family's most prominent members would be seen to align themselves "extraordinarily

Introduction

strongly" (*ausserordentlich stark* in German) to Hitler and Nazism, but there were equally extraordinary exceptions to this within the family (Niemann 2000: 332). As enthusiasm for Hitler increased, a parallel cohort within the family experienced growing doubts and distaste for Nazism; as the reality of Hitler's vision for Germany unfolded, this revulsion matured into firm commitments to what has generally been referred to as the German Resistance. Only one or two members of the family remained indifferent to Nazism. This incredible combination of reactions and responses within the same family would understandably cause conflict, confusion, and mystification for members of both "sides" of the dynasty as well as outside observers; in later years some authors would mistake pro–Hitler members of the family for anti–Hitler plotters and vice versa (Teichler 1991: 111).

This most unlikely combination of responses to Nazism within one family nucleus led to fates that are surprising in their details but predictable in their tragic nature. Violent, dramatic, and sudden demises punctuate this story. Tisa von der Schulenburg herself commented, with a degree of understatement, that the family was united by pain and divided by politics (a phrase used as the title of Chapter 2 of this book), a poignant and fitting description of a family which, uniquely in the history of Nazi Germany, comprised the most committed and fierce extremes of pro–Hitler fanaticism and anti–Hitler resistance, with both opinions being heartfelt even unto death. While one of Tisa's brothers masterminded (and ultimately avoided answerability for) appalling Nazi atrocities (investigated here in Chapter 5 through declassified wartime archive documents), another of her brothers (discussed here in Chapter 6) coordinated recruitment for the bomb plot to assassinate Hitler (for which he did not escape punishment), becoming one of the most important figures in the Resistance (Mommsen 2009: 152). Their cousin, meanwhile (discussed here in Chapter 3), viewed events from the unique perspective of being one of the Third Reich's most senior diplomats while harboring no sympathy for Nazism. Tisa herself, for her part, did not refrain from choosing a side in all this, though without losing the ability to love and cherish her family as a whole, as explained here in Chapter 7. Her family, after all, had been full of contradictions and eccentricities long before the Hitler years, not least in its fascination with the English-speaking world and its ancestral ties to the English throne, thanks to one Schulenburg's marriage to a Hanoverian King.

Many aspects of the Schulenburg story trace back to their nobility, and the whole topic of the German aristocracy's dealings with Nazism

Introduction

is a fascinating one, as the saga within these pages starkly demonstrates. Nobles and Nazis were not perfect bedfellows; Hitler's plans did not include reviving the monarchy or restoring the aristocracy's influence. Within the military, which was historically a bastion of the nobility, aristocratic ties, traditions, and attitudes would create divisions at senior levels and interfere with decision-making. The nobility—and people—of Germany, of course, were all divided over Nazism, not just the Schulenburgs. In theory, the nobility enjoyed no special status in Nazi society, but the creators of the "new" Germany under Hitler could not deny that the aristocratic families held a solid claim to true Germanness, being the heirs of German history. The Schulenburgs were close blood relatives of the Bismarcks, the Bülows, and the Arnims, among others; since every true German could lay claim to that heritage and that history, then the noble families could surely lay claim to it in a special way. As a very old, very high Prussian, quirkily internationalist, staunchly Nazi, and incorrigibly rebellious family, the Schulenburgs are a reminder of the inherent complexity of family itself, not just a German one, aristocratic or otherwise. Their story—in reality a set of interlocking and parallel stories that have never been analyzed in an integrated narrative—is an important one that sheds additional light on a crucial period in history, one that we continue to strive to understand. The Schulenburgs' is also a cautionary tale about making black and white judgments.

Some histories clearly defy generalizations and throw up a barrage of contradictions, such as German royals seated on English thrones, a German author with a French name, Prussian nobles with English tastes, an SS general with a Jewish son-in-law, or a twice-divorced Catholic nun. Goethe appeared to be keenly aware of the paradoxes of the German people when he described them as "so estimable in the individual and so wretched in the generality," but Goethe was surely playing a trick of flawed logic on the reader; the more one tries to assess the implications of his dichotomy, the more it begins to resemble one of Escher's impossible objects. No individual, Goethe seems to say, is so estimable that they cannot be part of a wretched people, and no people is so wretched that they cannot be estimable, one by one. German philosophers of the nineteenth century attempted to break free from the constraints of Cartesian dualism, part of their wider revolt against the domination—and philosophical principles—of Catholic Europe, which had not been kind to Germany after the Napoleonic Wars. But German thinkers' fascination with contrasts and paradoxes, the conflict between science and nature, dark and light, good and evil, led inexorably back to thinking in dualities. The Nazis, as stated above, hated Erich

Introduction

Maria Remarque's book for exposing the "other" Germany of the post–First World War era—disillusioned, realist, and reflective—in contrast to the image of a people of destiny—purposeful, heroic, unemotional—that they wished to create, a nation of people, ultimately, who were superhuman rather than human. Any binary analysis risks falling into another trap like Goethe's, however; there were not two Germanys, but one, and, as Goethe wrote, there was one German people, which, like the Schulenburgs and like most families, was both estimable and wretched at the same time.

1

"Bewitched by English Ways"
The House of Schulenburg, 1865–1933

"What experience and history teach is this; that nations and governments have never learned anything from history."—Georg Wilhelm Friedrich Hegel, *Lectures on the Philosophy of World History,* 1830

"Live with your century, but do not be its creature." —Friedrich Schiller, *On the Aesthetic Education of Man,* 1794

The Schulenburg name belongs to an ancient dynasty of the German nobility; the family can be traced back with certainty to the thirteenth century and with diminishing certainty well beyond that time. In the case of recent generations, the Schulenburgs are also descendants of the more famous Bismarcks, no less, and they are also connected to the Arnims, the Bülows, the Helldorffs, and several other prominent aristocratic families. Most modern readers, experts and non-experts alike, instantly recognize the key identifying marks of a noble German surname, written in its entirety, especially the prefixes "von" and "der" when the person's full name is given, making the Schulenburg surname "von der Schulenburg," meaning "of the Schulenburg(s)." Other recognizable features of a German noble family include the titles used by the male family members—in the Schulenburgs' case "Graf," which is usually translated as Count, though it is not a direct equivalent—and the less-famous titles for female family members—in this case "Gräfin," usually translated as Countess—both of which, since a 1919 law, actually form part of the surname. It would be expected that such an aristocratic family would have ties, at least historically, to a recognized castle, though they may no longer live there. The name of the castle can also be used to identify the branch of the family, and it may be joined onto the family name by a hyphen. The branch of the Schulenburg family whose story is told here belonged to the castle at Tressow. Schloss Tressow, or Tressow Castle—an imposing, square, and rather plain white building in its day; wide, long, and surrounded on three sides by forest—is located on a hill overlooking Tressower See (lake) in the district of Bobitz, Mecklenburg region (modern-day Mecklenburg-Western Pomerania). The castle is approximately seven and a half miles (twelve kilometers) southwest of Wismar, roughly halfway between Lübeck and Rostock near the northeastern coast of Germany.

The obvious identifying signs of the German nobility, however, do not really help to tell the story of the Schulenburg-Tressow family; fortunately, they were blessed with more idiosyncratic and colorful identifiers. Most of the male family members, almost according to aristocratic stereotype, bore the classic dueling scars on their cheeks, but the Schulenburgs also had their own special quirks. Perhaps the most notable of these quirks was their Anglophilia; they nurtured an unusual and enduring affection and affinity for all things English, or Anglo-Saxon. This Anglophilia was felt to be rooted in the family's ancestral links to the British throne; it was therefore certainly well-founded, historically, but it was also part of a much broader and older tradition of friendship between Britain and Germany. The same King George I, who sits in the Schulenburg family tree, was the first British king of the German House of Hanover; he was, in fact, German-born, like his Queen, Princess Melusine von der Schulenburg. King George's Germanness, far from being considered incongruous, was seen as part of a vital Anglo-German bond that lasted for three hundred years, until 1914. This bond was first cemented with the marriage of George I's maternal grandparents; Friedrich V (1596–1632), Elector Palatine of the Rhine in the Holy Roman Empire from 1610 to 1623, and briefly King of Bohemia from 1619 to 1620 (earning him the derisive sobriquet of The Winter King) and Elizabeth Stuart (1596–1662), second child and eldest daughter of James VI and I, King of Scotland, England, and Ireland. Friedrich and Elizabeth were born just seven days apart, and they were married on St Valentine's Day in 1613, when they were sixteen years old. The union was popular and greatly celebrated. This marriage of the two great European powers was more than symbolic; it was hoped that the alliance would ensure peace in Europe and bestow credibility on the idea of Protestant rule, affirming its legitimacy. The twelfth child of that marriage was Princess Sophia (1630–1714); Sophia of Hanover by her marriage, which joined the House of Hanover to the lineage of the British thrones.

Thus began a reciprocal and seemingly indestructible exchange of regard and admiration between the two countries. It has been pointed out that no two countries in Europe possessed a stronger, more fruitful, and

1. "Bewitched by English Ways"

more connected history of cultural and familial sympathy, shared dreams and aspirations, and mutual trust and respect, though this assertion may strain credulity nowadays (Seymour 2013: 8–9). The Schulenburgs considered themselves to be at the heart of that historic relationship, with considerable justification. The young Melusine von der Schulenburg was maid of honor to Princess Sophia of Hanover, and in this capacity she met and began her relationship with Sophia's firstborn, the future King George I. Sophia passed her royal succession to George after the death of her cousin, Queen Anne, in 1714 (Sophia herself had died just two months previously). To these events the Tressow branch of the Schulenburgs owed not just their proud links to the British throne, but also their aristocratic title itself. The Habsburg Charles VI, Holy Roman Emperor, granted noble status upon Christian Günther, nephew of Princess Melusine, de facto Queen of England, when he made him a Count (Graf) on December 7, 1728. The granting of the title was ratified the following year by Friedrich Wilhelm I of Prussia, and in subsequent years by the Electors of Saxony and Hanover.

Christian Günther's great-great-great-grandson, Friedrich Bernhard Karl Gustav Ulrich Erich Graf von der Schulenburg, of Tressow Castle, succeeded to the title on April 18, 1880. Friedrich was born on November 21, 1865, the second child and first son of Werner Ludwig Ernst Karl Heinrich Achat Graf von der Schulenburg (1832–1880) and his wife Marie Cäcilie Hedwig Sophie Pauline, nee Freiin von Maltzahn (1843–1900). Friedrich's birthplace was registered administratively as Bobitz, Mecklenburg; however, as this location is less than four miles (less than six kilometers) from Tressow Castle, as the crow flies, it is very likely that he was actually born at the ancestral home. The expectations placed on him would be the familiar ones for a firstborn son of an important European dynasty at that time, the duties of landowner and heir, as long as the boy's health, physique, and general demeanor made an active, public role desirable. As the issue of a prominent and ancient Prussian aristocratic family, Friedrich was born as part of the German Empire's ruling class. This class was defined by the two pillars of that imperial state, the military and the senior civil service, the diplomatic corps; one or both of them, in turn, would define the young nobleman's career path. He became the sixth Graf von der Schulenburg rather unexpectedly, aged only fourteen, upon the untimely death of his father. After briefly attending the University of Heidelberg, he joined the Second Guards Uhlan Regiment of the cavalry in 1888, garrisoned in Berlin. He then transferred to the more prestigious Gardes du Corps cavalry regiment, the Kaiser's own special life guards, in 1890. In 1894 he was appointed regimental adjutant of the Gardes du

Divided Over Hitler

Corps and, in 1897, personal adjutant or aide-de-camp to Duke Johann Albrecht (1857–1920) who had just become regent of the Grand Duchy of Mecklenburg-Schwerin, the Schulernburgs' home state of the German Empire (Ruvigny 1914: 1332, 1333).

Even by aristocracy standards, Friedrich was moving in exalted circles of royal protocol and governance, rather than being restricted to the normal duties of a cavalry officer, though he would never completely sever his ties to the military. The dividing lines between these pursuits would be increasingly blurred during the approaching new century, when the conventionally apolitical worlds of soldiering and diplomacy would become hopelessly entangled with the politics of the age, later in Friedrich's lifetime. At the end of the nineteenth century, however, everything was proceeding happily and according to tradition for Friedrich. On July 21, 1897, the then-first lieutenant married Freda Marie Gräfin (Countess) von Arnim, who was eight years Friedrich's junior. She was the daughter of Georg Werner Graf von Arnim of Boitzenburg Castle, part of the ancient Arnim dynasty, one of the oldest extant Prussian noble families. The following year, on June 5, 1898, their first son and Friedrich's heir was born at Schwerin; they named him Johann-Albrecht Werner Adolf Hermann-Moritz, the first two names being given in honor of the reigning Duke whom Friedrich served. Johann-Albrecht would grow up into the same timeless and comparatively sheltered life of a true firstborn aristocratic heir, just as his father had been prepared for, overseeing the family estate as landowner and Count, and raising a family in order to provide a future heir of his own. Johann-Albrecht would grow up to serve in the cavalry like his father, attaining the equivalent of the rank of captain (Rittmeister, rather than the more common Hauptmann, according to the historic rank system of the Prussian cavalry), and he would later sit in the provincial legislature of Mecklenburg. Johann-Albrecht's time-honored feudal lifestyle, tending to the ancestral property, would contrast with the modern and mobile life of his younger brother, Friedrich and Freda's second-born son.

Wolf-Werner Graf von der Schulenburg was Friedrich and Freda's second-born son, born on September 14, 1899, at Muskau; he would be known as "Wolfi" among family and friends (Heinemann 1994: 3–4). Friedrich, at that time still a first lieutenant, had been posted to the historically important defensive town of Muskau in Saxony; today it is a spa town, accordingly renamed Bad Muskau, and it sits on the modern-day German-Polish border. Muskau is the ancestral home of the Arnims, Countess Freda's family. Wolfi was, in fact, named after Freda's favorite

1. "Bewitched by English Ways"

younger brother, Wolf-Werner Graf von Arnim (1876–1904), who was killed in combat a few years later at the Battle of Waterberg in Germany's southwest African colony (modern day Namibia), and the choice of name would not be a good omen. Wolf-Werner's first birthday saw his father, Friedrich, promoted to captain (Rittmeister) and assigned to assist the Higher General Staff in Berlin. The following spring, on May 25, 1901, a third son, Adolf-Heinrich, who would be known as "Heini" in family circles, was born in Muskau, shortly before Friedrich was posted overseas with his young family; Friedrich had been granted the prestigious appointment of military attaché to the German Embassy in London, a move that predictably enhanced Friedrich's personal affinity for the country. Throughout these years, in keeping with the traditions of the German nobility, the children (three sons at the time of their move to England) were first educated by a series of private nurses and governesses; later, Friedrich would select private tutors, with a preference for English-speaking ones, even after their return to Germany. He was said to be truly "bewitched by English ways" and he persuaded his wife that they should transmit this dual heritage to their children (Seymour 2013: 142, 203).

After their first year in London, a fourth son was born to Friedrich and Freda, on September 5, 1902, and they named him Fritz-Dietlof. The four boys were then joined, a year later, by a sole sister, named Elisabeth Karoline Mary Margarete Veronika, on December 7, 1903; Freda returned to Tressow Castle for the birth. Elisabeth would be known as "Tisa" from infancy and for the rest of her long life. Fritz-Dietlof was the only one of the siblings to be born in England and the only one not born in Germany. To what extent and in what ways he absorbed and processed, psychologically, this sense of being different, being the odd one out, we can only speculate, but there is no question that "Fritzi" was set to follow a unique path in life. As a child he was already considered something of a loner, in a growing family where company was never in short supply (Krebs 1964: 31). The child being the proverbial father of the man, he would grow up to be conventional and conservative in his own ways, but with a profound sense of moral conviction and individual freedom; this combination would be well expressed in the title of a biography of him, *A Conservative Rebel [Ein konservativer Rebel]* by Ulrich Heinemann. After five years, the family's sojourn in England was coming to an end, but the affinity with England would remain. This affinity was now tinged with a certain wariness; despite his own ties with, and considerable affection for England, Friedrich perceived that the "flame" of anti–German feeling could easily flare up there (Singapore Free Press 1930: 8). The expansion of the German navy,

Divided Over Hitler

under the Kaiser's direction, was no secret; Germans were divided over this, with some seeing it as unnecessary baiting of the British, who seemed to be justified in pursuing an entente with France, who in turn already had a pact with Russia (Herwarth 1981: 19). As early as 1906, Friedrich, as he and his and family were preparing to leave England, clearly saw the opposing sides lining up for the future war, developments that would leave Germany feeling dangerously isolated. In March 1907, Friedrich's efforts were rewarded with promotion to major, and he resumed his work with the Higher General Staff in Berlin. In 1913, he was appointed to the command of the Gardes du Corps regiment. At the same time, Kaiser Wilhelm II appointed him his aide-de-camp, with promotion to lieutenant-colonel (Ruvigny 1914: 1333).

Tisa soon remembered nothing of her childhood stay in London, but she was always aware of the distinct Anglo-Saxon family legacy; their home at Tressow Castle was now filled with English mementoes—chintz covers, carpets bought at East India Docks, tweed coats, bone china—collected by the devout Anglophiles, not to mention the English nurses and governesses. Daily life at home was effortlessly bilingual, and the family bookshelves contained English and German books in equal quantities. Tisa's unpublished memoirs—she would live until the age of ninety-seven, incidentally—describe a blissful childhood at Tressow, where the local people venerated Tisa's mother for her kindness, which would become even more evident in the dark years to come. Tisa, as well as being the only girl, would be unique among the siblings in many ways, both in breaking with old conventions and exploring new ones; much later in life she would discover religion, which played only a symbolic, traditional role in the Schulenburgs' nominally Lutheran upbringing (Seymour 2013: 142, 203). Childhood at Tressow Castle was also coming to an end, however; in line with Friedrich's increasingly important royal and military promotions, the family would now be housed in Potsdam, the prestigious and historic royal garrison town.

In the fateful summer of 1914, Friedrich was a forty-eight-year-old lieutenant-colonel. Breeding and class, coupled with unswerving commitment and patriotic devotion, had secured him a series of high-level appointments and steady, rather than meteoric, progression through the officer ranks. He was also a father of six by that time: Johann-Albrecht was sixteen years old, Wolf-Werner—Wolfi—was nearly fifteen, Adolf-Heidrich—Heini—was thirteen, Fritz-Dietlof—Fritzi—was eleven going on twelve, Elisabeth—Tisa—was ten, and the sixth and final sibling, born after a long gap, was a boy named Wilhelm, probably born on February

1. "Bewitched by English Ways"

15, 1914. Some sources give Wilhelm's date of birth as February 1904, only two months after Tisa's birth; this may be the result of an ancient error of transcription, or it may be due to a mistaken assumption that the unusual ten-year gap between births must be wrong. The Marquis of Ruvigny, however, in his meticulous work *The Titled Nobility of Europe,* published in 1914 but finalized in the previous year, does not yet list the baby Wilhelm among the Schulenburg children. It is almost certain, therefore, that Wilhelm was born in 1914. Fritzi, always the outsider, was described as a thin and tender boy with a brooding demeanor, absorbed in his books; his manner contrasted with the surroundings, the martial environment of Potsdam and the fast-developing military aspirations of his older brothers. Attending school as the outbreak of the First World War approached, Fritz-Dietlof personally resolved to reject the traditional Schulenburg family career path into the army, while the majority of his contemporaries longed to graduate in time to prove their manhood by serving the Kaiser and fighting in the coming war (Krebs 1964: 31).

The assassination of Archduke Franz Ferdinand of Austria placed the whole of Europe on a war footing. Friedrich von der Schulenburg was devastated by the prospect of war, already mourning the breaking of the bond with his beloved England, and fearing, correctly, that the special relationship between the two countries was rapidly passing into history. With the official declarations of war between Britain and Germany, their three-century-long friendship was effectively terminated. Many families' histories were interwoven with the fortunes of both countries, many of them had bonds that were stronger and more emotional than the Schulenburgs had, and these families now faced divisions of loyalty that would tear them apart (Seymour 2013: 8, 203). Reservations put aside, Friedrich dutifully departed for the war, in the relatively safe role of staff officer, though he was not always far from combat. In 1915 he was promoted to colonel, and in August 1916 he was appointed Chief of Staff of the Sixth Army, under Crown Prince Rupprecht of Bavaria (Heinemann 1994: 2). After only three months in this role, however, he was appointed Chief of Staff to Crown Prince Wilhelm of Germany (Malaya Tribune 1923: 2). Crown Prince Wilhelm commanded the eponymous Army Group German Crown Prince, which from February 1917 was engaged in intense defensive battles on the Aisne and in Champagne. After a large-scale French breakthrough attempt was repelled in April 1917, Friedrich and the Crown Prince arrived at the conclusion that while a repeat of this success could not be guaranteed, it could indeed be used as political leverage to bargain for an armistice—effectively quitting while they were ahead—aiming

Divided Over Hitler

"to bring the war to an end ... albeit with sacrifices." They suggested that Germany should renounce her claim to Alsace-Lorraine and broker "a wise and far-sighted peace with Russia" that excluded all talk of territorial annexations and reparations (Dellmensingen 1930: 192). In summary, Friedrich and the Crown Prince began to realize that a German victory was impossible. As if to compound this view, it is worth recalling that April 1917 also saw the entry of the United States into the war.

The eldest two Schulenburg brothers, Johann-Albrecht and Wolf-Werner, reached military age in the latter half of the war. They were eager to serve, and like many boys of their generation they risked frustration if they did not get into the army in time. Johann-Albrecht turned eighteen in the summer of 1916, and, as the heir to Tressow Castle, his officer's commission in the cavalry was assured. It was still a custom in the nobility, though in its waning years, that the firstborn son should serve until reaching the rank of captain (Rittmeister) before resigning to take care of the family estate (Herwarth 1981: 21). Wolfi turned eighteen in September 1917, when talk of armistices—and revolutions—was already in the air. He felt a distinct sense of urgency to qualify as an officer and see action in the war. Heinrich Himmler, Wolfi's near-contemporary, also endured a tense year beginning around this time, finding himself in a similar situation. Himmler's father used his connections to get his son enlisted as an officer candidate with a reserve battalion in December 1917, but while Himmler's older brother served on the western front, saw combat, and was decorated with the Iron Cross, Himmler was still in training when the war ended (Longerich 2012: 20–26). The same thing happened to Hans Frank (1900–1946), future Nazi Gauleiter of Poland. Wolfi and other boys his age feared this kind of trick of fate; it was imperative to get into uniform quickly and avoid disappointment. Many German youths born a little later than Wolfi, in the early years of the twentieth century, would feel cheated by fate because they did not reach military age in time for the war (Herwarth 1981: 24).

In the event, Wolf-Werner acted promptly enough to complete his training in a reserve regiment, like Himmler's, and get to the front. He enlisted voluntarily in the reserve in August 1917, while still at school, and was eventually appointed Lieutenant and declared fit for battle in September 1918. He was just in time to gain limited combat experience at the very end of the war; long enough to be quite badly wounded, and sufficient to merit the award of the Iron Cross, second class (Hammerstein-Equord 1966: 110). Friedrich, meanwhile, was promoted to major-general in June 1918 (Heinemann 1994: 2). Freda, the new major-general's wife, was acutely

1. *"Bewitched by English Ways"*

aware of the war's devastating effect on the German home front, where many people were left destitute. In a country that still, nevertheless, venerated its military and their uniforms, there cannot have been many general's wives who responded as Freda did, cutting up the family's collection of old uniforms and flags to re-stitch them into overcoats, smocks, and everyday clothes for the poor and homeless. Eighty years later, Tisa still recalled the impression her mother's gesture made on her. At that time, young Tisa was sent to a school for the daughters of the nobility, housed in the ancient Stift zum Heiligengrabe, historically a Cistercian convent. The school was strict, but it was a positive experience for Tisa, which may have sown the first seed of her later conversion to Roman Catholicism.

On November 9, 1918, at the Germans' final war council at Spa, Friedrich was the only one present to advise the Kaiser not to abdicate, or at least to step aside temporarily but not flee (Singapore Free Press 1939: 12). The Kaiser's generals and counselors had already bombarded him with advice that ranged, according to some assessments, from the rabid to the unreal; "fanatics" like Friedrich von Berg, General Erich Ludendorff, and Major-General Friedrich von der Schulenburg thought that the Kaiser should go seek an honorable and heroic death, leading the charge at the head of his men, before it was too late; only Friedrich, however, actually dared to suggest this out loud (Hull 2004: 290). In desperation, Friedrich pleaded with the Kaiser for a gallant final gesture; if not leading the last attack against the Allies then perhaps a march on Berlin to suppress nascent "Bolshevik" revolutions and uprisings there, some of which, but not all, were inspired by the Russian Revolution. Friedrich was privately scathing of the Kaiser and Crown Prince Wilhelm's "defeatist" attitudes; nevertheless, when a fellow aristocrat publicly called the Kaiser a coward the following year, Friedrich challenged him to a duel. Friedrich was transferred to the army reserve of officers on December 28, 1918, and released from active service on March 29, 1920, keeping his rank of major-general. It was, of course, a dismal end to the war for all Germans; the various ranks, honors, and Iron Crosses taken home by the Schulenburg men must have seemed like small compensation. In a particular way, the war's end was an enormous blow for the German aristocracy, whose centuries-old traditions and conservative values could not keep them safely detached from the ensuing mayhem; now, with the abolition of the monarchy, that system of traditions and values was on the brink of collapse, like the nobility itself. It was a demoralizing and radicalizing experience for them, in which any heartfelt proposal to restore Germany's greatness and influence could appear attractive. The Schulenburg family ruefully reported a great reduction in its wealth, though many nobles' claims of living austere lives around that time were questionable; such pleas of poverty were considered affectations, or attempts to distance themselves from what aristocrats saw as the middle class's undignified struggles to live well amidst the postwar chaos, which the aristocracy dismissed as finagling and profiteering (Malinowksi 2020: 3, 9–10, 74, 83, 249).

In one of his last conversations with Crown Prince Wilhelm, about what each of them would do next, Friedrich apparently mentioned going into the tobacco business; a previously unthinkable step-down for a nobleman (Singapore Free Press 1930: 18). Money was undeniably tighter than before; Wolf-Werner was able to begin studying law at Göttingen, but only thanks to an assistance program for returning veterans (Krebs 1964: 42). He turned twenty in September 1919 and became active in the "Corps Saxonia" traditionalist student fraternity. His father had briefly been a member of the Corps Saxo-Borussia Heidelberg, while at the University of Heidelberg in 1887–88. While these university fraternity "corps" were principally dedicated to gentlemanly pursuits, such as dueling, many of them now also formed volunteer units as part of the Freikorps Oberland. The Freikorps was a paramilitary volunteer force that was being expanded across Germany to counter the various postwar insurrections taking place. In the case of Wolf-Werner's unit, they would be dispatched to fight against Polish separatists and their ultimately successful Silesian Uprisings of 1919–1921, during which the Freikorps would gain notoriety for clandestine murders of opponents and of those considered traitors in far-right circles (Möller 2004: 152). Wolf-Werner appears to have served for at least six months in the Silesian campaign, long enough to be awarded the Silesian Eagle (Schlesischer Adler) medal, first class (Hammerstein-Equord 1966: 110). A vast number of Freikorps awards were instituted, but only two were later permitted to be worn on uniforms of the Third Reich, after the 1935 ban on unofficial medals; one of these approved medals was the Silesian Eagle medal. It would not be Wolf-Werner's last decoration, nor was it the last of his awards to be associated with highly questionable conduct.

Tisa, in her memoirs, described how she and her classmates at their strict boarding school responded with joy to the announcement of the new republic, decorating their hair with red ribbons and refusing to curtsey to their teachers; they definitely did not mourn the fall of the monarchy. At home, the teenage Tisa frightened her mother's old-fashioned maid by singing a ditty that went "smear the guillotine with the aristocracy's fat." She also noted that local insurgents in the postwar years posed no threat to the family home, as they well remembered Freda's kindness to the local

1. "Bewitched by English Ways"

populace during the war. Tisa was determined to become an artist, and she begged for permission to get involved with the burgeoning Bauhaus movement. The Bauhaus, inspired by leftwing values and with permissive undertones, was not acceptable to Friedrich, who at that time was becoming seriously involved with the conservative DNVP—the German National People's Party (Deutschnationalen Volkspartei)—but he compromised and consented to Tisa studying art and sculpture elsewhere, but only when she turned twenty-one. Living in Berlin in the 1920s, Tisa's unconventional personality, striking looks, and bold artistic talent brought her to the attention of the similarly rebellious leftwing and liberal intelligentsia of the Weimar years. In a rebellious counterculture that would make the 1960s seem tame, influential figures like Hugh Simon operated a revolving door policy at their art-filled homes; a whirlwind of parties famed for free expression and free love. Tisa became friends with the Mann brothers, Thomas and Heinrich, and the philosopher Ernst Cassirer, as well as mixing socially with Bertolt Brecht, Erich Maria Remarque, and even Albert Einstein. In this environment, Tisa would meet and begin a relationship with Fritz Hesse, a charming, open-minded, and very rich Jewish art collector. Her relationship with her father, surprisingly, would not only survive her embarking on an art career, but also the shock of her engagement to Hesse, who was, apart from being Jewish, nearly twenty years her senior and divorced. Tisa later recalled that in spite of his disappointment—and anti–Semitism—Friedrich treated his future son-in-law with impeccable courtesy (Seymour 2013: 231–32, 263–64).

The first of the Schulenburg siblings to wed, however, was the third son, Adolf-Heinrich—Heini—of whom relatively little is known. Born in 1901, he was part of that generation that was too young to win their spurs in the war, and the first generation of young aristocrats for whom commerce was an acceptable career. At the age of twenty-two he married another young noble, Jutta Freiin von Barnekow, nicknamed "Schnuz," who was just nineteen years old. They married on June 29, 1923, and would have two children, one of whom later settled in the United States. In December 1924, Friedrich was elected to the Reichstag for the People's Party (DNVP); he served for a term of nearly three and a half years, at a time when the DNVP was at the height of its influence, with more than a hundred Reichstag seats (Klee 2005: 565). Wolf-Werner had meanwhile complemented his military achievements with a degree in law, qualifying him to broker commercial contracts. He turned his hand to business, specifically import and export with Brazil and Argentina. Sometime in the late 1920s he met a woman three years his junior, Gisela Elisabeth Louise Therese Freiin von

Divided Over Hitler

Stralenheim, from Dresden; it would seem that Wolf-Werner's commercial interests took him to Dresden, where they appear to have met and become engaged. Gisela, appropriately, came from the German nobility, and as the unmarried daughter of a Freiherr (literally "Freeman" and roughly equivalent to an English Baron) she bore the title of Freiin. Being the daughter of a Freiherr certainly qualified Gisela as true German aristocracy, but at a distinctly junior level to the Graf rank of the Schulenburgs. There was no shame in this, of course, and it was commonplace for senior families to give junior nobility a "step up" through marriage; Wolf-Werner's own paternal grandmother, Marie Cäcilie, began life as Freiin von Maltzahn. Gisela's English-sounding middle names, Elisabeth Louise, while not unpopular in Germany at the time (Tisa's birth name was also Elisabeth), offer a clue to yet another Anglo-Saxon family connection. In Gisela's case, her mother was actually American, born Helen Hudson Leavitt in 1864, in Berkshire County, Massachusetts, a county that in the late nineteenth century, as now, was a preserve of the elite. With no apparent hard feelings over the war or the ongoing Allied occupation, Wolf-Werner acquired an American mother-in-law when he married Gisela in Dresden on Tuesday, November 12, 1929.

Honeymoon over, the groom returned to his business, but these were years of increasing politicization in German life. The Weimar republic failed to live up to its promise for many people, feelings that were intensified by the worldwide economic collapse. Friedrich quit the People's Party (DNVP) in favor of a short-lived, more moderate, and more monarchist spin-off party, the Conservative People's Party (Konservative Volkspartei or KVP). Federal elections were held on Sunday, September 14, 1930, Wolf-Werner's thirty-first birthday. The results, both at the time and in retrospect, have been seen as a barometer reading of the age; the center-left Social Democratic Party (SDP) lost ten seats, but in spite of this slight bruising it remained the largest party in the Reichstag, winning one-hundred and forty-three of the five-hundred and seventy-seven seats. More tellingly, the National Socialist German Workers Party (Nazionalsozialistische Deutsche Arbeiterpartei, or NSDAP), already better known as Hitler's Nazis, dramatically increased its quota of seats from twelve to one hundred and seven. Hitler was as surprised as anyone (Shirer 1960: 138). Just as significantly, the communist KPD also increased their parliamentary share, gaining twenty-three seats and becoming the third-largest party in the Reichstag (Nohlen and Stöver 2010: 762, 790).

Germany's original communist party, ironically, was actually the now center-left SDP; long-established in the homeland of Karl Marx, the SDP

1. "Bewitched by English Ways"

had historically been the largest Marxist party in the world, but decades of parliamentary negotiations and compromises had softened the party line considerably. In the wake of 1917, and the subsequent Marxist-inspired uprisings across postwar Germany, the appetite for a new, non-revisionist, uncompromisingly communist political party had grown; the newer Communist Party (KPD) was therefore the antagonist of the SDP, and there was no prospect of an alliance between the two, not even a pact of convenience in order to thwart a common enemy. The SDP, in fact, preferred to govern through a grand center-right—not center-left—coalition, and it had attempted to do this after the previous elections, in 1928, but this coalition was so full of internal divisions that it only led to the new elections of 1930 (Evans and Jenkins 1999: 83, 88). Wolf-Werner was one of many Germans who felt compelled to make their position clear at this time. The Nazis would have to be taken seriously from now on, as the first serious non-communist contender for the SDP's primacy. Hitler also seemed readier to work with small conservative and monarchist parties, but most importantly he was anticommunist. This was enough for Wolf-Werner, and on Saturday, November 1, 1930, he joined the Nazi party (Teichler 1991: 111).

Wolf-Werner's younger brother, Fritz-Dietlof—Fritzi—meanwhile, had stayed true to his rebellious schoolboy convictions and resisted the family tradition of military service. After graduating from high school in 1920, he followed his older brother to Göttingen to study law, before transferring to Marburg. Like Wolf-Werner, he joined the Corps Saxonia fraternity, though apparently avoiding the military aspect. Fritzi did, however, take part in the traditional dueling with swords, and he sustained prominent lifelong scars on his cheeks, an aristocratic custom. After university he embarked on a civil service career, which was an appropriate and acceptable alternative to the army, for a son of the aristocracy. He was first appointed as a clerk (Gerichtsreferendar) in 1923 and then as an advisor in training (Regierungsreferendar) in 1925, both at the courthouse (Landratsamt) in Kyritz. He was then promoted to the role of administrator and sent to Recklinghausen in the Ruhr region. Fritzi's individualism made him a controversial figure in a context where convention and conformity were valued and expected. His transparency tended to elicit extremes of trust and distrust from people, while his liberal views earned him the nickname "Roter Graf"—the Schulenburg family's black sheep had apparently become the "Red Count"—though the insinuation that he was a hard left-winger is probably an exaggeration. Like his older brother, Fritzi began to take a serious interest in the Nazi party—which, like him, was by no means strictly conventional, conservative, or conformist—though he would forever engage with politics on his own terms. Fritzi veered, predictably, towards the more socialist, northern-based brand of Nazism, led by the brothers Gregor Strasser (1892–1934) and Otto Strasser (1897–1974). This more grass-roots and worker-oriented wing of the Nazi party had a bigger membership than the southern-German rightwing incarnation of Nazism, and the Strassers' political activity was much more focused on policy and persuasion than on agitation and militancy. The popularity of this distinctive northern approach to Nazism infuriated the southern-based Hitler, and both of the Strasser brothers were placed on his blacklist. Even so, the years of inclusion in the coalition government after 1930 seemed like a good omen for all sides of the Nazi movement. Fritzi's position and influence in the civil service steadily increased during this time, despite clashing with some of his superiors, such as the Nazi Erich Koch (1896–1986), infamous Gauleiter of East Prussia (Meding 1997: 116).

Fritz-Dietlof's superiors and colleagues were not all committed Nazis like Koch, though there were obviously some adherents and supporters of Hitler working within the civil service of the early 1930s. Some civil servants calculated that the benefits of a future Nazi government would outweigh those elements of the Nazi party program that they found unsettling, while others utterly despaired of what was to come and left the country. Some civil servants, finding that they definitely did not agree with Hitler's vision, decided to just stay quiet and retreat into a kind of "exile in plain sight," while some others protested openly. On the whole, however, it was not difficult for the Nazis to win support from civil servants, including university lecturers and their students; most of them had backed conservative political parties, which, though ultimately ineffectual, had been hostile to the Weimar republic, and these were sore points that the Nazis could play on. Enthusiasm for the proposed renaissance of traditional German values was widespread on university campuses, which gave rise to anti–Semitic policies in student fraternities and the persecution of professors who were considered unpatriotic. These features of university life would later be formalized as Nazi legislation. The situation in the military contrasted with that of the civil service; the army's leaders were aware, until quite a late stage, that they could fairly easily overthrow any future Nazi regime, if they so desired, so the extent to which they cooperated with Hitler was therefore a more open and conscious decision, rather than a case of caving to pressure. This troubled the consciences of a significant number of high-ranking army officers, but it would take years for their

1. "Bewitched by English Ways"

reservations to mature into actual opposition to the Nazis and, crucially, for their resolve to converge with those of dissenting civil servants, aristocrats, and diplomats. This convergence of dissenting resolve would require a widespread realization that the path set out upon by Hitler was going to lead to the nation's certain destruction, unless he was stopped. While many Germans faced dilemmas in response to the spread of Nazi views and the rise in Hitler's popularity, however, it is important to acknowledge that many others did not. For a wide variety of reasons—not necessarily fanatical adulation of Hitler or calculated self-interest—many German civil servants, soldiers, and private citizens embraced, promoted, and sought to realize Hitler's vision (Kershaw 1993: 117).

Wolf-Werner followed up his new Nazi party membership with enrollment in the SA on February 1, 1931 (Teichler 1991: 111). The SA, or Sturmabteilung—literally "Storm Detachment"—was the Nazi party's paramilitary wing. It played a significant role in Adolf Hitler's rise to power within the party by establishing him as an effective leader in public; the SA's primary purposes were to provide protection for Nazi rallies and assemblies, to disrupt the meetings of opposing parties, and to fight against the paramilitary units of the opposing parties, especially the Roter Frontkämpferbund (the "red front" combat association) of the communist KPD and the Reichsbanner Schwarz-Rot-Gold (the black-red-gold "national banner") of the SDP. The SA also devoted itself to intimidating trade unionists, Romani, Jews, and numerous others. More broadly, the status and power of the SA demonstrated Hitler's intention to supplant the state and replicate its institutions; the Nazi party was already being organized as a shadow state apparatus and it therefore needed its own army (Shirer 1960: 119–21). SA members were colloquially called brownshirts (Braunhemden) in similarity to Benito Mussolini's blackshirts (Camicie Nere), the official uniform of the SA being a brown shirt with a brown tie. The color came about because a large shipment of shirts, originally intended for colonial troops in Germany's former East African colonies, was purchased in 1921 for use by the Freikorps paramilitary units, and these later became available for the SA. The SA developed pseudo-military titles for its members, with ranks that were later adopted by other Nazi organizations, most notably the Schutzstaffel (SS), which originated as a branch of the SA. Wolf-Werner's younger brother, Adolf-Heinrich—Heini—who was by then a businessman and financier, became the second Schulenburg brother to join the Nazi party, on March 1, 1931, and he too then joined the SA. The firstborn son and heir, Johann-Albrecht, joined the Nazi party seven months later, on October 1 of the same year, and at around the same time he took over the running of Tressow Castle. Only the youngest brother, Wilhelm, apparently showed no interest whatsoever in the Nazi movement (Seymour, 2013: 263).

Within the family, the only strong reaction against the rise of the Nazis, up to that point at least, came from Tisa, now a successful artist. She was still busy enjoying the exciting social whirl of a decadent counterculture, rubbing shoulders with leading Marxist and socialist thinkers and writers, especially at the permissive and star-studded house parties of Hugh Simon and other socialites and culture vultures. The Schulenburg family actually moved their regular residence from Tressow to Tisa's beloved Berlin in 1932, but by that time Tisa was somewhat estranged and certainly detached from the main events of family life (Seymour 2013: 263–64, 357). Like his three eldest sons, Friedrich now joined the Nazi party, cutting his former ties to both the DNVP, the People's Party, and its offshoot, the KVP, the Conservative People's Party. He would later return to the Reichstag for a term, this time as a Nazi party deputy. Friedrich also took his sons' lead in joining the SA; as a veteran major-general of the imperial army he was highly valued, perhaps more for the prestige and legitimacy he could lend to the movement, rather than as an expert on military matters, though his endorsement did little to improve army leaders' opinions of the unruly SA. Nevertheless, his most significant contribution to the cause was astute, timely, and far-reaching; Friedrich suggested the creation of an elite corps, more specialized than the SA, which should pledge its allegiance directly to the Reich chancellor, just as Friedrich's own old regiment, the Gardes du Corps, had sworn personal allegiance to the Kaiser. This vision would eventually be realized with Hitler's reform of the existing Schutzstaffel (Protection squadron) or SS. Previously an entity of the state, following Friedrich's suggestion the SS would henceforth only be answerable to Hitler, and plans were drawn up to formally separate it from the rag-tag rabble of the SA (Haupt 2001: 111).

Friedrich's enthusiastic adherence to the Nazi cause may be slightly surprising, coming from the royalist, traditionalist, aristocratic patriarch of the Schulenburg family. It could be seen as a political about-face for the ageing knight, who was still broodingly resentful of the Kaiser's abdication and had long maintained faith in a restoration of the monarchy. By the early 1930s, however, Friedrich had arrived at the conclusion that Wilhelm II's abdication inflicted a "broken neck" upon the monarchy, from which it would take at least a lifetime to recover. Furthermore, the Weimar republic and communism were, in his view, clear and present evils that urgently needed to be quashed, even if it took an anti-monarchist to do

1. *"Bewitched by English Ways"*

it; "only a Titan can master the situation," he wrote (Malinowski 2020: 86, 87). Friedrich's previous term in the Reichstag, representing the rightwing DNVP, was perhaps more congruent with his monarchist and conservative positions, but the People's Party, like its offshoot the Conservative People's Party (KVP), was largely sympathetic to the Nazis anyway; moreover, the more traditionalist conservative parties helped to promote and diffuse the view that Hitler might just be the imperfect "Titan" that Germany sorely needed (Malinowski 2020: 211).

Friedrich did not give up on the monarchy, therefore, but he regarded Nazism as the only possible route to a restoration; in the circumstances, supporting the imperfect option of the ruffian Hitler was the truest patriotism, a necessary sacrifice. Having patriotism as the priority went with the territory, of course, as the Schulenburgs were from the class of knights, royal aides, statesmen, and cavalry officers, counting among their number generals, diplomats, and winners of the highest decorations, but what patriotism meant in practice was the great dilemma of the age. Most Schulenburg family members allied themselves to the Nazi cause with apparent conviction, but certainly not all, and at least one of those who did join the Nazis (and almost certainly others) clearly wrestled with their consciences (Niemann 2000: 332). Each individual Schulenburg's broader aspirations and orientation in life may have been somewhat disparate, but none of this appeared incompatible with a sincere and heartfelt commitment to the Nazi movement. Part of the strength of Nazism, it has often been pointed out, was just that; the ability to unite disparate and even dissonant factions and individuals in a common cause, mainly by presenting them with common enemies to loath (Malinowski 2020: 14, 211).

2

"United by Pain, Divided by Politics"

The Schulenburg Family and the Reich, 1933–1939

"Only a titan can master the situation."—Friedrich Bernhard Graf von der Schulenburg, quoted in Malinowski, *Nazis and Nobles,* 2020

"I solemnly prophesy that this accursed man will cast our Reich into the abyss and bring our nation to inconceivable misery. Future generations will damn you in your grave for what you have done."—attributed to General Erich Ludendorff, quoted in Kershaw, *Hitler,* 2008

The Reichstag elections of 1932 resulted in yet another unstable and ineffective coalition government, but this time it was led by the Nazis. Germany's president, Hindenburg, was successfully pressured into appointing Hitler as chancellor on Monday, January 30, 1933. This has conventionally been given as the date of the Nazi "seizure" of power, though it is well established that the takeover process was more a case of horse-trading than coup d'état. Far from being inevitable, Hitler's accession to power depended on cunning, bartering, good timing, and, on the part of his opponents and rivals, poor judgment (Bullock 1962: 253). For Hitler, however, the work was only just beginning, and he urgently needed to protect his new position and defend against potential counterattack. The roles of the paramilitary SA, and of Hitler's preferred loyalists, the SS, were going to have to change, in line with the suggestion of Friedrich von der Schulenburg (Haupt 2001: 111). The SS, led by Heinrich Himmler, was going to rise to predominance, while the SA would lose its prestige and would no longer be considered the uniformed vanguard of the Nazi party. The SS was to be formally detached from the SA, once and for all, as soon as Hitler

2. "United by Pain, Divided by Politics"

had carried out an internal party purge of his rivals, opponents, and critics, during which the SA's senior figures would be culled. This event would become known as the Night of the Long Knives. The disgrace of its murdered leaders would work to discredit the remaining SA; bereft of its leaders and stripped of its political relevance, the organization would strive to reinvent itself as the Nazis' sports and leisure club, organizing galas and tournaments in various games and athletic disciplines. An agreement would be reached with the Nazi party, through which the now-innocuous SA would be given responsibility for running strictly military-themed sporting activities, aimed at interested members of the public; meanwhile, the new German Reich Association for Physical Exercise would take care of the general physical education of the populace and all competitive sports organizing. This enormous state intervention in sport would provide significant professional opportunities for those of the Nazi party faithful who were eager to make a fuller contribution to the Third Reich, like Wolf-Werner Graf von der Schulenburg.

To understand exactly why the world of sport should have been the focus of so much attention and investment in the development of the Third Reich, from as early as April 1933, it is necessary to step back and look at the broader picture. Putting sensationalist interpretations of the Nazi "coup" aside, Hitler had actually achieved no more than a rather tenuous hold on power, against which the opposition parties, had they been inclined to work together, could still have mounted a serious challenge. Hitler's solution was to turn Germany's existing instability into total chaos, thereby ramping up the anxiety and creating a slate of pretexts for clampdowns; the first concentration camp, it must be remembered, opened within weeks of Hitler's appointment as chancellor, not years. This chaos of Hitler's making would not be an end in itself, therefore, but an opportunity to impose order, Nazi style, and the all-important visible manifestations of this order would be employment, rearmament, and national physical prowess. Achievement in sport was to be the glue that held the Nazi public image together, with its intrinsic—and quite genuine—implications for military greatness, personal development, social improvement, and national pride; sport was therefore central to the perceived order that was designed to emerge from Hitler's orchestrated chaos.

The fuse of this chaos was lit, symbolically and literally, on the evening of February 27, 1933, in Berlin, when the nation's parliament building, the Reichstag, was destroyed by fire. Within minutes, Hitler capitalized on this opportunity to denounce the communists and swear revenge. The suspected arsonist was apprehended and confessed that he had worked alone,

Divided Over Hitler

but the Nazis swept aside his admission; they were not interested in an individual scapegoat. Hitler was focused on eliminating his biggest threat, and he immediately ordered the arrest of anyone with links to the communist KPD. Within just a few days, four thousand KPD members and their leaders had been thrown into hastily arranged temporary prisons and, the novel solution, concentration camps. By the end of March, less than two months since the Nazi takeover, the number of detainees had rocketed to twenty thousand, and by the first summer of Hitler's Reich it would be one hundred thousand. By that time, the summarily detained included Social Democrats, union officials, and other supposed "radicals" in addition to the original communists. The question of whether any of these people could have had anything to do with the Reichstag fire, incidentally, was of no concern to the Nazis, and neither was the important matter of identifying those truly responsible for the fire that had served Hitler's purposes so well. The only thing that mattered was that the reign of chaos and fear had begun (Evans 2005: 11).

In the immediate wake of the Reichstag fire came a volley of new legislation, beginning with "emergency decrees" designed to justify, legitimize, and authorize—retroactively—the outrageous actions already being taken; arrest without due cause, imprisonment without trial, and summary suspension of civil rights. The decrees' deliberately intimidating titles—"For the Defense of Nation and State" and "To Combat Treason Against the German Nation and Treasonable Activities" for example—were designed to stoke further fear and silence objections. Incredibly, in the midst of all this, on March 5, just six days after the fire, another election was held, which the Nazis hoped would consolidate their control of the still-smoldering Reichstag. The Nazi party won two hundred and eighty-eight seats and nearly forty-four per cent of the votes. The communist deputies won eighty-one seats, but they faced immediate arrest if they dared to show up and claim them. Other opposition parties also won significant numbers of seats; the SDP took one hundred and nineteen seats and eighteen-point-three per cent of the votes, and the Catholic Center Party won seventy-three seats, with more than eleven per cent of the votes. Combined, the opposition's wins continued to pose a problem for the Nazis, but even at that stage, regrettably, the opposition parties still distrusted each other, almost as much as they feared the Nazis.

The Nazis' next step was to outlaw criticism of the government and its leaders—the Malicious Practices Act—and indeed dissent of any kind; this included "gossiping" about or "poking fun" at government officials, and could be punished by prison or concentration camp. This was followed

2. "United by Pain, Divided by Politics"

by the Enabling Act, which enabled the chancellor of Germany to unilaterally identify and punish "enemies of the state" as he perceived them. Ninety-four Social Democrats voted against this Machiavellian law, but most of the opposing deputies were by then in hiding, in prison, in concentration camps, or in exile. The Nazis' campaign of intimidation, which was clearly no bluff, had been rolled out in a very short arc of time, and it continued with the dissolution of labor unions, which were replaced by a single Nazi workers' organization, and then the outlawing of the SDP. The DNVP, which was still part of Hitler's coalition government, dissolved voluntarily after being threatened with attack; most of its former members joined the Nazis. By July 1933, the Nazi party was the only legally permitted political party. Obviously, not everyone was prepared to accept these developments, and the exodus of tens of thousands of Germans began almost immediately. The majority of Germany's sixty million inhabitants, however, either through choice or through lack of choice, began to adapt to the new Germany, in which every entity in society had to be brought under Nazi control or disappear (Allen 1973: 214). Many professions in Germany were already traditionally government-controlled, and this would facilitate the identification, expulsion, and exclusion of liberals, militant Catholics, erstwhile Social Democrats, and other "undesirables" from those professions. To protect their jobs, amidst what was still, after all, an ongoing unemployment crisis, one point six million people joined the Nazi party between January 30 and May 1, 1933 (Evans 2005: 14).

On April 28, 1933, as part of their determination to bring all aspects of German life and society under their control, the Nazis announced the appointment of a new Reich Commissioner for Gymnastics and Sport (Reichskommissar für Turnen und Sport). The new appointee was Hans von Tschammer und Osten (1887–1943), a Reichstag deputy for the Nazi party and a Gruppenführer (group leader) in the SA. During his time as a Reichstag deputy, he was already notable for his involvement in the national sports scene, but after the Nazis took power he condemned all existing sports associations as "bourgeois." On May 30 of the same year, Tschammer und Osten published his guidelines for the Reconstruction of German Physical Exercise. With immediate effect, according to the published guidelines, some element of outdoor or military-oriented sport and exercise became compulsory in all state-recognized entities and associations. Existing professional sports associations immediately came under Tschammer und Osten's direct control. This meant that the German Gymnastics Association would be designated "Bureau One" of the Reich sports commission, the German Football Association (which included cricket and rugby) became Bureau Two, and so on. Even the German Motorists Association (Bureau Twelve), the German Sports Medical Association (Bureau Thirteen), the German Sports Press Association (Bureau Fourteen) and the German Sports Teachers Association (Bureau Fifteen) were taken over. Power over all staffing appointments within the Bureaus went to Tschammer und Osten, though in practice he was encouraged to maintain stability and limit the number of sackings and new appointments during his first three years in office. This was primarily in the interest of facilitating the comprehensive security and intelligence arrangements in the run-up to the 1936 Olympics; the event was expected to be a target for protests, demonstrations, and possible sabotage, and it would have to be as tightly controlled as the German sport world itself. In August 1933, Tschammer und Osten, as "Reichssportführer" automatically became president of the German National Olympic Committee (Timpe 2017: 45, 57).

This concentration of power into Tschammer und Osten's hands set the scene for the formation of the German Reich Association for Physical Exercise (Deutscher Reichsbund für Leibesübungen) or DRL, which, with further Nazification, would be renamed the National-Socialist Reich Association for Physical Exercise (Nationalsozialistischer Reichsbund für Leibesübungen) or NSRL in 1937. With the official establishment of the DRL came the need for a vast and complex national bureaucracy, in order to reach the whole population, including Germans in the diaspora, and to cover every possible aspect of sport and exercise. As mentioned above, this provided jobs for a large number of Nazi party members, organized around the Gau system. The ancient term Gau, meaning an administrative region, had been revived by the Nazis; each Gau was further subdivided into Kreise, or districts. For organizational purposes, international branches of the DRL, catering for Germans resident overseas, were together considered one Gau. Third in the national hierarchy, therefore, after Reichssportführer (Tschammer und Osten) and Reichsfachamtsleiter (National Heads of Department, or Bureau) came Gauführer (Region Leaders) and Gaufachamtsleiter (Regional Head of Department), and into this latter level of Nazi sports organization stepped Wolf-Werner Graf von der Schulenburg (Teichler 1991: 134).

Relatively early Nazi party members like Wolf-Werner, the first one in his family to join, could look forward to comfortable and interesting employment within the DRL hierarchy. He was also a member of the less-influential SA, which was now no more than an innocuous sports-oriented organization, but this would not go against him, as the

2. "United by Pain, Divided by Politics"

SS was about to endorse every decision and appointment that the DRL made. The SS, in contrast to the discredited SA, was one of very few state organizations that retained the legal right to organize its own program of national competitions, but even the SS voluntarily chose to acknowledge the DRL's authority from the outset. This meant that the sports clubs of the SS were also signed-up as regular member clubs of the DRL. Cooperation between the SS and the DRL was cemented when senior SS figures also took important positions in the DRL; these included SS Brigadier-General Richard Herrmann, head of the SS sports office and until 1942 Head of Department for Handball and Basketball in the DRL, and from 1938 also President of the International Handball Federation, and SS Standard-Leader Dr. Karl Ritter von Halt, Head of Department for Athletics in the DRL and later Reichssportführer of the whole DRL. The intended message was unity, organization, strength, and absolute seamless cooperation between Nazi entities. With the Berlin Summer Olympics just around the corner, sport was a crucial part of the image that Nazi Germany wanted to project upon the world (Bullock 1962: 355).

The organized, legalized chaos of day-to-day life in Hitler's Germany was a well-established routine long before the Olympics, and those who still upheld the idea of Nazism as a cultured, principled, socialist movement were little short of fooling themselves. Public politically-motivated violence was normal, and the involvement in this violence of police auxiliaries and party paramilitaries—the SA and the SS—was routine. The boundaries between official police and political paramilitaries were completely blurred in fact, with the paramilitaries having the upper hand; it was generally considered safer to endure a robbery or assault in silence rather than to risk calling the police. The more urgent police priorities, as far as the Nazi leadership was concerned, were the harassment, disruption, and annihilation of any kind of rival influence. Despite everything, however, erudite and educated Nazi party members like the Schulenburgs managed to see the Olympics as an affirmation of Nazism's positive social ideals and capacity to restore Germany's greatness. Such events, involving a diverse range of individuals, allowed them to feel reassured that, after all, their movement still valued and integrated a wide variety of viewpoints, in harmony with the Schulenburg family's international cultural heritage. Soon, however, it became clear that the quasi-messianic cultish adulation of the Nuremburg rally, following closely on the heels of the Olympics, was the truer face of Nazism (Bullock 1962: 262–63, 273–78).

The Schulenburg family was by then irreparably divided over Nazism, and their individual fates were already inseparable from the extreme,

Divided Over Hitler

polarized reactions to Hitler with which all of German society would sooner or later be caught up. As individuals, the Schulenburg family's members experienced misgivings and doubts, though most of them would remain ostensibly committed to the Nazi cause. All but one of the Schulenburg brothers, as well as their father, were members of the Nazi party, and three of them were members of the SA. The Nazi party was not a particularly natural home for them; aristocratic roots afforded no special route to progression within the institutions of the Third Reich. Even so, the education, international connections, and cultural acumen often attached to nobility were very useful attributes; such qualities boosted many a Third Reich career, as they did for Wolf-Werner working at senior levels of the DRL. Additionally, membership of the upper class generally inculcated a sense of patriotism that easily found its expression in Nazi ideals. This was even true in the case of someone like Fritz-Dietlof, who had eschewed military service and had carved out a reputation as something of a non-conformer and class rebel; these traits, after all, were expressions of German identity as well. The case of the "Red Count" in fact highlights an often-misconstrued aspect of Nazism, namely the existence of the left wing of the Nazi party.

The early twenty-first century is described as a new age of political polarization, and the fact that the Nazi party was the National "Socialist" German Workers Party is sometimes used to frame modern-day socialists, with priorities such as universal free healthcare and liberalized family and reproductive values, as the ideological heirs of the Nazis. These socialist movements start innocently, critics suggest, but the curse of socialism is ever poised to trigger a nation's descent into the moral abyss. Regardless of the merits or demerits of the modern left, however, history defies these simplistic interpretations. While the purported socialism of the Nazi party may be used as a stick to beat present-day socialists, the Nazis' adoption of the word Socialist is the subject of both a complex process of political marketing and a widespread misunderstanding. The Nazi party was founded as the National German Workers Party (NDAP); the adjective National obviously referred to the party, because it would be nonsensical as well as ungrammatical, in German, to refer to a person as a "National German" or a "National German Worker." The controversial inclusion, in February 1920, of the word Socialist added enduring confusion to the party's name, but it was not designed to alter the meaning significantly; just as the original party name did not refer to "National Germans" the new party name did not intend to invent something called a "National Socialist." While in English (and some other languages) the word "socialist" can

2. "United by Pain, Divided by Politics"

be a noun, in the name of the NSDAP it is the second of two adjectives to describe the party. But this grammar confusion is just one way in which the inclusion of the word "socialist" can be misunderstood.

As well as being controversial among large parts of the existing membership, the decision to include the word "socialist" in the party name was by all accounts calculated and opportunistic, rather than ideological or even strictly political; it represented a strategy to broaden the Nazi party's appeal, rather than a genuine political orientation (Kershaw 2008: 87). The cynicism of this move can perhaps be overstated, but it is clear that early Nazi party leaders wanted to attract potential Communist Party (KPD) supporters and others who may have been alienated by the formerly–Marxist SDP's abandonment of the revolutionary path. Hitler did not approve of this strategy, preferring to establish the Nazi party's unequivocal anticommunist credentials from the outset, but he was overruled (Mitcham 1996: 68). He was right to suspect that the use of socialistic terminology would lead to intentional or unintentional mischaracterizations of the Nazi party, a fact borne out to this day with the disingenuous approximation of modern far left viewpoints with Nazism, in order to score political points. Hitler's opposition to the amendment of the Nazi party name had an even more urgent logic behind it, however; there was in fact a significant wing of the Nazi party that did sympathize strongly with actual socialism. This was the sizeable faction that grew around the Strasser brothers in northern Germany; Hitler, Hermann Göring, and Rudolf Hess, on the other hand, were Bavarian—southern— Germans, either by birth or by adoption. The Strasserite grouping became the most successful wing of the Nazi party, to the great chagrin of Hitler and to the great relief of liberal Nazi supporters like Fritz-Dietlof von der Schulenburg. The northern Nazis were less concerned with displays of militarism and authoritarianism and more keen on developing a comprehensive social policy program and a strong labor movement that would appeal to the working class, the bulk of German society. Not all of the northern members appreciated being labeled leftwing or socialist, in reality, but this image won them enough support among traditional leftwing voters to make it a bitter but highly effective pill to swallow. As popular as leftwing Nazism may have been, however, the northern Strasserite faction had no-one in their ranks with the persuasive power of the great orator Hitler; consequently, it is extremely difficult to imagine what the outcome would have been, had this faction remained the dominant wing of the Nazi party.

Fritz-Dietlof, convinced that there was a significant element of the diverse Nazi movement that resonated with his liberal political outlook, formally joined the Nazi party in February 1932. An early member by broader German standards but slightly late by Schulenburg standards, Fritz-Dietlof's membership came as a relief to his immediate family, at least three of whom were already party members (Mommsen 2009: 154). He further satisfied his family's expectations by opting to get married, to twenty-three-year-old Charlotte Kotelmann, on March 11, 1933 (Meding 1997: 116). By the time of his marriage, Fritz-Dietlof was head of the political office of the controversial East Prussian Gauleiter (region head) Erich Koch (1896–1986), to whom he also acted as personal assistant; the two men clashed, though they were not without things in common. Koch was hypersensitive to any form of unorthodoxy or dissent, and this was possibly due to his own background as an opponent of Hitler's domination in the party, or indeed because of his unorthodox status as one of the few openly Christian senior Nazis (Shirer 1960: 127). Fritz-Dietlof was already sufficiently respected and well-liked in civil service circles to be able to maneuver himself into different jobs around East Prussia, which allowed him to avoid too much contact with Koch. He managed to get himself appointed as district administrator (Landrat) at Fischhausen, for example, though according to some accounts this move was actually brought about by Koch, seeking to rid himself of Fritz-Dietlof (Gregory 2018: 88).

Until 1933, it was apparently still possible to see the Nazi party as a reassuringly diverse and surprisingly big political "tent" that accommodated a broad range of viewpoints, including the left, with a shared goal of the common good for Germany. This harmonious balance of powers (plural) and influences within the Nazi party, however, was not what Hitler wanted, and much of the Nazi party, correspondingly, did not particularly want Hitler. It may seem odd, looking back, that the most decisive and homicidal opposition to Hitler would ultimately come from committed Nazi party members like Fritz-Dietlof, but in fact opposing Hitler was as old as the movement itself. It was not that these opponents later revised their views, necessarily; rather it was the Nazi party that gradually ceased to accommodate their positions. For open-minded progressives and idealists like Fritz-Dietlof, the all-embracing and all-inclusive character of the Nazi movement was a major part of its strength and appeal (Mommsen 2009: 155). He believed that "everything [in Germany] that still had faith, will, self-sacrifice, and willingness to act was concentrated in [the Nazi party]." He was not immune, either, to the overblown idealistic rhetoric of the Nazi party, even calling it "the incarnation of the faith and will of the German people" (Steinau-Steinrück 2020). In 1933, high ideals gave way to stark reality; nothing would accelerate disillusionment with Nazism as

2. "United by Pain, Divided by Politics"

effectively as Nazism itself. Some party members, including Fritz-Dietlof, began to have their doubts, but they still had to contend with a Nazified society in which their lives were already completely entangled.

It is important not to underestimate the increasing pressure placed upon those like Fritz-Dietlof who were members of the civil service, which was a much broader sector of employment in Nazi Germany than in most modern societies; it included schoolteachers, university staff, court staff, judges, and many other professions. The Nazis' campaign to align all facets of society with their party's goals—Gleichschaltung, meaning coordination, and effectively Nazification—was central to Hitler's vision of dictatorship. It would be brought about through a mixture of incentives, threats, legislation, terror, and brute force. Individuals and institutions were forced to weigh up the dangers and advantages posed by dissent or cooperation with the new regime (Evans 2005: 14). Fritz-Dietlof had always been aware that support for Hitler among his civil service colleagues was manifested in many different forms and degrees, and he regarded this as healthier than uniformity. There was ample room for his own brand of careful, critical optimism, and many shared his belief that Nazism could be channeled for good. This open-minded and basically supportive assessment, though only mildly critical of the Nazi party, was suddenly considered intolerably subversive, and the space for ideological movement within the civil service was about to become much smaller. The 1933 Civil Service Law (with parallel legislation for the armed forces) demanded that civil servants take an oath of personal loyalty to Hitler. The Law for the Restoration of the Professional Civil Service, in the same year, expelled all Jews and political opponents of the Nazis from government employment. The oath of fealty to Adolf Hitler in person replaced a previous oath taken to the Weimar constitution and to the office of president. The goal of these moves was a twofold one; to consolidate the Nazi dictatorship and to make individual Germans accomplices in Hitler's rule, under the guise of generously involving everyone in a great national revival (Kershaw 1993: 117).

The Schulenburg family on the whole was ready and willing to join in with the somewhat forced mood of national celebration in 1933. They had some reasons for celebration of their own; Friedrich's heir and firstborn son, Johann-Albrecht, finally wed at the age of thirty-five, to Angela Freiin von Schönberg, who was eight years his junior. They married in the cavalry chapel in Potsdam, on December 2, 1933, and would have six children over the next eleven years. Hitler sought to include more and more individual Germans—and "true" German families like Johann-Albrecht's—in his national project, but the concerns of thinking Nazis like Fritz-Dietlof,

Divided Over Hitler

who until recently had still spouted Hitlerian rhetoric, was a reminder that simmering divisions inside the Nazi party had not been quelled. In 1933, many Nazi party members, not least in the highly militant massed ranks of the SA, continued to believe in the revolutionary socialist promise of Nazism; now that power had been obtained, they expected the Nazi regime to take radical economic steps such as breaking up the vast landed estates of the aristocracy. One faction or the other was going to be bitterly disappointed; many disillusioned leftwing Nazis would in fact quit the Nazi party when the revolutionary talk ceased, which, in retrospect, was probably the safest course of action for them (Bullock 1962: 74–76). The loss of this portion of the membership was no minor setback. The very existence of the Nazi party in the north of Germany, the Schulenburgs' home territory, was owed to Gregor Strasser, the de facto leader of the party's left wing, but by 1933 he was hopelessly out of sync with the Hitlerite vision (Shirer 1960: 123). Hitler partly addressed the impasse, firstly, by unapologetically sidelining the SA, which had grown too powerful for his liking; the unruly SA also jeopardized his attempts to woo the conservative leaders of the official, conventional army. Hitler also resolved, meanwhile, to greatly enhance the influence and powers of the Schutzstaffel—the SS—which had begun as an adjunct of the SA, but had evolved, in line with the suggestion of Friedrich Graf von der Schulenburg, to be more directly and fanatically loyal to Hitler, and even less scrupulous in its methods than the sidelined SA (Kershaw 2008: 304–306, 309–314).

These actions did not really address the fundamental differences of orientation between left and right within the Nazi party. Strictly in terms of politics, Hitler still had to find a way to placate those Nazi party members who remained committed to conventional leftwing ideas—the self-declared revolutionaries and socialists—or conventional rightwing ideas—the conservatives and monarchists. On this occasion, no stroke of genius was forthcoming, and the strategy Hitler opted for was simple obfuscation and equivocation; he rather feebly claimed that the Nazi party was not exclusively for any one social class and that Nazism favored neither left nor right, preserving "pure" elements from both schools of thought (Domarus and Romane 2007: 171–73). Actions spoke louder than words, however, when Hitler violently purged his opponents from the movement in July 1934. At least one hundred, or, according to some calculations, hundreds of Hitler's perceived enemies were murdered, with most estimates ranging from four hundred to a thousand (Shirer 1960: 223). The vast number of dead included the upper leadership of the SA, starting with Gregor Strasser and other senior figures in the leftwing faction of the Nazi

2. "United by Pain, Divided by Politics"

party, but also critical senior conservative figures with no connection to the SA. This would go down in history as the Night of the Long Knives (die Nacht der langen Messer) (Evans 2015b: 98).

The Night of the Long Knives, therefore, was not just about purging or incapacitating the SA; many of the victims had simply been engaged in grudges or personal squabbles with Hitler or others, and a number of random Jews were also murdered, just to take advantage of the situation. A connection to the SA was certainly no indispensable requirement for being added to the hit list, and nor was simple membership of the SA necessarily the mark of death (Bullock 1962: 305). Even so, the evident targeting of the SA, which provided a home within the party for many left-leaning Nazis, sent out a stark message. It was well known that Fritz-Dietlof, though not a member of the SA, was, politically speaking, a Strasserite, and it is not clear exactly how close he came to elimination on the Night of the Long Knives (Mommsen 2009: 157). The path of the left-wing Nazi party member, even (or especially) one with position and influence such as Fritz-Dietlof, was not going to be straightforward from then onwards; such members would be forced to either reassess their stance or fade into the background. For Fritz-Dietlof this conflictive situation mirrored the profound and growing dissonance within his family. Even at that early stage, very few prominent families in the Third Reich presented such contrasts between siblings as the Schulenburg family did. There were, no doubt, many families that were divided on the subject of Hitler and Nazism, and then, later, on the subject of the war, euthanasia, the Jews, and the concentration camps; many families surely harbored both pro-Nazi and anti-Nazi elements; but the Schulenburg case was already developing into a scenario of absolute extremes, in which the individuals would be prepared to act upon their convictions.

Tisa von der Schulenburg was the only girl in a brood of five boys, and she had been a rebel since adolescence. So far, her relationship with her family had survived the dual shock of her rather decadent art career and marriage to a much older, divorced, Jewish art collector, Fritz Hesse. The Hesses' art world lifestyle in the Berlin of the late 1920s and early 1930s brought them into regular social contact with the leftwing and liberal intelligentsia of the Weimar years. They counted Brecht, Remarque, Zweig, and the Mann brothers among their friends and acquaintances. At home, Fritz provided Tisa with her own private gym, a personal art studio, and a houseful of astonishingly valuable art treasures. She still saw herself as leftwing, however, and shared her radical views with anyone who was ready to listen, suggesting that a sense of irony was perhaps not the young Tisa's strongest suit. Almost as soon as it started, however, the party lifestyle seemed to be drawing to a close; Fritz and Tisa, like Brecht, Zweig, and many others in their social circle, interpreted the signs of the times accurately and fled from Germany in 1933 and 1934. The Hesses settled in Highgate, London, where they found support from local Quakers, before gravitating towards the picturesque artists' enclave of Walberswick, near Southwold in Suffolk. The initial struggles, privations, and inconveniences of exile came as a shock to Tisa, who had never experienced anything resembling real poverty or scarcity before; it was the beginning of a time of reckoning, in which Tisa's leftwing sympathies were finally being put to the practical test (Seymour 2013: 263–64, 357–60).

It was the beginning of a time of reckoning for the rest of the Schulenburg family too; their political disagreements, which had been largely unspoken until then, started to become more evident now that the estranged, socialist Tisa had gone into exile. By 1935, Fritz-Dietlof was actually striving to decelerate his own rise within the Nazi party, feeling that he could more effectively mitigate the extreme effects of the Nazi regime from a lowlier, middle-ranking position, while also protecting himself. He was still by no means a confirmed anti-Nazi, but he was deeply troubled by the Nazi ways of getting things done—nepotism, duplicity, lawlessness—that had emerged, and he wanted to see himself as a moderating force, limiting Nazism's negative impact. It was too early to confide this to any of his siblings. On March 16, 1936, Friedrich, as if to eliminate any vestigial doubt as to the Schulenburg family's allegiance, resigned from the SA, and, at the sprightly age of seventy, was taken on as an Oberführer (colonel) in the ultra-loyal unit he himself had ideated, the SS. This was, coincidentally, the day on which Hitler established the Wehrmacht long service medal (Wehrmacht Dienstauszeichnung) in four classes, with its distinctive cornflower-blue ribbon, which was duly added to Friedrich's many prestigious awards. Friedrich had made history once again, as the only senior SS officer to have a socialist daughter and a Jewish son-in-law, both living in exile from Nazism. Friedrich would be rapidly promoted twice within the SS, first to Brigadeführer (brigade leader) and then to the senior two-star general's rank of Gruppenführer (group leader) (Haupt 2001: 111).

Wolf-Werner was also rising up; on June 13 of that same year, 1936, just six weeks before the start of the Olympics, he was appointed Gau leader of the Overseas Gau of the national sports association, and international advisor (Auslandsreferent) for the entire DRL (Teichler 1991: 111). He was not without convincing credentials for overseeing international relations,

2. "United by Pain, Divided by Politics"

after all; brought up in a bilingual household, he had lived for several years in England, his wife was half–American, he had done business internationally as a commercial lawyer and businessman, and his father's first cousin, Friedrich-Werner Graf von der Schulenburg, was Germany's ambassador in Moscow. Furthermore, Wolf-Werner's credentials as a German patriot—wounded wartime volunteer, Iron Cross recipient, Freikorps veteran, notably disdainful of Weimar, and early Nazi party member—were impeccable, according to Nazi standards. The Olympics promised to be, and indeed was, a tremendous spectacle of pageantry and pomp, showcasing Nazi Germany before thousands of foreign visitors and the world's press. Ordinary Germans did their best to resist the overt politicization of the event, offering a tumultuous welcome to all the international athletes without discrimination; above all, Germans appreciated this contact with the outside world, after several isolated years of national stir-craziness (Herwarth 1981: 106). At the state level, however, the Olympics was ultimately a grand theatrical performance, a public-relations sleight-of-hand, designed to pull an elaborate veil across the real goings-on inside Nazi Germany. It made an enormous international impression, topped only by the lavish Nuremburg rally of the following month (Bullock 1962: 355).

Tisa, exiled in Suffolk, England, had rekindled the Schulenburg affection for the Anglo-Saxon world, right at the moment when the new German vision rendered such dual affiliation unpatriotic. She would later recall her years in 1930s England as being among her happiest. She made friends with the sculptor Henry Moore (1898–1986) and, as a result of giving art lessons to unemployed miners, she formed an unlikely but lifelong association with the Durham mining community. At the same time that her beloved father and some of her less-beloved brothers were increasing their commitment to the Nazi cause, Tisa joined an "Artists Against Fascism" group in London. Rather predictably, the one brother with whom Tisa would always have a good relationship was Fritz-Dietlof. Being close in age, and with neither of them experiencing the pressures of being first- or second-born sons of the nobility, Tisa and Fritzi enjoyed an affinity that sustained them through the grim first postwar years. Tisa, though the younger of the two, had taught Fritzi English, and they had excitedly hatched a plan for Fritzi to claim British citizenship, having been born in London; this was their childhood fantasy for escaping the dark drudgery of postwar Germany (Seymour 2013: 252). Tisa had an affectionate though less close relationship with Wilhelm—the baby of the Schulenburg siblings and the only other non–Nazi apart from Tisa—and she suffered a long and inconsolable mourning when he was killed in a car accident in 1936. The grief only seemed to make the Schulenburgs' unspoken divisions even bitterer in Tisa's eyes; she lamented the irony that the family was united by pain and divided by politics (Seymour 2014). Tisa's difficulties were only just beginning, however; after ten years of marriage she and Hesse divorced in 1938, but by that time she had established herself in her own right, artistically and socially, in English society, which she always associated with personal and political liberty. It was Fritz-Dietlof's attachment to those same principles that increasingly drove him towards opposition to the Nazi regime; it was a protracted process to be sure, but the scales were steadily falling from his eyes. His slow maturation to opposing Nazism may be bewildering today, but it is not easy to imagine the psychological power wielded by the myth of a national renaissance, a cultural reawakening that had been longed for since those bleak early postwar years; these were aspirations that Nazi propaganda relentlessly exploited (Mommsen 2009: 159).

The Nazis' popularity was not solely built on intimidation and theatrics, and there were convincingly tangible benefits on offer, but this was not enough to fool perceptive, reflective people like Fritz-Dietlof forever. The Nazi party pledged to do what no other party had managed to do; extract Germany from the Depression and get Germans back to work, and thanks to good timing it appeared to be achieving just that. Right at the time of Hitler's appointment as chancellor, economic support programs launched by previous administrations were finally starting to alleviate the huge unemployment problem, and Hitler claimed the credit. Leaving nothing to chance, however, the Nazis also doctored the official unemployment statistics in order to convince the public of their success (Evans 2005: 329, 334–35). There were some genuine and transparent moves to encourage new businesses and to provide authentic, decent jobs, but the Nazis' job creation program was less about economic recovery and more about rearmament, both military and ideological. This had an added advantage; concealing rearmament behind terms like "job creation" in all public and private discourse helped the Nazis' to hide violations of the Treaty of Versailles, which was designed to severely limit the rebuilding of the German military. Defense contracts soon accounted for more than half of all iron, steel, engineering, and motor vehicle production, and the number of people employed in aircraft manufacture multiplied twentyfold. The Krupp conglomerate began production of "large tractors"—in reality tanks—and several major firms turned to producing "sporting goods"—actually firearms—for the state. While rearmament certainly did create jobs, it primarily advanced the Nazis' true longer-term goal of reestablishing

2. "United by Pain, Divided by Politics"

Germany as a European military power, and through deception the Nazis achieved this in a way that evaded censure and avoided alerting the other powers. Domestically, however, facts were still facts; Hitler effectively honored his pledge to solve the unemployment problem within four years of taking office, and the incessant triumphalist propaganda, the constant bleating that the "battle for work" had been won, was both well-received and difficult to refute. Many erstwhile doubters and skeptics were won over, and the Third Reich's existing supporters received a huge confidence boost (Evans 2005: 333, 338–41). Some doubters, however, were only disconcerted even more.

Reflecting on the superficial patriotism and fanatical atmosphere of the first four years of Nazi rule, Fritz-Dietlof saw that his moral objections had met with incomprehension from his fellow Nazi officials, rather than actual suspicion. He had shown an unfathomable (in retrospect) willingness to give Hitler and the Nazi leadership the benefit of the doubt, while doing his best to humanize the regime from within it; now, he began to conclude that Nazism was irredeemable. "To begin with" he wrote, "I looked for opportunities to remedy this evil by reform. But gradually I came to realize that reform would no longer do any good, since everything is interlinked and based on fundamental facts which are immutably bound up with the nature of the system" (Mommsen 2009: 163). Fritz-Dietlof's conflicts with his superior, Erich Koch, had intensified as the decade progressed, but he had managed to dodge any serious confrontation through a succession of sideways career moves within the Reich Interior Ministry. In 1937 he was posted to Berlin as vice president of police; there is a suggestion here too that this move was actually Koch's final, successful attempt to rid himself of his unorthodox subordinate (Gregory 2018: 88). Fritz-Dietlof's immediate superior was now the Berlin president of police, Wolf Heinrich Graf von Helldorff (1896–1944) who, despite their families being related, had long contrived to avoid having the controversial Fritz-Dietlof assigned to his jurisdiction. Contrary to their own expectations, however, the two men got along well, and Fritz-Dietlof would later stand in for Helldorff, briefly, as Berlin's police president (Mengden 1980: 73). The reason for the two men's affinity may come as no surprise; Helldorff was also in the process of turning against the regime, and he too would eventually pay the ultimate price for his opposition. In 1937, however, Fritz-Dietlof and his secret inclinations were temporarily safe.

On April 1, 1938, on the occasion of the fiftieth anniversary of his joining the army, Friedrich was made an honorary full four-star general of the cavalry. During his long career he had received such an utterly bewildering array of chivalric orders, knight's crosses, decorations, and medals, that the honorary generalship was one of the few remaining honors he did not already possess. Both Friedrich and Freda were seriously ill, however—he suffered symptoms of tuberculosis while she had had a stroke—and Tisa received letters from her mother, pleading with her to come home. Tisa was torn, and Freda's letters grew insistent. Reading the signs of the times, from the vantage point of peaceful Walberswick, was increasingly difficult, in fairness to Tisa. Hitler's remilitarization of the Rhineland and annexation of Austria—the Anschluss—alternated with the supposed success of the Munich agreement—promising "peace in our time" but sounding more like "placation for the moment"—so that, on the whole, it was hard to be optimistic about the future (Seymour 2013: 417, 418). The Rhineland, the Berlin Olympics, the Anschluss, and German participation in the Spanish Civil War all kept Hitler in the international news in the late 1930s. While some marveled at Hitler's achievements in reenergizing Germany, many foreign observers inside Germany itself developed a very different view of the man and his party. Some of them finally began to see all of the Nazis' efforts as part of orchestrated preparations for war, and it seemed that many Germans broadly approved of the more-or-less unspoken plan to make their nation a world power once again. Many young Nazis openly expressed their enthusiasm for militarization, and, far from denying the prospect of a war with chemical, bacteriological, and even supersonic weapons, they actually relished it. Myths of German invincibility were widespread, and the Nazis encouraged them (Moskin 2013: 371). If, however, war turned out not to be imminent after all, foreign observers believed, it would be difficult to rein-in the warlike spirit of young Germans and channel their violent energies into socially positive endeavors. War, for good or ill, seemed to be the only logical outlet for this build-up of violent energy (Gillette 2011: 32).

By 1938, however, the erstwhile uncritical enthusiasm for Nazism felt by a significant number of Germans was beginning to wane, and most people merely sought to keep going on with their daily lives and survive. They superficially went along with the Nazis' various programs, campaigns, and initiatives, to be sure, but an increasing number of Germans grew indifferent to and even bored of the constant parades, propaganda, and other staged public displays of adulation and hysteria. Nazi officials noted that contributions to Hitler's birthday present were suddenly very poor; only half of potential subscribers had donated anything to the fund. The remainder would, of course, be forced to pay up, but the fact that they had not done so voluntarily was troubling to the Nazis. The Italian ambassador

2. "United by Pain, Divided by Politics"

in Berlin felt that Hitler enjoyed little real popularity among the capital's residents, which seemed to be confirmed by the lukewarm crowds at Hitler's birthday celebrations of 1937 and 1938. In general, there seemed to be some reluctance to take part in rallies and parades; even Nazi party conference celebrations, which were naturally aimed at party members, met with limited enthusiasm. All the more logical then, that ordinary people found the endless ceremonies and speeches dull and repetitive, and few were keen to make the trip to attend the Nuremberg rally again (Bankier 1992: 57). No such halfhearted participation would be tolerated on April 20, 1939, however. Hitler turned fifty years old, and a wave of honors and appointments were bestowed upon the faithful, demonstrating the Führer's special birthday magnanimity. Friedrich von der Schulenburg became one of only a handful of people ever promoted to the three-star general rank of Obergruppenführer in the SS, the highest achievable rank, second only to the Reichsführer-SS, Heinrich Himmler. The appointment was backdated to take effect from January 30, presumably because of Friedrich's state of health. Just one month later, on May 19, 1939, he died of tuberculosis, aged seventy-three (Seymour 2013: 418).

3

"A Statesman Bent Upon Action"

Diplomacy and Dissent in the East, 1934–1941

"All war represents a failure of diplomacy."—Tony Benn, to the British parliament, February 28, 1991

"All diplomacy is a continuation of war by other means."—Zhou Enlai, quoted in the *Saturday Evening Post,* March 27, 1954

General and SS-Obergruppenführer Friedrich Bernhard Graf von der Schulenburg's death in 1939 provoked some interesting and significant responses, beginning with a state funeral being ordered by Hitler for May 24, with instructions that the military cortege first pass through the traditional army citadel of Potsdam. Hitler, Himmler, and Field Marshal Walther von Brauchitsch, the army commander-in-chief, attended. The subdued pageant was intended to underline the martial dignity and historic continuity of the new Germany, demonstrating a sobering solemnity that contrasted with Hitler's recent lavish birthday celebrations (Singapore Free Press 1939: 12). Tisa had returned to Germany in time to say a last goodbye to her father, and remained for the funeral, but both she and her mother vowed to eschew the funereal military parade in Potsdam. This was the first clear sign that the widowed Countess Freda's enthusiasm for Hitler was less than total; it was her subtle gesture of sympathy with Tisa and Fritz-Dietlof. Himmler, however, pushed for a second funeral procession to be held at Tressow Castle; he intended to trumpet this as a strictly SS event, and, as it would take place at their castle home, even the dissenting Schulenburgs could hardly shun it. The forced symbolism of the new regime, with the SS publicly saluting the Prussian general, the Kaiser's former attaché and advisor, who had dueled for the honor of Germany,

3. "A Statesman Bent Upon Action"

was blatant. Friedrich was one of the old guard, an outspoken supporter of the aristocracy and the monarchy, who had also—eventually, and perhaps not entirely without reservation—endorsed the new order. In the person of Friedrich, the old Germany had seamlessly blended into the new Germany, and the Nazi leaders were understandably falling over themselves to celebrate his life. In retrospect, knowing that this was only three months before the outbreak of war, the irony is particularly strong (Seymour 2013: 418).

The following month, June 1939, Hitler ordered that the Mecklenburg Black Guard, the local Tressow regiment, be renamed the Friedrich Graf von der Schulenburg Regiment in homage to the late Count (Singapore Free Press 1939: 12). The whole matter of the Schulenburg patriarch's passing was kept deliberately high-profile, which, while obviously focused on honoring the ancient warrior who had accepted Nazism, inevitably also drew public attention to the Schulenburg family, and this, in light of the growing dissidence of some family members, would have been a cause for concern. In 1939, however, as the prospect of war in both east and west became increasingly real, the most publicly recognizable Schulenburg was not a member of the immediate family nucleus headed by the late Friedrich; it was his cousin, Friedrich-Werner, Germany's ambassador to the USSR. As well as being near-namesakes, the two cousins were born almost exactly ten years apart; Friedrich was born on November 21, 1865, and his cousin Friedrich-Werner was born on November 20, 1875. Friedrich-Werner Erdmann Matthias Johann Bernhard Erich Graf von der Schulenburg was the second son of Bernhard Friedrich Wilhelm Graf von der Schulenburg, who was born on May 10, 1839; he was the younger brother of Werner Ludwig Ernst Karl Heinrich Achat Graf von der Schulenburg, Friedrich's father. An older brother to Friedrich-Werner, named Friedrich, had been born the year before him, and had died before reaching the age of one. This relentless repetition of the same names—Friedrich, Werner, Bernhard, Ludwig, Wilhelm—can be a source of confusion nowadays, but at the time it was an important method of paying homage, and a vital display of family unity and continuity. First cousins in the aristocracy were considered "second brothers" and they were accordingly given similar names; given the scope for confusion, it is no surprise that several German texts refer to Friedrich-Werner as being the uncle of Tisa, Fritz-Dietlof, and Wolf-Werner, rather than their first cousin once removed and their father's first cousin (Heinemann 1994: 167).

For the two noble cousins, Friedrich and Friedrich-Werner, reaching

Divided Over Hitler

adulthood in the final decades of the nineteenth century, the available choices of profession were predictable; the "arts" of war and diplomacy, sometimes regarded as opposites, were the career staples of the German aristocracy. Until the collapse of the imperial hierarchy after the First World War, sons of the nobility risked estrangement if they dared to consider a career in anything as lowly and mundane as business or even what would today be called company management. Even a legal career, as honorable as the law was in principle, risked exposing a young man to the tawdriness and conniving of ordinary life, unsuitable for an aristocratic son. Party politics, meanwhile, was far too modern and novel a concept and far too grubby a pastime to interest young nobles. The aristocracy, it was felt, was called by divine will to lead society through moral rectitude, not through bartering, politicking, or the mere accumulation of wealth, and their secular professions should reflect the timeless mystique of this higher calling. The only public roles upon which the fates of states really hung were the military and the diplomatic corps. Joining some administrative branch of the vast civil service would hardly make a young man's pulse race, but it was an acceptable alternative for a third- or fourth-born son, perhaps. Apart from these career options there were of course the duties associated with owning land, if they were lucky enough to inherit any, and this role generally belonged to the firstborn son. Much changed after 1919; business, law, government, teaching, and even journalism would become acceptable careers for aristocrats. Friedrich himself, worried about money, considered going into the tobacco trade, and his children, the younger generation of Schulenburgs, fully adapted to the career choices available, through force of history rather than their personal eccentricities. Friedrich, however, in his youth, was earmarked for the army. Friedrich-Werner's branch of the family was apparently less wealthy than Friedrich's, and when he took the first steps towards a diplomatic career he veered towards the less glamorous and highly bureaucratic consular service, rather than the prestigious and romantic diplomatic corps itself, which required a more costly degree of social mobility, physical mobility—travel money—and education (Herwarth 1981: 91).

The young Friedrich-Werner completed his compulsory one year of service in the army, serving with the First Guards Field Artillery Regiment, and then studied law in Lausanne, Munich, and Berlin, while remaining in the officers' reserve of his regiment. He entered the consular service in 1901, which sadly coincided with his father's illness and then death the following year. His early consular career took him to

3. "A Statesman Bent Upon Action"

Barcelona, Lemberg (Lviv, Ukraine), Prague, Warsaw, and Tiflis (Tbilisi, Georgia). His years in Warsaw left a particularly strong impression on him; he would retain a lifelong affection for the Polish people, and their suffering would have a decisive influence on his later choices. On May 12, 1908, Friedrich-Werner began a short-lived marriage to Elisabeth von Sobbe (1875–1955), who gave birth to their daughter, Christa, on December 29 of the same year. They divorced in 1910 (Ruvigny 1914: 1333). When the First World War broke out in 1914, Friedrich-Werner returned to the army, serving with the First Guards Field Artillery Regiment at the First Battle of the Marne. He was promoted to captain in October 1914 and given command of an artillery battery. In 1915 he was appointed as liaison officer to the Third Army of the Ottoman Empire, Germany's ally, stationed on the Armenian front. By October 1915 he had effectively returned to a diplomatic role, first in Turkey and then in Georgia. He was instrumental in launching the Georgian Legion, a unit devised for political ends, as they aimed to destabilize Russian imperial rule and fight for Georgian independence. Friedrich-Werner's wartime service earned him the Iron Cross and several honors from the Ottoman Empire. After the defeat of both the German and Ottoman Empires in 1918, he was interned by the British on the island of Prinkipo (Büyükada), near Istanbul. At this time he learned that his mother had died. After returning to Germany in 1919, he was appointed German consul in Beirut. Having risen up through the consular service for twenty years, in 1922 he was named German ambassador to Iran, where he served for nine years before being transferred to Romania in 1931, and finally to Moscow (Stackelberg 2007: 1964).

Friedrich-Werner arrived in Moscow in the autumn of 1934, when he was nearly fifty-nine years old. With his considerable experience, professional apoliticality, and personal credibility, he brought with him an air of reassurance at a time of growing uncertainty. Initial impressions of the new ambassador among the Moscow diplomatic set confirmed his reputation as the very model of a true diplomat; one who accepts the status quo that he or she finds and aims to work within it as well as possible, looking for opportunities to do the right thing. Friedrich-Werner was considered cautious, friendly, fair, and likeable. He had acquired a vast cultural acumen and an incisive knowledge of the East, the Levant, the Caucasus, and the Balkans. In his dealings with the locals, he seemed to represent the version of Germany that Russians had historically always liked, not the new Nazi version. Looking back, it can be difficult to imagine an atmosphere of mutual respect and cordial affinity between Germany and

Divided Over Hitler

Russia, especially in the 1930s, but, in fact, German-Soviet cooperation, up until 1934, was much more extensive than history often records. The German armed forces had at least three semi-secret bases on Soviet soil, carrying out tank testing, pilot training, even joint chemical weapon trials alongside the armed forces of the USSR, and these are only the military collaborations that were well known-about. The benefit to Germany, of course, was that these projects circumvented the restrictions of the Treaty of Versailles. Stalin, meanwhile, was keen to monitor developments in Germany, but when Hitler came to power in 1933, both leaders turned towards animosity rather than affinity. This was despite the fact that Hitler initially vowed no change to German foreign policy with Russia; the reality could hardly have unfolded more differently (Herwarth 1981: 56–58, 89–90).

Despite the gradual freezing of international relations after 1933, there was still a high degree of cooperation and communication between the various embassy staffs present in Moscow. Being somewhat remote from the rest of the world and also somewhat excluded from local goings-on, a type of "ghetto" atmosphere developed among members of the diplomatic community. This environment fostered some exceptional and long-lasting friendships between British, German, American, and Italian staffs, in obvious stark contrast to the growing hostility between those countries. Life for diplomatic personnel in 1930s Moscow was not all good and not all bad; consumer goods were scarce, and embassy staffs resorted to the black market, even for things like currency exchange, but many diplomats were able to devote their time (and funds) to collecting extraordinary antiquities and rare books. There was also a lively social scene, encouraged by senior diplomats like Friedrich-Werner; he was no bon vivant himself, but he was socially popular, especially with younger staffers who valued the opportunity to mix and find new friends. Christa, Friedrich-Werner's somewhat estranged only child, made an appearance in Moscow; the father-daughter relationship was frosty, but, seeing how fond people were of her father, Christa discovered a new affection for him; Friedrich-Werner felt that he had regained his daughter. With regard to the future outlook and the inevitable question of politics, a fairly wide variety of views were represented among the young German expats, though hardly any of them were really committed Nazis. A key member of the German staff was Hans-Heinrich Herwarth von Bittenfeld (1904–1999), more often known as Johann or Johnnie von Herwarth; he was strongly anti–Nazi and had been so, instinctively, from the beginning. Herwarth, whose memoirs provide a truly unique record of events in Moscow and, later, in the German

3. "A Statesman Bent Upon Action"

Resistance, had been in Russia since 1931, first working in the consular section before being appointed secretary to the ambassador. Viewing events in Germany from afar, Herwarth had experienced short-lived joy at the reelection of Hindenburg in 1932, only to see his hopes dissolve with the appointment of Hitler as chancellor. In 1933, his concerns increased when the then-ambassador showed little patience or skill in dealing with Hitler. The potential volatility of the whole situation worried the staff, and the newly arrived Ambassador Schulenburg's gentleness and passivity led many to believe that he too would crumble if the going got tough (Herwarth 1981: 11, 33, 60–63, 70–79, 84, 92–100).

Friedrich-Werner did not have an overriding personal vision for his diplomatic mission, but he adhered to the line that maintaining good relations between the USSR and Germany, or at the very least the absence of conflict, was essential for the future good of his country. He was, and would remain, an optimist with regard to the two countries' joint future, reasoning that apart from the First World War relations had mostly been good for well over a century, and that, ultimately, countries usually do what is in their best interests (Herwarth 1981: 112–13). This may sound naïve nowadays, but the general consensus was that Germany and Russia flourished when they got along and suffered when they did not, and Friedrich-Werner concurred with this assessment. Back in 1922, in fact, he had been a driving force behind the Treaty of Rapallo, which had, against considerable resistance, cemented Russo-German friendship in the face of the somewhat overbearing victors of the First World War (Bullock 1962: 515). There was reason to believe, in fact, that a certain forcefulness of character lay behind Ambassador Schulenburg's eager-to-please exterior, and to the surprise and relief of many he handled meetings with Hitler calmly and forthrightly. Others, including Schulenburg's predecessors, were easily provoked into losing their temper with the Führer. If Friedrich-Werner had anything resembling early Resistance sympathies, however, he gave no hint whatsoever, and he would have been absolutely opposed, as a matter of basic principle, to the idea of forcibly removing any head of state. He was devoted to law and order and he was also a man of religious faith, though apparently not an assiduous churchgoer. His Christian beliefs were thought to explain his practice of being somewhat indiscriminately courteous and respectful, regardless of who was present, and this impartiality, along with a few mild eccentricities, sometimes irritated his staff. Nevertheless, when the moment finally came to show what he was made of, Friedrich-Werner did not disappoint (Herwarth 1981: 66–68, 88).

Divided Over Hitler

Since 1933, a number of Jews had fled Germany to seek refuge in the USSR; it was not the most popular choice of destination, but for some, whether for reasons of family, practicality, or political sympathy, it offered an emergency solution. In general, the Jews were not made especially welcome in the USSR, partly, perhaps, because their motives were considered suspect—they were still Germans, in the eyes of the world, as well as Jews—and partly because the local authorities in Russia feared a coming onslaught of refugees. Whatever the precise reason, many Jewish refugees felt uncomfortable and wanted to leave the USSR. This presented them with a significant problem, because in many cases their passports had either expired or been invalidated, while others had fled Germany without proper papers to begin with. Being allowed to take refuge in the USSR had not been a problem, but moving on to a third country would require a valid German passport, and German diplomatic missions had received a standing order that Jews requesting the issue or renewal of passports or documents must be turned away. Herwarth was approached in semi-secret by a Jewish refugee of his acquaintance, and Herwarth in turn explained this dilemma to the ambassador. It was a turning point for Friedrich-Werner. He agreed to provide the Jews with passports, and the practice would continue in secrecy for several years (Herwarth 1981: 66–68, 88).

History had thus provided Friedrich-Werner von der Schulenburg with one of those decisions that would launch a ripple effect. A similar situation to the Jewish dilemma presented itself in the case of certain notable and less-notable political dissidents, including some German communists who had fled Germany since 1933. For one reason or another, whether personal, political, or practical, many of them were disillusioned with life in the USSR and wanted to leave. Friedrich-Werner, once again with the support of Johnnie von Herwarth, was disposed to assist them, just as they had done with the Jews. From one perspective, this most certainly constituted disobedience to Hitler's lawful directives, but it must also be said that when Herwarth made discreet enquiries about these German political dissidents, the response from Berlin was that Germany was not interested in having them back, not even in order to punish them. The actions of Schulenburg and Herwarth were all the more commendable, therefore, because they were not actually required to do anything for these German refugees. Inaction would have been the "patriotic" thing to do, officially. The right thing to do, in practice, ended up being the deciding factor. It was not ideology, politics, or radicalization that would gradually transform Friedrich-Werner into an opponent of Nazism, but rather the simple realization that people—families, civilians, Jews, Poles, children,

3. "A Statesman Bent Upon Action"

grandparents—were suffering; it was an idea that he could not bear and would not be a part of. It aggrieved him as a Christian, as an aristocrat, and perhaps most strongly as a human being. Johnnie von Herwarth witnessed the transformation of his superior with a mixture of satisfaction and trepidation. Schulenburg was no longer "a loveable but passive Eastern sage," Herwarth recalled, "where he had once been a skilled observer and diplomat, he now became a statesman bent upon action" (Herwarth 1981: 66–68, 95–96).

Even before Friedrich-Werner's arrival in Moscow, there was an unspoken diplomatic policy of resisting interference from the Nazi party. At the embassy, the morning round of "guten Tag" was never replaced with the officially required "Heil Hitler." The Nazi party had its own "embassies" of sorts, in the organization for Germans living abroad—Auslandsorganisation—which included the sports representation mentioned earlier, for which Wolf-Werner von der Schulenburg was responsible. These overseas party representatives had no understanding of foreign policy work as such, and they tactlessly tried to pressure the embassies into publicizing Nazism, as though Nazism were synonymous with Germany. Friedrich-Werner repelled these efforts. He also managed to convince the Nazi hierarchy that opening a Nazi party branch in communist Moscow would be a waste of time; the Nazis, as it turned out, cared little about Russia and felt no urge to bestow their great "culture" upon the ungrateful "subhuman" Slavs. Moscow, diplomatically speaking, was considered a hardship posting, which is probably why a non-Aryan like Johnnie von Herwarth, who was a quarter Jewish, got away with staying there for so long, while other non-Aryans were purged. Herwarth would eventually be the only non-Aryan remaining in the entire government foreign service. Schulenburg did concede to having an individual Nazi party representative stationed at the embassy, but he or she was to be chosen from among the existing staff, and approved by the ambassador. As a result of their careful choice, Nazi party events such as fundraisers and rallies were never held at the embassy. Those chosen as party representative tended to be fairly convinced Nazis, though somewhat confused and ill-informed ones, not militant, and they could easily be shielded from sensitive embassy business. More troublesome Nazi party members did visit the embassy, for various reasons, whether on official or commercial business, and there were concerns that they would report the various infractions of rules, large and small, such as the absence of "Heil Hitlers" at the embassy. However, these Nazis were conscious of being mere visitors in a potentially—or even tangibly—hostile country, and they knew that they might

Divided Over Hitler

regret making enemies at the embassy, which was their only lifeline in case of trouble. Common sense won the day, therefore, and even very committed visiting Nazis turned a blind eye to anomalies in embassy discipline (Herwarth 1981: 97–100).

Before long, Friedrich-Werner developed an approach that would prove providential; he sought to emphasize the safeguarding of Germany's normal economic relations with the USSR, and vowed to use this emphasis to keep the channels of communication open at all costs. As a diplomat, he was aware of which matters he could effectively influence, avoiding the quagmire of ideological politics, and which topics would be best kept at arm's length, such as defense. His military concerns were limited to reporting, sincerely, that Soviet defense seemed to be focused on just that, defensive measures, and he perceived no aggressive military ambitions. This report was intended to defuse warlike sentiments in Berlin, but it may have had the effect of encouraging the view of Russia as a potentially easy prey (Stackelberg 2007: 1964). Enmity between the two nations, in fact, appeared to be increasing, and the broader European picture was far from reassuring; this situation would lead Schulenburg to become a passionate supporter of a non-aggression pact between Germany and the Soviet Union. In 1936, the alliances that were to fight the Second World War, three years later, were not established or obvious. Britain's allies of the First World War, Japan and Italy, were equivocal in their loyalties and ambitions, while the orientation of the USSR was something of a mystery to all.

The Spanish Civil War, which quickly descended into a fascist-versus-communist proxy war, with Germany and Italy against the USSR, added no clarity to the situation. The British and the French exerted themselves to stay out of it, but this was complicated by the fact that individuals from Britain and France, not to mention the USA and Canada, organized volunteer units to fight in Spain against fascism. Meanwhile, with regard to Central and Eastern Europe, the Munich conference in September 1938 was destined to be both a clarifier and a catalyst. Britain and France aimed to avoid confusion by not inviting the USSR to Munich, but they did not foresee the impact of this exclusion and the message that it sent to Stalin. The West—the British and the French—were now definitively cast as the appeasers of Hitler, arrogating to themselves the power to permit him to do as he wished in the east; the Munich conference actually allowed for only a partial German annexation of Czechoslovakia, but this was regarded as a "gateway" concession. The synthesis of all this was that no Western power, it seemed, would consider standing beside faraway Russia in their wildest

3. "A Statesman Bent Upon Action"

dreams, whatever Hitler might do. Britain and France's hinting at pledging eventual guarantees to support Poland and other countries merely looked to Stalin like arbitrary lines in the sand; Hitler, meanwhile, could not afford to ignore the possibility of those Western pledges being formalized, as long as there was an outside chance of the British and French actually keeping their word. Neither Hitler nor Stalin now had a serious and powerful friend in the West (Kershaw 2008: 487–90).

Hitler's displeasure with the situation after Munich, especially the prospect of British and French pledges to support Poland, triggered a rapid overhaul of German policy towards Moscow. At the Berghof, his vacation home in the Bavarian Alps, Hitler gathered his inner circle and talked openly of a potential alliance or pact with the USSR, and he even found one or two positive things to say about Stalin. Joachim von Ribbentrop (1893–1946), Hitler's foreign minister, was given the go-ahead to pursue negotiations with Moscow; when consulted, Schulenburg assured the foreign minister that Stalin was open to a rapprochement, which he was, and this was the insider encouragement that Ribbentrop needed (Kershaw 2008: 488–89). There were vital practical reasons for pursuing a deal as well as strictly political ones; trade with the West was likely to deteriorate or cease entirely, so it made perfect sense to court Germany's existing provider of raw materials in the east. Both nations, in light of the international situation, had military ambitions of sorts, whether defensive (USSR) or aggressive (Germany), and these ambitions necessitated an exchange of raw materials from the former and advanced engineering from the latter. As a result, trade talks began in late 1938, in the wake of Munich. Schulenburg was already in tune with the emphasis of these talks, as he had long considered trade to be the main—and safest—basis for German-Soviet diplomacy. Schulenburg wanted a pact based on business, not war. By the following spring, Britain and France had cemented their pledges to aid Poland, Belgium, Romania, Greece, and Turkey, formalizing this as a military alliance; Hitler in turn repudiated the 1934 German-Polish non-aggression pact and scrapped the 1935 Anglo-German naval agreement (Shirer 1960: 476–77, 492–94).

The prospect of an agreement (it was never an alliance as such) between the USSR and Germany was, and would always be, undermined by the two nations' mutual distrust, which, paradoxically, seemed to have increased in proportion to the likelihood of a pact. This animosity was reinforced by rash public statements affirming the two nations' supposedly deep-rooted enmity; after all, the destruction of Bolshevism had been a staple of Hitler's oratory for two decades. His speeches, including those at Nuremberg, not only violently attacked the USSR but also floated outrageous territorial claims, such as seizing the Ukraine and the Urals; this was highly provocative considering that Hitler had already acted on similar territorial claims, such as the "reoccupation" of the Rhineland (Herwarth 1981: 107). Against logic, therefore, the strongest basis for driving forward to a pact could only be the two leaders' personal goals, which trampled upon all other considerations, limitations, and warnings; Stalin needed to avoid a war that he had no reason to believe he could survive economically or militarily, while Hitler's priorities were to isolate Poland and neuter the threat from the Western powers (Kershaw 2008: 489). Understandably however, given the residual bad feeling, the Russians did not seem eager to begin negotiations. Schulenburg had it on good authority that Hitler, too, was worried about paying the price for his reckless threats and demands, but his attacks on the USSR were largely tolerated because trade between the two countries was already successful; Germany even extended generous credit to the USSR, who paid well and paid in gold (Herwarth 1981: 108).

Both sides, therefore, were apparently willing to live with the inconsistencies in their relationship; it was like an unspoken pact, to precede the formal, written one. Behind the bluster and rhetoric, Hitler actually prioritized economic recovery over ideology, at least in the immediate term, and so did Stalin. In this sense, Hitler's vision was similar to Schulenburg's, except that, for the ambassador, peacemaking was an end in itself, not just a means. Both sides still struggled, however, to paste over the cracks in German-Soviet relations, and attacks in both nations' press continued. Schulenburg was deeply committed to the idea of the pact, and he proved himself to be indispensable in achieving it. Quintessentially diplomatic and characteristically subtle, he approached Maxim Maximovich Litvinov (1876–1951), Stalin's foreign minister—or People's Commissar for Foreign Affairs—shortly after Munich, with a proposal; they would use their influence, personality, and connections to persuade their respective countries' press to cease attacking Stalin and Hitler. This "gentlemen's agreement" was credited with vastly improving relations between the two countries and removing a major obstacle to the pact; it is now an almost-forgotten piece of brilliant diplomacy (Herwarth 1981: 108, 142).

It suddenly emerged that the USSR was still exploring other options and were in talks with Britain; this revelation unnerved the Germans and weakened their negotiating verve. The USSR, Britain, and France, despite other differences, shared a common wariness of Hitler's expansionism, but they could not agree on what to do about it. Informal "tripartite"

3. "A Statesman Bent Upon Action"

consultations began in April 1939, with formal talks beginning the following month. Hitler countered this by sending word through diplomatic backchannels to assure the Russians that Germany would beat any deal offered by Britain or France; in fact, the Russians struggled to find any reason to trust the capitalist Western powers over Germany (Bullock 1962: 515–17). One way or another, a choice had to be made; if Stalin was to achieve his goal of avoiding war, he needed an alliance with someone. Unconvinced by the West, he told them he would settle for nothing less than an ironclad alliance, with guaranteed military intervention in the event of a German invasion; it would then become a two-pronged counterattack on Germany (as eventually had to happen in 1944–45). Stalin's priority was of course the defense of the Soviet Union rather than Europe-wide peace or foiling Hitler, but in any case Britain and France so thoroughly doubted the USSR's ability to fight that they still regarded the general avoidance of war to be the more valid objective. The French, being located on the continent, were actually more willing to satisfy Stalin than Britain was, as the French were more conscious of the dangers of a pact between the Russians and the Germans. Stalin drew the conclusion that the West was trying, and would continue to try, to goad Germany into attacking Russia, and he viewed Hitler as quite susceptible to being goaded. Stalin knew that Hitler's priority was to have Poland at his mercy, but Stalin also had to consider the threat from the Japanese in the Russian Far East (Kershaw 2008: 488). Japan and China had already been at war for several years, and it was clear to no-one how far Japan's expansionism would go (Herwarth 1981: 113).

These contrasting considerations, shifting stances, and complex political calculations largely explain why the USSR has often been described as cynically playing both sides against each other during 1939, conducting open negotiations for a military alliance with Britain and France while secretly considering propositions from Germany. In reality, Stalin's bargaining position was one of desperation and urgency rather than strategy and strength. So far, however, no side had exactly triumphed. The sluggish progress and ultimate failure of the tripartite negotiations meant the loss of a great opportunity to prevent German aggression. Britain and France's half-heartedness was evident, which only encouraged Hitler to believe that a German-Soviet isolation of Poland would expose Britain's pledges as worthless. By July 1939 it was clear that Germany and the Soviet Union were determined to reach an agreement. The Germans honed their strategy once again; in order to maximize the chances of clinching a foothold deal, they switched the emphasis from political and military cooperation back to Ambassador Schulenburg's recommended priority, economics; the trade agreements would be signed and sealed first, then they would move onto the topic of "non-aggression." Friedrich-Werner felt increasingly vindicated and justified in emphasizing trade as the basis of German-Soviet relations; his trade-based approach long predated the current negotiations, and it now had two increasingly appealing features; as war seemed likely, all states had to consider the impact of sea blockades and closed borders on their vital supply lines. More than ever, close and powerful neighbors would be necessary. The main arguments for momentarily putting aside political and military negotiations were equally obvious; the extent of the ideological gulf between Germany and the USSR was becoming increasingly evident through the negotiations, while German-Soviet military cooperation, which had once been excellent, was practically non-existent, having passed its peak by 1933 (Shirer 1960: 492–94; Kershaw 2008: 488, 489).

Hitler, through Ribbentrop, began to constantly pressure Schulenburg to drive home the deal quickly; secretly, the Führer was now fixated on a late-summer invasion of Poland, and he wanted the pact to be firmly in place first. They did not pressure Schulenburg daily, Johnnie von Herwarth recalled, they pressured him hourly. The ambassador complied, with such an enthusiasm for non-aggression that Hitler began to wonder where his loyalties really lay. The disparity in the two men's goals—peace for the sake of peace, and peace to buy time for war preparations—was not a secret within the circles of diplomacy and governance, but the mounting pressure increased the risk of Schulenburg being exposed as a doubter or condemned outright as an anti-Nazi (Herwarth 1981: 144–45, 152). Stalin, who was also under pressure to show seriousness and commitment to achieving an agreement, suddenly fired his long-serving foreign minister, Litvinov, and replaced him with Vyacheslav Mikhailovich Molotov (1890–1986). Litvinov was Jewish and, influenced by having served as ambassador to the USA, he was an advocate of rapprochement with the West. Molotov, meanwhile, was a member of Stalin's Politburo, unlike Litvinov, and he fully appreciated the pressing usefulness of bringing the talks with Germany to a successful conclusion. One of Molotov's first acts was to personally warn Schulenburg that negotiations were about to become tough, and to assure him that they would ultimately be successful (Kershaw 2008: 488–89). By early August 1939, in fact, Germany and the Soviet Union were working out the last details of the new trade deal, and with its signing on August 19, attention could now turn to the potential political and military agreement. Officials from both sides began by seeking

3. "A Statesman Bent Upon Action"

to explain-away their erstwhile hostility, and emphasize their common ideological ground in opposition to Western capitalism. German delegates studied and echoed Schulenburg's long-held theory of a "convergence" between German and Soviet aspirations and interests (Herwarth 1981: 117–18).

The official suspension of the tripartite talks coincided with Hitler's assurance that Stalin's demands for a Soviet sphere of influence would be acknowledged militarily and politically; the deciding factor in their "non-aggression" pact was, ironically, the setting of agreed limits on each side's aggressive ambitions. Stalin responded clamorously to this assurance, announcing that the USSR was now willing to sign the pact, and that he would personally receive Ribbentrop in Moscow (Shirer 1960: 520–28). On August 23, 1939, two Focke-Wulf Condors (one of them Hitler's private airplane), each packed with around twenty German diplomats and officials, led by Ribbentrop, descended into Moscow. The Nazi emissaries disembarked to the strains of "Deutschland über Alles" played by the military band of the Red Army Guards division. No detail was overlooked for the staging of this diplomatic coup; the red flags' hammers and sickles brushed against the black swastikas of the red and white Nazi banners (they were made for a Soviet propaganda film and had been borrowed from the nearby studios for the occasion). Ribbentrop was warmly greeted by Ambassador Schulenburg and led to a waiting NKVD (internal affairs police) limousine, heading to Red Square. Emerging near Stalin's office, the Germans were led up a flight of stairs to a long room with lavish Tsarist-era furnishings. True to his word, Stalin, waiting with Molotov, welcomed the visitors warmly and in person, much to the Nazis' surprise. It was well known that Stalin avoided meeting foreign visitors, and his presence reflected the paramount importance of the occasion in the leader's eyes. It was a good omen. Stalin did not beat around the bush; he reaffirmed that the bad blood between the two countries was forgotten, and he bluntly set out his territorial aims once more, namely Finland, the Baltic States, and Bessarabia. Ribbentrop countered by reiterating the demarcation of the planned new Polish frontier. Apart from minor queries, which were almost immediately clarified with a call to Berlin, the pact was sealed right there (Kershaw 2008: 498–99).

The agreement of territorial demands had closed the deal, but within that closure the seeds of the pact's failure were germinating. Those would not be the last of the territorial demands for either side, meaning that the mistrust, second-guessing, and horse-trading would continue throughout the remainder of 1939 and into 1940. Hitler, of course, wasted no time

Divided Over Hitler

in exercising the powers accorded to him by the pact, which he saw primarily as Stalin's endorsement of the invasion of Poland. The speed of the German advance across Poland surprised everyone, including the USSR; Hitler tried hard, through Schulenburg, to encourage Stalin to join in. Encouragement soon turned to pressure, but, as Schulenburg was forced to admit, the Russians still mistrusted the Germans' intentions. Schulenburg personally felt that Hitler would keep to the limits of the agreement, but each side watched for the other's next move with trepidation (Shirer 1960: 621–30). When Stalin made his moves, not only advancing into Poland as requested but then, before very long, doing the same in Finland, Hitler was perturbed. By the following spring, Stalin was looking towards his promised prizes in the Baltic, and although Hitler was fully occupied in the west, both sides found time to accuse the other, repeatedly, of violating the terms of the pact. What the pact could never provide, clearly, was peace of mind. Increasingly a source of annoyance, the Molotov-Ribbentrop Pact was demoted, in Hitler's mind, to the ploy it is remembered for being; a cheap strategy for stalling the USSR while Germany concluded its business in the west. If all else failed, the Nazis reflected, the pact could at least be presumed to have killed and buried the possibility of the USSR ever joining the Allies. There was clearly still some scope for wishful thinking (Shirer 1960: 632, 801–812; Kershaw 2008: 584–87).

The bickering between the two parties to the Molotov-Ribbentrop Pact went on, in classic diplomatic fashion, but Hitler's planned next move was becoming increasingly obvious by the start of 1941. Germany had a million troops in the Balkans and Hitler now ordered a similar build-up on Poland's new eastern frontier. The Nazis had seized Yugoslavia, Greece, Romania, Bulgaria, and Hungary, but many, like Schulenburg, whether living in hope or in denial, still believed that war with Russia could be avoided. Schulenburg was convinced, and with good reason, that Stalin's goal was still to avoid war. Even Schulenburg, however, was beginning to see through the haze; he referred, in writing, to the "Stalin government" for the first time, as though acknowledging the illusory nature of the USSR's collective leadership, and recognizing that perhaps all was not what it seemed. For the sake of avoiding war, Schulenburg had backed the idea of a German-Soviet agreement from the start; ultimately it only served Hitler's cause, rather than the cause of peace. Now a global war was underway, but Schulenburg persisted with his priority of working to avoid a Russian front (Shirer 1960: 839–42). The final months of peace in the east were filled with rumors of imminent invasion. Stalin's bonhomie, including towards Friedrich-Werner personally, was ramped up, with bear hugs

3. "A Statesman Bent Upon Action"

and pledges of unending friendship. Schulenburg may have accepted Stalin's warmth at face value—Stalin truly did not want war, after all—and he may also have believed that Hitler wisely preferred not to fight in Russia. Outwardly, it appeared that this may be the case; Hitler made a point of ensuring that trade with the USSR continued completely uninterrupted, right up until the last moment, but it was a calculated charade. A further important trade agreement, in fact, was signed at the start of 1941, which would have allowed Germany to circumvent the British blockade indefinitely. On the surface, it looked like part of a war-winning strategy, but Hitler had made up his mind. From around March, Schulenburg stopped receiving instructions on how to proceed with dialogue. By May, Schulenburg's embassy was almost inactive, and across the once-thriving Moscow diplomatic community people were packing up and leaving (Herwarth 1981: 188–92).

Chilled by the prospect of war, Friedrich-Werner, for the first time, altered the focus of his arguments for keeping the peace. He had previously stressed Russia's desire for peace as the main factor, and he had also not discouraged the opinion that the USSR was not even capable of waging a war. But times had changed, and the exchange of goods and services with Germany, especially machinery and engineering, had served Stalin's army well. Schulenburg now hinted that war against the USSR would be wholly unwise, considering the inexhaustibility of Soviet manpower, their vast industrial reserves, and their emerging military defensive capability. Schulenburg spoke with foundation, but in Nazi eyes he sacrificed his credibility with this line of argument; his insistence led to his fall from grace, but, in any case, his usefulness to Hitler was already close to its expiration date. Schulenburg was so personally invested in keeping the peace with Russia that he was unlikely to be able to accept, espouse, and commit himself to a new status quo that involved an eastern war. One of Friedrich-Werner's principal traits was consistency, and this was not a quality that was appreciated by or endearing to the Nazi hierarchy. On April 28, 1941, he met with Hitler and assured him, yet again, that there was still no danger of Russian aggression. He repeated these assurances on June 6 and 7, personally handing a typed memorandum to Hitler. Schulenburg was, as before, correct about Russia, but by that time Hitler was only interested in finding pretexts for invasion. He filtered Schulenburg's words, looking for anything he could use to justify the forthcoming attack. For years, the Führer had unequivocally considered Schulenburg to be his top expert on Soviet affairs; now he curtly thanked him for his "most interesting" comments, slipped the unread memorandum into a drawer, and limply shook the ambassador's hand for the last time (Herwarth 1981: 115–16, 187, 191). Schulenburg was, incredibly, not even informed about Hitler's invasion plans, and he only knew for certain that the invasion was going to take place a few hours before German boots touched Soviet soil (Bullock 1962: 646–48).

The question inevitably emerges as to whether Friedrich-Werner was simply duped, whether Hitler abused the ambassador's immense gifts of diplomacy and well-earned reputation for fairness, to broker a deal that allowed Hitler to stab both East and West in the back. "In one sense I have achieved my goal" Schulenburg admitted when the pact was first signed, "[but] I didn't really achieve anything" he added, recognizing, tragically, the catastrophe he had helped to bring about. "Up to now, the brakes which keep the train of Europe from plummeting down the track to war have held. With this treaty, they will be released" (Herwarth 1981: 166). Short of actually assassinating Hitler with a paperweight, it is difficult to imagine what else Schulenburg could have done. Had the Molotov-Ribbentrop Pact not been concluded quickly by Schulenburg, the negotiations may have simply dragged on until Hitler was ready to attack the USSR. The pact's conclusion could not prevent war, and it is hard to believe that its hypothetical abandonment would have significantly altered the events of 1939 to 1941. Stalin, too, badly needed to buy time to prepare for battle. From this perspective, it is possible that the pact served the Soviets in equal or greater measure and ultimately shortened the war by making the USSR a highly effective Ally. After the German invasion began on June 22, 1941, Schulenburg was interned for a few weeks and then transported to the Soviet-Turkish border for repatriation. He was gently escorted to the crossing point by a squad of the NKVD, who waited to wave him off on his way; their affectionate respect for Friedrich-Werner was as incongruous as it was evident (Herwarth 1981: 81). On his return to Germany, he was placed in charge of the Russia desk at the foreign office; an ineffectual role, partly devoted to preparing propaganda materials aimed at the minority ethnic groups corralled into the USSR. The intended effect on Schulenburg was to neutralize him but keep him busy; in fact, his work inadvertently brought the Nazis' atrocious conduct in the east to his attention, and, appalled to his core, he took the fateful step of contacting members of the conservative German Resistance (Stackelberg 2007: 1964).

4

"The Land That Is in Need of Heroes"

War and Resistance, 1939–1943

"A thousand years will pass and the guilt of Germany will not be erased."—Hans Frank, before he was hanged at Nuremberg in 1946, quoted in Shirer, *The Rise and Fall of the Third Reich*, 1960

"The Germans must bear responsibility, but responsibility is not the same as guilt."—Willy Brandt, in *Verbrecher und andere Deutsche (Criminals and other Germans)*, 1946

Count Friedrich's high-profile state funeral in 1939, in the presence of Hitler and several of his lieutenants, drew the Schulenburg family together for what was, unbeknownst to them, the final time. The event also drew dangerous scrutiny upon this ostensibly model Nazi family, which was in reality profoundly split over Nazism. At the funeral, Fritz-Dietlof took Tisa to one side, away from the others, and confided in her that he was already in contact with circles of organized opposition to the Nazi regime. As close as Fritzi and Tisa may have been, making this admission out loud was risky. This could absolutely not be revealed to their brothers, who at the very least struggled to understand Fritz-Dietlof, Tisa—and their mother's—lack of commitment to the Nazi cause, but could tolerate it as long as Fritz and Tisa were perceived as eccentric liberal moralists rather than subversive anti–Hitler activists (Seymour 2013: 418). Fritz-Dietlof was officially regarded as politically untrustworthy but not a serious threat. As vice-president of police in Berlin, he had been one of the few senior Nazis to voice disapproval over Kristallnacht and similar incidents, joining the handful of senior figures mockingly labeled "Jew lovers." His views were considered naïve, bizarre, and unfashionably leftwing, rather than ideologically combative with the regime, but he would nevertheless soon be excluded from the Nazi party; it is unclear whether or not he was actually expelled from the Nazi party or simply declared persona non grata and kept at arm's length (Gregory 2018: 88). The result was that Fritz-Dietlof was sent to Silesia to serve as acting Oberpräsident, or provincial governor; a grand-sounding title, but in reality an archaic office that the Nazis had progressively stripped of any real power, which was Hitler's express intention (Shirer 1960: 200; Bullock 1962: 272; Mommsen 2009: 152).

The battle lines within the family were therefore clearly drawn, if still necessarily unspoken, by 1939. Tisa, perhaps, understood the dilemma better than anyone, seeing three of her brothers—Johann-Albrecht, Wolf-Werner, and Adolf-Heinrich—on one side, with their various positions in the Reich, their Nazi party memberships, and their SA officers' ranks, and on the other side listening to Fritzi confess his first tentative steps into the Resistance, and even learning of their widowed mother's disdain for Hitler. Ten days after the funeral, Tisa returned to England, flying from Cologne, only to be refused entry at Croydon Airport, south of London. She arrived at lunchtime on June 3, still dressed in black from head to foot, and was detained for questioning by officials. She stated her intention to return to Durham, where, she explained, she had been working with the Community Service Council—an organization for the unemployed, made up of trade unions, churches, and social service centers—who apparently denied that she was actually employed by them; it was assumed that she had perhaps worked under another name, or that she was perhaps known by her married name (Singapore Free Press 1939: 12). It seems more likely, however, that Tisa was not formally employed by the Community Services Council, and was probably offering her services for free. The British officials were not interested in these subtle distinctions. It was Tisa's opinion that she had made an enemy inside the British border authorities; not for reasons of politics or nationality, but because she had rebuffed an impromptu marriage proposal (Seymour 2013: 419).

Tisa politely protested her detention at the airport, but to no avail. Among her possessions, she apparently carried with her a German newspaper report about her father's funeral, and the British officials were startled to discover photos of Hitler as a mourner. As Tisa herself later described the situation, "the British thought I was a Nazi and the Germans thought I was a communist" (Gowrie and Rea 2001), but she had no choice except to turn back. At teatime she was escorted to a Belgian plane, which then departed for Cologne via Brussels. Tisa was condemned to spend the war years in a kind of home exile in Germany. Arriving in Cologne, she first stayed with her brother Adolf-Heinrich—Heini—though their

4. "The Land That Is in Need of Heroes"

relationship was by no means close. Heini was a businessman, financier, and a first lieutenant (Obersturmführer) in the SA. From Cologne, Tisa went to Travemünde to stay briefly with her mother, who had suffered several strokes; she died a few weeks later, on August 25, 1939, just three months after her husband. Heini was to die of colon cancer the following year, aged thirty-nine, leaving a widow, Jutta, and two children. In the space of quite a short time, therefore, the family was whittled down to just three brothers and Tisa. For Fritz-Dietlof, the string of four bereavements—both parents, two brothers—over four years was Death's way of signaling the end of the family as they had all known it (Heinemann 1994: 208). The Schulenburg parents, at least, had been spared all of the horrors yet to come.

In terms of position and standing in the regime, the number one spot in the Schulenburg family was now taken by Wolf-Werner. The start of the Second World War found him working as director of the overseas department and international advisor (Auslandsreferent) of the NSRL—Nationalsozialistischer Reichsbund für Leibesübungen (National-Socialist Reich Association for Physical Exercise)—the Reich's all-embracing national sports body (Mengden 1980: 63). He had been a high-ranking advisor since 1936 and continued as Gau leader of the overseas section after the Olympics. A little later he also became head of the foreign department attached to the office of Reichssportführer Hans von Tschammer und Osten himself, advising him and representing him on foreign policy issues. He also managed the ethnic German association within the office. In March 1938, after the "Anschluss," Wolf-Werner was sent to Vienna as special Reich commissioner for sport, to coordinate the integration of Austrian sports organizations into the Nazi system (Marschik 2020: 440). He then took a lead role in organizing the Winter Olympics, planned for 1940, which obviously never went ahead. He kept a relatively low profile in the now vaguely disreputable SA, being only a junior officer, though with the approach of war he applied for and was accepted for elite parachute training (Teichler 1991: 111, 270, 377). He was one of the most able and influential people in the NSRL, and his reputation both highlighted and benefited from his family connections, including "uncle" Friedrich-Werner, his late father's cousin, the ambassador to Moscow (Mengden 1980: 73).

The importance of Wolf-Werner's position should not be underestimated, in the context of a government apparatus that placed great political and ideological significance on the nation's sporting prowess. It was also considered politically important to nurture a healthy rivalry with fascist Italy, a nation equally committed, ideologically, to sustaining a myth of athletic greatness, personified in Hitler's increasingly vital ally, Mussolini. It was fortuitous that Wolf-Werner found a friend in his Italian opposite number, General Giorgio Vaccaro (1892–1983). Vaccaro was Secretary General of CONI, the Italian National Olympic Committee (Comitato Olimpico Nazionale Italiano) from 1933 to 1939. The two men had several things in common; they were both veterans of the First World War, and they were both loyal members of their respective political parties. Their work in sport was, to put it mildly, as much about politics as it was about sport, but with the outbreak of war imminent, Wolf-Werner had to consider his longer-term prospects in the Nazi regime, with the possibility of even more consequential future roles. In August 1939, Wolf-Werner prepared to join his military unit full-time. The SA had by this time been reinvented, once again, as a network of military training units—officially styled as SA Wehrmannshaften, or personnel units—to supplement the regular armed forces. Successful SA trainees would be shipped out to fill gaps in army units, which further weakened the home-based SA itself. As he left to join his unit, Wolf-Werner was replaced at the NSRL by the much better-qualified Carl Diem (1882–1962). Diem organized his first athletics club at the age of seventeen and led the German team at the Athens Olympics in 1906; thirty years later he masterminded the 1936 Summer Olympics in Berlin (Teichler 1991: 111, 127).

A degree of egalitarianism governed the transition from peacetime to wartime Nazism, and Wolf-Werner's seniority in Third Reich sports did not translate into senior rank or fast promotion in the military; nor was this guaranteed by his noble title or impressive connections. Hitler never wanted the development of his Nazi movement to be impeded by divisions of class, aiming instead to appeal to all social classes. From the earliest days, in fact, individuals from many different sectors of society were welcome to join the Nazis, as long as they nourished some form of brooding discontent or resentment, ideally towards one of the other sectors of society (Bullock 1962: 76). Being a member of the nobility was clearly no impediment to joining the Nazi party, or even to joining emphatically working-class party organizations such as the SA, but aristocratic birth provided no fast track to high rank either, as would be illustrated in the cases of the Schulenburg brothers. At the start of the Second World War, Wolf-Werner had already served for nearly ten years in the SA, alongside his increasingly prominent political roles, but he began the war as a humble lieutenant. Fritz-Dietlof, similarly, though certainly considered a controversial figure by 1939, was nevertheless influential in government, aristocratic, and social circles, yet he too was not afforded any higher rank

4. "The Land That Is in Need of Heroes"

than lieutenant during the war. Age, incidentally, did not make any difference either; Wolf-Werner turned forty at the start of the Second World War and Fritz-Dietlof was thirty-seven, both much older than the average lieutenants of the time. The same thing is observable in other noble families at that time, and it is certainly possible that unspoken prejudice was in operation to keep the civilian nobility from attaining too-high military rank. Their father, Friedrich, had joined the SA and been immediately raised to a senior rank, but this was in recognition of the rank he had achieved in the regular army, it was not on account of any social or class superiority. The outbreak of war did bring small changes for Wolf-Werner; he was soon promoted to captain, though in the SA, slightly confusingly, rather than the regular forces. Membership of the SA and membership of the armed forces now ran parallel but separately to each other; members of the armed forces who originated in the SA retained a nominal rank in the SA, which may be different to their military rank. Wolf-Werner effectively remained a lieutenant, for now (Scherzer 2007: 688).

As mentioned above, whether it was in order to avoid further scrutiny, to deflect suspicion from his dissident activities, or simply out of genuine patriotism, Fritz-Dietlof joined the army shortly after the outbreak of war. Though he had already communicated with figures in the German proto-Resistance, Fritz-Dietlof still saw opposition to the Nazi regime mainly in terms of working within it to reverse its irregularities and excesses, and he may even have perceived the war as an opportunity for Nazism to right itself (Mommsen 2009: 162). His army destination was Infantry Regiment 9 (IR9), garrisoned in the cradle of the Prussian army, Potsdam, which had been the Schulenburgs' second home since the First World War. He was aware that this was a significant step down in status, mixing with fellow officers nearly two decades his junior (Mommsen 2009: 153). His fellow officers, including future West German president Richard von Weizsäcker, would in turn remember "Fritzi" as "a peculiar and outstanding personality, … down to earth, provocative and, my goodness, very courageous" (Kimmelman 2009). Fritz-Dietlof's no-nonsense style could also come across as brusque and somewhat arrogant, though this was perhaps just the habitual demeanor fostered by his environment, or possibly even a black sheep's defensive tick (Mommsen 2009: 153). IR9 was rich in aristocratic tradition; humorists nicknamed it "IR 'von' 9" or "Graf Neun" (Count Nine) because of the high quota of aristocrats in its ranks, accompanied by their trademark hubris. Today it is mostly remembered for the fact that nineteen of its officers and former officers were later involved in conspiracies against Hitler, far more than in any other regiment; IR9's Major-General Henning von Tresckow, along with Fritz-Dietlof, were to become particularly central figures in coordinating the German Resistance. The man whose name would become almost synonymous with the July 1944 bomb plot to kill Hitler, Colonel Claus Schenk Graf von Stauffenberg, did not belong to the IR9, though the credit for convincing him to join the Resistance goes to one of the IR9's junior officers; none other than Fritz-Dietlof (Kramarz 1967: 72, 126).

Wolf-Werner's active military service had resumed in dramatic style when he was selected, at the age of thirty-nine, for parachute training; he received the coveted Parachutists' badge—Fallschirmschützenabzeichen—after successfully completing the required six practice jumps. He was assigned as adjutant, under Major Bruno Bräuer, of I (first) Fallschirmjäger regiment of the first Fallshirmjäger division (then called the Seventh Air Division or Flieger division) with which he would take part in the first major campaigns of the war, starting with the regiment's arrival in Poland on September 14, Wolf-Werner's fortieth birthday. Their first task was the disappointingly mundane one of occupying and guarding Polish airfields (McNab 2000: 39). The Fallshirmjäger were the new paratroop sub-branch of the German armed forces, and they were part of the Luftwaffe—the air force—rather than the army. They were among the first paratroop units in history to be deployed in large-scale airborne operations, and they would remain active throughout the Second World War under their commander General Kurt Student (1890–1978). The idea of airborne deployment of large numbers of troops had in fact been mooted during the First World War, but it took the developments in aircraft and aviation technology of the interwar period to really unleash military planners' imagination. Among the first countries to begin developing the potential of airborne forces were Italy and the Soviet Union. The static-line parachute, preferred by the military, was developed in Italy in the 1920s, whereby parachutes were attached to the inside of the aircraft and deployed automatically upon exiting. This technique, which began to be referred to in German as the Rückfallschirm, Zwangablösung—backpack-parachute, static-line—allowed jumps at low altitudes, which limited exposure to enemy fire and provided a tighter drop-zone grouping, compared to the more widely-known individually deployed rip-cord type parachutes (Ailsby 2000: 12–16).

Building on Italian technology, the Soviet Union first demonstrated the military potential of airborne infantry in the 1930s, with a series of major maneuvers starting in 1935. Though the parachute jumps themselves were somewhat crudely executed—troops crawled onto the fuselage and along the wings of their Tupolev TB–3 transport planes before jumping in

4. "The Land That Is in Need of Heroes"

unison—the vast exercise succeeded in landing no fewer than one thousand troops by parachute, followed by a further two and a half thousand soldiers with heavy equipment delivered via aircraft landings. Once on the ground, the gathered forces proceeded to carry out conventional light infantry attacks with the support of heavy machine guns and light artillery, which had all been landed by air, to the amazement of invited onlookers. Among the foreign observers present at these maneuvers was Hermann Göring; it is worth remembering that German-Soviet military training cooperation had been good up until this time. Göring was immediately converted into a fervent advocate of airborne infantry tactics and vowed to develop the same capability for Germany; he was especially determined that this should be his own pet project. Before his appointment as minister of aviation, Göring had served as Prussian interior minister, with command over his own specialist police unit; this unit, devoted to protecting Nazi party officials, was called Landespolizeigruppe General Göring. The unit carried out conventional police duties, but it was Göring's intention to create a force that would ultimately withstand comparison to the elite units of the Wehrmacht and be a rival to Himmler's SS. Between March and April 1935, Göring transformed his Landespolizei General Göring into Germany's first dedicated airborne regiment, giving it the military designation Regiment General Göring (RGG) on April 1, 1935. Hitler, who had reintroduced conscription just two weeks earlier, was happy to support any surreptitious expansion of the armed forces, and ostensible police units were not restricted by the Versailles prohibitions. Göring's unit was incorporated into "his" newly formed Luftwaffe—not the army—on October 1 of the same year, and eventually renamed (Ailsby 2000: 16–22).

The word Fallschirmjäger is derived from the German words Fallschirm—parachute—and Jäger—hunter—the latter of which was also traditionally used for the light infantry units of the Prussian army; the precise translation of Fallschirmjäger would therefore be Parachute Light Infantry. As a new component of the armed forces the Fallschirmjäger was officially inaugurated on January 29, 1936, with an order of the day calling for more recruits, including general volunteers as well as active and reserve Luftwaffe personnel. Wherever the volunteers hailed from, whether from existing Luftwaffe units or from other branches of the armed forces, whether they were officers or enlisted men, all of them were required to successfully complete six jumps in order to receive the Luftwaffe Parachutists' badge—Fallschirmschützenabzeichen—instituted on November 5, 1936. The first Fallschirmjäger division was formed in 1938 and was originally named the Seventh Air—Flieger—Division. The I (first) Fallschirmjäger regiment gradually added first, second, and third battalions during 1938 and 1939, in the run-up to the outbreak of war. They absorbed a mixture of individuals, from members of Göring's original RGG unit, to Luftwaffe reservists and volunteers from the army, including the replenishment units provided by the SA, like Wolf-Werner's. After their initial short deployment to Poland in 1939, Wolf-Werner and his unit would have to wait until the following spring for a chance to see action, serving in Denmark and Norway (Ailsby 2000: 22–26).

It was not until May 1940 that General Student's Fallschirmjäger would really be put to the test, with the airborne invasion of the neutral Netherlands. Wolf-Werner had just been promoted to first lieutenant (Oberleutnant). Between four-thirty and five o'clock on the morning of May 10, 1940, preceded by a large aerial bombardment, some of the first ever mass parachute drops signaled the start of the battle, as Fallschirmjäger units sought to secure strategic points in advance of the land invasion. There was no declaration of war, but in spite of the surprise attack the Dutch fought back well. Outcomes were therefore mixed. The attack on The Hague was a failure, with great loss of transport planes, and with many paratroopers and air-landing troops being taken prisoner. Meanwhile, the assault on the extensive border defense complex at Eben Emael was a complete success, with over a thousand Dutch troops being captured, besides seizing the border fort itself, allowing the Germans to sweep into Belgium as well. The six-day battle for the Netherlands was ultimately a success for the Germans, but at considerable cost; hundreds were killed or wounded and a staggering one and a half thousand German prisoners were transported to England. Despite the mixed outcome of the Netherlands invasion, Wolf-Werner was given a double award of the Iron Cross, first and second class (it was his second award of the latter, the first being in 1918) and promotion to captain was on the way. He was then deployed with his unit to Norway for a second time, from May to June 1940, until the Allied defense collapsed and the country was occupied by Germany. It would be almost a year before the Fallschirmjäger would next see action, in the invasion of Crete, the largest and most populous of the Greek islands, which would make history in a number of ways and have an unexpected impact on the rest of the war (Böhmler and Haupt 1971: 99; Kurowski 1965: 81, 111, 113; Schreiber 1996: 153).

The Battle of Crete was the first occasion where Fallschirmjäger troops were used as the principal method of attack, rather than in support of a ground troop attack. It was, in fact, the first mainly airborne invasion

4. "The Land That Is in Need of Heroes"

in military history, and also the first time German troops encountered mass resistance from a civilian population, to the Germans' considerable shock. Crete was also, furthermore, the first occasion that the Allies made significant use of intelligence from decrypted German messages, thanks to the now-famous Enigma machine (Collier 2014: 74). The invasion began on May 20, 1941. While much has been written about the invasion of Crete, the emphasis has largely been on the capture of the town of Chania and the Maleme airfield, which ultimately held the keys to victory, while the concurrent action at the port city of Heraklion remained largely ignored for many years. This may be because the events of the arduous Battle of Heraklion, which mostly took place in the dead of night, were always shrouded in confusion and contradiction, making it difficult for historical narrators to interpret the progress of the battle. There were multiple perspectives on, and varying recollections of the battle, which produced several conflicting versions of events as a result. The battle consisted of fierce street-fighting, in total darkness, up and down the narrow alleys of the old town, numerous logistical blunders, heroic—and sometimes hopeless—attacks against well-fortified positions ensconced in the medieval walls, and, ultimately, heavy losses on both sides. Members of the most notable German aristocratic families, such as the Blüchers and the Bismarcks, perished; Wolfgang Graf von Blücher's entire platoon was cornered and annihilated.

Wolf-Werner Graf von der Schulenburg had been promoted to captain (Hauptmann) by the time he and his III / I Fallschirmjäger (third battalion of the first Fallschirmjäger regiment, of the first Fallschirmjäger division) dropped into west Heraklion at noon on May 20 (Böhmler and Haupt 1971: 99; Kurowski 1965: 81, 111, 113). The forty-one-year-old Captain von der Schulenburg, at this time, did not boast an impressive appearance; he was described as lanky and gaunt, with a hooked nose, but this unimposing impression contrasted with a trademark calmness and courtesy, even when demonstrating a certain talent for finding himself in the tightest corners (Mabire 1997: 105). He was not averse to challenges; Wolf-Werner had, after all, completed rigorous parachute training at nearly forty years of age, graduating alongside comrades fifteen or twenty years younger than him, and by the time he parachuted into Crete he had already served in three successful campaigns. On their descent onto Heraklion, however, the whole regiment suffered badly from Allied anti-aircraft fire, and in some instances Greek troops and armed civilians immediately attacked them once they were on the ground. The battalion commander, Major Karl-Lothar Schulz, gathered reports from his men, establishing that their location was within a large concentration of enemy forces, a short distance outside of the city (Kurowski 2010: 111–12).

Wolf-Werner managed to locate Schulz and reported heavy casualties among the third battalion, which had landed about a quarter of a mile (four hundred meters) further to the rear, near a village on the city's outskirts. He suggested attacking that village and using it as a route into the city, and Schulz agreed. House-to-house fighting ensued and the Fallschirmjäger were steadily taking control of the village, but as they neared Heraklion they came under increasing fire from British and Greek troops on the city walls. The Scottish snipers of the second battalion Black Watch (Royal Highlanders) were particularly efficient; they were regular peacetime soldiers, not wartime conscripts, who had served in Palestine before the war and had already seen action against the Italians in East Africa. Many Germans fell victim to the snipers' headshots, including a Fallschirmjäger medical officer, who was rushing to assist the wounded. As evening approached, the Germans had captured the village, but they were pinned down outside the ancient city walls; Schulz admitted to Wolf-Werner that the walls could not be climbed, and, being only paratroops without support units, they lacked the artillery or explosives to breach them (Kurowski 2010: 111–12).

Wolf-Werner suggested splitting up, and the major agreed; Schulz decided to attack from the west in order to circumvent the city walls, so he sent the third battalion, under Wolf-Werner, north to secure the port and seize the ancient Venetian fortress of Koules, while another group, under First Lieutenant (Oberleutnant) Becker, set off to probe around the area of the town hall, approaching from the sea. Schulz planned to navigate the steep cliffs to the west, giving his men a vantage point from which to pick off the snipers, allowing a descent into the city. Once inside the city, however, instead of swiftly capturing strategic points as planned, confused house-to-house fighting ensued, and this continued late into the night. Major Schulz attempted to regroup in the southern part of the city but was unable to gather all of those fighting in the labyrinth of narrow streets and alleys, and the small groups of men who got as far as the harbor were also unreachable. Schulz opted to withdraw from the city with whatever troops he could gather, to stymie further losses, and they made their escape for that day (Prekatsounakis 2017: 161–75). When General Student received Major Schulz's report from west Heraklion, and then an equally dismal report from Major Bruno Bräuer in east Heraklion, it became clear to him that all four of the day's parachute assaults—Maleme airfield, Chania town, east and west Heraklion—had failed. Determined to carve out a

4. "The Land That Is in Need of Heroes"

path to victory, Student ordered all further available resources to be concentrated on capturing the airfield at Maleme. As predawn winds swept across the island, those Fallschirmjäger who had landed around Heraklion were lost, isolated, or huddled in small groups; many of them were wounded, all of them suffered greatly from thirst, and some contracted dysentery from drinking stagnant water. Allied and Greek patrols hunted them through the night. Major Bräuer tried to attack again at dawn on May 21, hoping both to relieve a platoon that had been cut off on the hill the previous evening and also to gain a position with a view of the airfield in the distance. These assaults were poorly coordinated and subsequently failed, with heavy losses; the isolated platoon on the hillside was overrun by local forces at around midday (Kurowski 2010: 112–13).

Schulz and Schulenburg, in west Heraklion, were out of contact with Bräuer in the east, but they could hear his attempted attacks, and Schulz was inspired to try to capture the city again. A number of stragglers joined them, and after some interruptions the German air support resumed. The situation was tense and it was taking its toll; Wolf-Werner was seen looking increasingly disheveled and haggard, his face framed by a collar of dirty beard (Mabire 1997: 306). At last, the aerial bombardment of Heraklion began, allowing the III / I Fallschirmjäger to attack the shaken Greeks via the south and west gates of the city; they successfully broke into the city center and relieved some of the paratroopers who had been trapped there since the previous evening. With the Greeks running out of ammunition, the Germans again fought their way as far as the harbor, where the Greeks negotiated the surrender of the city. Before this could be put into effect, Allied reinforcements arrived along with large quantities of captured German weapons and ammunition, forcing the Germans to withdraw again. Following reports that the Germans were using civilians as human shields, the Greek military governor of Heraklion sent an emissary to demand that this cease, threatening to retaliate against German prisoners of war. Major Schulz agreed on condition that Heraklion surrender within two hours, which the governor refused to do (Hellenic Army History Directorate 1985: 245–51).

The confusion and stalemate dragged on and on over eight more days. German air support mistakenly dropped supplies and weapons to the Allies, facilitating further resistance attacks, in spite of the Germans' increasing reprisals against civilians. Elsewhere however, Student's plan to focus any additional resources on the original objectives of the Maleme airfield and Chania town proved successful. Possession of the airfield allowed for further reinforcements to parachute in safely and steadily,

Divided Over Hitler

forcing the exhausted Allies to evacuate (Hellenic Army History Directorate 1985: 259–60). A number of important conclusions were drawn by both sides in Crete, and these lessons would impinge critically upon the course of the rest of the war, specifically in the converse evolution of attitudes to airborne operations. The number of airborne casualties in Crete was reminiscent of the Fallschirmjäger's previous experience in the Netherlands, and this realization was demoralizing for the German forces. More significantly, Hitler and his generals were convinced that airborne attack would no longer benefit from the element of surprise, having now been used on a large scale in two key operations, both times with mixed results. Hitler was therefore reluctant to authorize further major airborne operations, preferring instead to employ paratroopers as normal ground troops (Beevor 1991: 229–30).

In stark contrast, the Allies were actually deeply impressed by the potential of paratroops displayed at Crete, and they urgently started to form airborne-assault and airfield-defense regiments, leading to the launch of units such as the British Parachute Regiment, in 1942. Another legacy of Crete, one that would involve Wolf-Werner directly, was that war crimes and atrocities against civilians, and their use as human shields and hostages, had clearly become standard practice for German military units such as the Fallschirmjäger. The subsequent German occupation of Crete was brutal, with thousands of civilians executed by firing squad and many more killed in reprisals and other serious crimes. Major Bräuer remained as German commander in Crete until July 1944. After the war, he was charged with war crimes by a Greek military court, convicted, and hanged on May 20, 1947, the sixth anniversary of the German invasion. Germans who witnessed or even took part in these types of wartime atrocities were generally divided over their legitimacy; in some cases such crimes were seen as a step too far, confirming hitherto latent reservations and doubts about the Nazi regime. Colonel Claus Schenk Graf von Stauffenberg, already mentioned above, found himself increasingly appalled by the indiscriminate killing of Jewish and Slav civilians, and of Russian prisoners-of-war. He was horrified by the SS units' apparently unbridled lust for murder, which began to have a corrupting and desensitizing effect on the army too; soldiers watched as criminal behaviors were modeled, excused, and legitimized by the supposed elite and then went unpunished. In response, Stauffenberg began his own personal rebellion by ignoring or changing orders, beginning with thwarting an order that all Russian prisoners-of-war must have an identifying mark tattooed on their buttocks (Kramarz 1967: 100).

4. "The Land That Is in Need of Heroes"

It is not clear whether it was in the Battle of Heraklion or in the preceding Netherlands invasion (or perhaps both) that Wolf-Werner was wounded, earning the award of the Wound Badge in addition to his previous decorations, as well as the Luftwaffe Ground Combat Badge and the cuff-band battle honor for Crete (Hammerstein-Equord 1966: 110). The I (first) Fallschirmjäger would next see action in the central sector of the eastern front, where, in the same period, 1941–42, Wolf-Werner's brother Fritz-Dietlof also served, while becoming increasingly critical of the Nazis' conduct of the war. He began the war thinking that the Nazi movement could still be purged of its negative aspects, and he actually embarked for Russia with considerable enthusiasm. Like many others, he saw the occupation of the east in ideological and idealistic terms, as a liberation from Bolshevism (Meding 1997: 117). This exaggerated form of anticommunism melded with a romanticized image of rural Russia, composed of pitchforks, oxcarts, maidens, and folk dancing. This vision was part of a "lite" imperialism that had been promoted by idealistic intellectuals since the 1920s, arguing for a return to rural lifestyles and a rejection of the modern; the invasion of Russia seemed to offer a chance to put this weird philosophy into practice. Fritz-Dietlof has been described as extremely naïve up to 1941, and in Russia he may have been ignorant of standing orders to kill all partisans and commissars on sight, but his process of detachment from Nazism was about to step up a gear. He was appalled by the realization that obscene crimes were being committed against Jews in the east, in widespread fashion, and while this realization alone was not yet enough for him to reject Nazism in its entirety, Fritz-Dietlof was convinced that something was fundamentally wrong. To what extent his army superiors were aware of his disaffection is unclear, as their handling of him was equivocal; he was decorated with the Iron Cross first class, but in early 1942 he was assigned to administrative duties, effectively a return to civil service. He turned down the offer of an administrative position in the occupied Russian lands, and also knocked back Himmler's offer of a senior post in the SS; he seemed determined to hold only a ministry civil servant role, based in Berlin, where he would be distant from the horrors perpetrated by the regime but strategically close to the heart of its operations, and those of the Resistance (Mommsen 2009: 153–62).

Fritz-Dietlof was affected by the treatment of civilians on the eastern front in a way that his brother Wolf-Werner, in Crete, clearly was not. Grotesque reprisals, summary executions, and the use of human shields, all to the detriment of civilians, had quite quickly become standard parts of the German army playbook. Such atrocious behavior was widely seen as the natural military application of Nazi ideology, and it did much to galvanize the opposition to Nazi forces in the invaded countries; any opposing troops or resistance fighters who may still have had doubts about the righteousness of their own non–Nazi cause, or who were still in two minds about the ideological alternatives presented by their own flawed leadership, were soon convinced by seeing the Germans in action. The standardization of atrocity did not sit well with all citizens back home in Germany either, of course, and popular opposition to Nazism was growing. Contrary to some perceptions, the organized German Resistance consisted of small, loosely-connected groups or cells with a fluctuating membership. Resistance members were only really united in their opposition to the Nazi regime, and this opposition varied in degree, orientation, and application; some individuals were morally repulsed by Nazism in its entirety, while others saw a potential to patriotically reform the regime and save Germany from ruin; there were monarchists, militarists, clergy, artists, and mystics in the mix (Bullock 1962: 735). There were also, of course, more than one Schulenburg in the German Resistance, not just Fritz-Dietlof, who would eventually be classed as more of a pragmatist and a motivator than a mystic, despite his apparent naiveté. In increasing numbers, patriotic pragmatists formed the opinion that, politics aside, it was at least necessary to halt the war, simply in order to salvage something resembling Germany from the wreckage. Stalingrad, predictably, did much to help form this opinion. Many of those who had served at the front knew that defeat and disaster were inevitable, while others, like Stauffenberg, were primarily morally appalled by the routine murders of civilians and prisoners (Mommsen 2009: 260–61).

Fritz-Dietlof's opposition must have been painfully obvious to his superiors by this stage, and he would never again be placed in a position of trust. At the same time, he was clearly cautious enough not to provide a solid pretext for arrest. He was sent back to the reserve battalion at the IR9 in Potsdam, to sit out the war where he could do no harm, or so it was thought. From that vantage point near Berlin, he continued to observe the lawlessness of the Nazi regime with growing disgust and resolve. The army consigned him to the oblivion of the reserve, and this gave him crucial time to think. His training in law told him that hopes of reforming any society had to presuppose some degree of recognition for basic and unshakeable legal principles, and these were being openly trampled upon in Nazi Germany. His understanding and assessment of the Nazi problem was therefore radically transformed at this time; while he had certainly harbored reservations about the Nazi movement for several years,

4. "The Land That Is in Need of Heroes"

he had tended to see the problem as a moral one of leadership and direction, the hope being that society's stable institutions—including the military—would ultimately halt the excesses of Nazism and steer it onto the right path. The Russian front, however, had exposed Fritz-Dietlof to the reality. He saw that supply, logistics, manpower, strategy—everything, in fact—was in chaos, and that the chaos was being systematically covered up by deception, misreporting, and subterfuge. Far from applying order to a chaotic situation, the Nazified state institutions, including the undermined, complicit military, were collapsing into disorder as well, while feverishly working to cover up the mess. In summary, Fritz-Dietlof saw that the Nazi regime was fundamentally dysfunctional as well as morally misguided, that this dysfunction was uncontrollably contagious, and that Nazism could not be redeemed with a change of leadership. As long as Hitler and Nazism persisted, none of society's institutions alone—whether law, aristocracy, military, church, academy, or intelligentsia—any longer enjoyed sufficient confidence or influence to apolitically guide the nation back in the right direction (Meding 1997: 117).

Fritz-Dietlof concluded that a secret coalition of the clear-sighted and genuinely patriotic must replace the Nazi leadership root and branch, starting at the top; the ambivalent Hitler, who alternated between feebly permitting and ferociously encouraging the Nazi disorder, had to go immediately. Being in Berlin allowed Fritz-Dietlof to develop his like-minded contacts and encourage them to draw the right conclusions; he already had a large number of friends and acquaintances, including many fellow aristocrats, spanning various political, ideological, and philosophical spectrums. He finally accepted that his vocation, duty, and destiny was to network among all circles and groups, promoting resistance and advocating for the forcible removal of Hitler and his regime. Fritz-Dietlof's role as networker and recruiter for the German Resistance was also effective among his young fellow officers at Potsdam. One such twenty-one-year-old officer was Richard Karl Freiherr von Weizsäcker (1920–2015), future two-term President of Germany, who remembered Fritz-Dietlof with awe. "He was the one to tell us what was needed," Weizsäcker recalled. "Fritzi was the one who inspired us, the one who reminded us that we could not possibly wait until this terrible war found its own end" (Kimmelman 2009). Long before the 1944 plot, dissenting officers in the IR9 mooted more than one scheme for assassinating Hitler, but for one reason or another none of their plans came to fruition (Gregory 2018: 19). Some would posit, in retrospect, that a key cohesive factor, the right person for the terrible task, was missing up to that point; after some considerable persuasion, Colonel Claus von Stauffenberg was recruited into the Resistance by Fritz-Dietlof, who was a friend of his uncle, Nikolaus Graf von Üxküll-Gyllenband (Kramarz 1967: 72, 126).

Official suspicions surrounding Fritz-Dietlof never really abated, but the personal risk was now greatly elevated; he was no longer merely rubbing shoulders with fellow disgruntled Nazis, he was now a central part of an actual plot to assassinate Hitler. He always covered up his activities well, but he was nevertheless questioned by the Gestapo on at least one occasion, as they "fished" for punishable offences (Gregory 2018: 19). For both Fritz-Dietlof and his wife Charlotte it was a rather secretive, anxious, and lonely existence, though Tisa could always be relied upon for meaningful support. Tisa, stranded in Germany for the duration, kept moving around aimlessly during the early war years; she was clearly unlikely to find, in wartime Germany, the kind of stimulating and rewarding environment that she was used to, and equally unlikely to find suitable outlets for her artistic work. During the war her art came to a standstill, except for a few sketches. By 1943 she was living at the Klein Trebbow estate, about nine miles (fifteen kilometers) south of Tressow Castle. Klein Trebbow belonged to Tisa's second husband's family, the Barners, who were also childhood friends of Tisa, and the Barners invited Tisa to take over the management of their estate. Fritz-Dietlof and Charlotte seized this opportunity to be based far from inquisitive eyes, and they also went to live temporarily on the Klein Trebbow estate; it was inevitably transformed into a kind of haven for the Resistance. Tisa was the first person that Fritzi had confided in, apart from his wife Charlotte, at their father's funeral; now, along with Fritzi and Charlotte, Tisa would be privy to key developments in the German Resistance.

Tisa herself, therefore, also became involved in the Resistance in small ways, and she even provided assistance to escaped prisoners of war, but her main contribution was surely providing a safe place for plotters to meet. A small pavilion or summerhouse in the grounds of the Klein Trebbow estate, surrounded by trees and known as the teahouse, guaranteed an additional layer of security for Resistance meetings. The teahouse was considered "bug-proof" but in any case a walk in the grounds was the preferred setting for the most sensitive discussions. One of the most memorable visitors was Claus von Stauffenberg, who by 1944 had been selected to become Hitler's assassin. At Easter of that year, the visiting Stauffenberg effortlessly bewitched everyone at Klein Trebbow, with the staff almost fighting over who would help the handsome, war-wounded Count to cut up his meat at dinner (Meding 1997: 119). Charlotte and Tisa

4. "The Land That Is in Need of Heroes"

did their best to entertain their charismatic and captivating guest, despite the impoverishments of wartime; the sisters-in-law dressed themselves up as best they could in the tatty and outdated evening gowns available, and sacrificed their last measure of gin to prepare a cocktail for their dashing guest. It was Stauffenburg's combination of erudition and gaiety that most impressed Tisa; he talked expertly about Goethe and Shakespeare, but their conversation was interspersed with roars of laughter. "I have never known anyone with such a capacity for laughter," she later recalled of Stauffenberg (Seymour 2014). Somehow managing to provide a fleeting evening of laughter in times of such profound sadness and adversity, when the Schulenburgs and all of the German people were at their lowest ebb, was undoubtedly a precious gift; it is a poignant tribute to one of modern history's great heroes. The words of Tisa's old acquaintance, Bertolt Brecht, in his *Life of Galileo*—"unhappy the land that is in need of heroes"—had never been more resonant.

5

"The Positions Will Be Held; If Necessary, to the Last Man!"
War and War Crimes, 1943–1944

> "The man of action is always unconscionable; none but the contemplative has a conscience."—Johann Wolfgang von Goethe, Maxim 241 in *Maxims and Reflections*, 1833

> "Never before in the history of warfare have so few been commanded by so many."—General Mark W. Clark, in his personal diary, January 23, 1944

Halfway through the war, as it may be described with hindsight, the outlook was not good for the Nazis. If North Africa was the more militarily strategic and honorable defeat, Stalingrad was the emotional and spiritual heartbreak for Germans of all persuasions. Doubters and dissidents like Fritz-Dietlof needed no more convincing by 1943, but even the most fanatical Nazis struggled to fool themselves any further that the war was going well. Wolf-Werner had had a successful war up to that point, but the prestigious reputation of his Fallschirmjäger was tarnished; not so much by the war crimes committed in Crete, as might be expected, but by the fact that their daring mass parachute assaults had outlived their usefulness in Hitler's eyes. As mentioned previously, Hitler and his generals' confidence in airborne invasions had evaporated; rather than guaranteeing the element of surprise, these attacks seemed to only guarantee heavy losses. To the dismay and frustration of proud paratroopers such as Captain von der Schulenburg, airborne units would henceforth be used as mere ground troops (Beevor 1991: 229–30). From Crete, Wolf-Werner and his men were sent back to Germany for brief retraining, and then to France in the area of Avignon, where the Fallschirmjäger had its regrouping base. Schulz placed Wolf-Werner in charge of the first battalion for their next destination, the central sector of the eastern front, and from

5. "The Positions Will Be Held; If Necessary, to the Last Man!"

the end of September 1941 they joined the invasion of Russia. In October the regiment was transferred by rail via Minsk and Vitebsk to Rudnya, near Smolensk, to take part in Operation Typhoon. At the end of October, the Fallschirmjäger division took over a fifty-six mile (ninety kilometer) wide combat zone on the Demidov–Dukhovshchina–Jarcewo line, to the north of Smolensk, in support of the ultimately futile drive towards Moscow. The failure of this three-month-long campaign was a crushing blow that demolished the myth of German invincibility. Germans, from Hitler down, began the autumn believing that Russia was finished, but by January 1942 the hope of a swift victory against the USSR was shattered (Shirer 1960: 853–65).

Wolf-Werner's regiment fought off Soviet counterattacks from their base near Smolensk, tasked with laborious anti-partisan warfare in the rear of the front line. Partisan activity, infuriatingly, seemed to increase daily; blowing up bridges, derailing trains, and ambushing German supply columns heading to the front. Smolensk was a hotbed of such activity, tying up twenty thousand German troops to contain it (Kurowski 2010: 206). The Fallschirmjäger were then deployed up and down the front line at Volkhov and Rshew, and were then transferred to Stalino in Ukraine, modern-day Donetsk, in the Don basin or Donbas. On November 9, 1942, Wolf-Werner was promoted to brigade leader—Brigadeführer—in the SA (Teichler 1991: 111). Their second Russian winter found them fending of counterattacks again around Vitebsk and Smolensk. From 11 to 20 January 1943, they were involved in heavy fighting at Welikiye-Luki, to the north of Smolensk, relieving army units that were trapped there. In the second half of February, Soviet forces attacked north from the Kursk area and broke through German positions south of Orel. The Fallschirmjäger were released from their positions north of Smolensk on February 27 and sent to the threatened section near Dmitrovsk. In a series of counterattacks at Alexeyevka, Stolbetskoe, Stepanovka and Nagornyj, the I, II, and III Fallschirmjäger halted the Soviet advance towards Orel by March 3. The more famous Battle of Kursk, a few months later, would definitively destroy Hitler's dream of conquering the Soviet Union. On March 30, Wolf-Werner's unit was withdrawn and sent back to France to recuperate again. At the beginning of June, the first Fallschirmjäger division was reinforced and then expanded to create a second Fallschirmjäger division in preparation for their next deployment, to Italy (Ailsby 2000: 66).

It was in Italy that Wolf-Werner's personal prestige reached its zenith on June 20, 1943, when he was awarded the Knight's Cross of the Iron Cross, the coveted swastika-adorned neck-cross, symbol of the very elite of Nazi warriors (Fellgiebel 2006: 318). Even his father, Friedrich, did not count the Knight's Cross among his more than two dozen orders and medals. The award recognized Wolf-Werner's accumulated war service, but particularly his conduct in action in the area south of Orel, and it made up for his less than astronomical rise through the officer ranks (Scherzer 2007: 688). Promotion to major was to follow swiftly, however, and with it a new command and a new battlefront. After their victory in North Africa, the Allies' attention turned towards the complete liberation of Europe and the retaking of Mediterranean control, starting, as everyone expected, in Italy. By the time Wolf-Werner received his prestigious medal, the Allies had already seized key strategic Italian islands, and the bombing of mainland targets was underway. The Germans correctly foresaw the collapse of the Italian leadership, in terms of both the military and the government. Not waiting for the demise of Mussolini's regime, German forces swept through the peninsula, pushing aside the chaotic Italian defense, and made Italy their new front line. The strategy, tactics, and politics of all this were disputed, and serious rifts began to develop between the OKW— Oberkommando der Wehrmacht, the Wehrmacht high command— and the unwieldy number of competing German field commanders; this multilateral squabbling would become an ongoing feature of the Italian campaign. On the ground, German units, including the first Fallschirmjäger regiment, first division, with Wolf-Werner's I (first) battalion, were joined—whether they liked it or not—by units fleeing North Africa after the Allied victory. The first Fallschirmjäger division took part in the July 1943 fight-back against the Allied invasion of Sicily, and they would be employed in the Italian campaign for the remainder of the war.

The men of the Fallschirmjäger felt chronically underused since the mixed results of Crete. Across northwest Europe and Russia, Hitler's elite paratroopers had seen the major fronts of the war, but their potential was unexploited, serving as ground troops or guarding transport, and waiting for a major operation that never came. Their modern methods of warfare were also largely frustrated by the clandestine tactics of the Russian partisans; this was antithetical to the Prussian military mindset, leaving staunch traditionalists like Wolf-Werner with a profound wariness and repugnance of unconventional warfare. By the time they arrived in Italy, therefore, the paratroopers' pride was severely dented, and their frustration must have been intense. The southeast of Italy, often identified as the heel of the boot, has sometimes escaped the attention of historians covering the Italian campaign, because the major landings occurred along the west coast, where the south-north road was always the focus of

5. "The Positions Will Be Held; If Necessary, to the Last Man!"

the main advance. Three of Italy's many important ports, however, were located in the southeast; the historic trading port of Bari, ancient gateway to the Levant and the Balkans, Brindisi further to the south, where the Italian royal family was exiled, and Taranto, the naval and petrochemical hub facing south to the Mediterranean basin. These ports would all soon be strategic objectives for the Allies. From the Allies' point of view, the grab for the southeastern ports also served the purpose of diverting German forces from the west, where they could have held back the Allies' progress after the bigger troop landings. The defense of Sicily collapsed on August 18, and more than fifty thousand Axis personnel were evacuated. Wolf-Werner's Fallschirmjäger were sent to a strategic inland point in the southeast, equidistant between the ports of Bari and Taranto; it was the sleepy, slow-paced town of Matera, whose unique and ancient stone and rock dwellings would provide the striking backdrop for several blockbuster movies in later decades. On Tuesday, September 7, Wolf-Werner's troops set up camp roughly a mile and a quarter (two kilometers) from Matera's downtown area. The unit consisted of around two hundred men, six junior officers, Wolf-Werner, and his second-in-command, whose name was variously reported as being either Schmidt or Schulze, but it was almost certainly Schulze, first name Georg (Ambrico 2003: 11; Andrae 1995: 77).

The unit was operating as a detachment, apparently with smaller groups of German troops—Panzers, stragglers from units hurriedly evacuated from Sicily—attached to them. The rest of the I Fallschirmjäger were spread out across southern Italy. On Wednesday, September 8, the day after the Fallschirmjägers' arrival in Matera, the interim Italian government announced an armistice, effectively meaning that the royal Italian armed forces were abandoning their German allies, although from some perspectives they actually switched sides. Demobilized Italian soldiers soon roamed the countryside, trying to make their way home and trying to avoid the Germans, adding to an already confusing situation (Ambrico 2003: 15–16). In this context, there were two main objectives entrusted to the Fallschirmjäger; find ways to impede the imminent Allied advance from Taranto, when the expected troop landings came, and then apply order to the inevitable German retreat. This latter task was realism rather than defeatism; retreat could be delayed, but not avoided, so it had to be facilitated, managed, and orderly. In connection with this, a third objective would soon emerge; coping with local insurrections, which were being timed to support the Allied advance (Ambrico 2003: 11–12). In addition to all this, Wolf-Werner received vague orders about detaining and

Divided Over Hitler

disarming any wandering Italian troops they might encounter, who could be planning to fight for the Allies, but the German leadership was divided on how to deal with this situation, and the orders were unclear. There were, in general, serious inconsistencies and contradictions in the German vision and management of the campaign. Hitler's commander in Italy was Field-Marshal Albert Kesselring, but his ability to command was subject to the OKW and Hitler's own military strategy, which obviously took precedence; Kesselring was there to balance conflicting views and stabilize the situation. Hitler actually understood the Italian situation well—partly thanks to Kesselring's reports, and also thanks to his own good intelligence channels—but his interference would ultimately impede the campaign (Sangster 2015: 73, 79, 95, 218).

On Thursday, September 9, the Allies landed at Taranto, and the situation in Matera became even more tense. By Saturday 11, the ports of Bari and Brindisi had already been liberated, and the landing force joined up with the 1st Canadian Infantry Division, moving across from Calabria in the west. There were rumors, which have still not been confirmed or refuted eighty years later, that at least one individual behind-the-lines Allied agent, was already operating among the populace of Matera, hoping to coordinate an anti–German rebellion as a prelude to the arrival of the Canadians. Local legend, uncorroborated, attributed the name Ganger to this Allied agent; whether this was supposed to be a surname, nickname, or codename is unclear. There were, certainly, numerous small acts of rebellion against the occupying Germans, who, having arrived recently and in heavy-handed fashion, stood little chance of winning sympathy or loyalty from the locals. The Fallschirmjäger, in fact, did as they pleased, taking items and commandeering property, and generally abusing the population (SIB 1944a: Exhibit U). Ultimately, their days in Matera were numbered, rebellion or no rebellion, and they knew it; the Allies were steadily taking nearby towns, day by day, meeting little or no resistance. On the following Tuesday, September 14, Wolf-Werner turned forty-four. Overnight on Thursday 16, the Allies took the airfield at Gioia del Colle, just twenty-two miles (thirty-six kilometers) from Matera, which gave them control of the airspace as well. Tensions in Matera reached a new high on Sunday, September 19, when a soldier of Wolf-Werner's second company was shot and seriously wounded; the shot came from a rifle, but beyond this the circumstances remain unclear. Reports described the shooting as being at close range and taking place close to the town center, in connection with an altercation, but this was not verified. Some time later, a further six soldiers of the third company were wounded by a hand

5. "The Positions Will Be Held; If Necessary, to the Last Man!"

grenade, and again the circumstances were unclear. The Allies at this point were almost within view. Wolf-Werner had already decided to take preemptive action, as a local insurrection seemed about to explode (Ambrico 2003: 11–12, 15).

The events that followed were later documented in a painstaking investigation by a special section of the British military police. The report, which was marked SECRET and then sealed until fifty years after the war, contains sixty-three depositions and consists of one hundred and thirty pages. It is dated November 7, 1944; Reference: SIB.67/WC/44.3; Subject: War Crimes at Matera—September 21 1943. The author was 252802 Captain William James Hutchins, DAPM (Deputy Assistant Provost Marshal) of 67 Section SIB (Special Investigation Branch), Corps of Military Police, CMF (Central Mediterranean Forces), who was reporting to the Deputy Provost Marshal, HQ SIB, AFHQ (Armed Forces Headquarters) CMF. Today, the report is housed at the National Archives, London, catalog number WO [War Office] 310/102 (the general war diaries of the SIB, meanwhile, are catalogued as WO170/3594); henceforth the report will be referred to as SIB 1944c. In the words of the report, "The results of these investigations show that two incidents occurred [in Matera] which undoubtedly may be classified as 'War Crimes'" (SIB 1944c: 1). The investigator, Captain Hutchins, details these incidents and attributes between seventeen and nineteen dead and two seriously wounded to the criminal actions of the German forces present in Matera (SIB 1944c: 1).

On the afternoon of Monday, September 20, 1943, three local men, including the "maresciallo"—station duty officer—of the police were arrested and detained at the barracks of the local MVSN unit. The MVSN (Milizia Volontaria per la Sicurezza Nazionale) was the national volunteer militia of fascist Italy, better known as the blackshirts; "blackshirt" was actually the official rank of ordinary enlisted men in the MVSN, not an informal term, as may be imagined. A detachment of Germans was now based at the barracks, which was a nondescript, modern, two-story building in Via Cappuccini. The three detained men were locked in a room, where they were soon joined by further detainees; five demobilized Italian soldiers, and then two local farmhands. The five soldiers and five civilians were interrogated by the German captain, who was not identified by name, but whose description—medium height, medium build, fair hair, fair complexion, two prominent front teeth, aged around thirty—matches contemporary descriptions of Captain Georg Schulze, Wolf-Werner's second-in-command. The Germans appeared to be in no hurry to release the men, and they did not give reasons for the detention (SIB 1944c: 21, 24–26).

The detained civilians stated that they were simply going about their daily business, while the arrested Italian soldiers said that they were making their way home after being released following the armistice. As mentioned above, the Germans' handling of Italians, whether in terms of what was officially mandated or in terms of what happened in practice, was a matter of confusion and inconsistency. Hitler's generals were in disagreement as to how to treat their former allies—or current friends, according to some interpretations—especially with regard to what to do about the Italian army. Kesselring was seen as taking the softer approach, allowing demobilized Italian soldiers to return home without hindrance, while Rommel advocated more forceful treatment; he ordered his men to detain and extract a pledge of loyalty from disbanded Italian troops, with deportation to Germany as forced labor if they refused. This confusion would not help the Germans' campaign, and although Hitler did not share Kesselring's positive view of the Italians he did consider Kesselring to be more politically reliable than Rommel; Kesselring's more generous treatment of the Italians was also thought to be more astute, as it gave individual Italians less motivation to defect to the Allies (Sangster 2015: 90–99). In Matera, Wolf-Werner and Schulze showed some uncertainty over what to do with their prisoners. They did not appear to have apprehended any leading troublemakers. As it was after eleven o'clock by the time they finished the interrogations, Schulze refused to let any of them go home, as there was a curfew in force, only to then relent and release three of the civilians; the police officer and the two farmhands. The detention in the militia barracks crept into its second day, with seven men still detained (SIB 1944c: 16, 21, 24–26).

On the morning of Tuesday, September 21, the Germans released the other two civilians who had first been arrested along with the police officer. The five Italian soldiers remained, soon to be joined by four more civilians. At some point during the night or early morning, a carload of four people was detained as they travelled from the direction of Taranto, which was now, of course, in Allied hands. Alarmingly, they had sped through a roadblock, were instantly fired upon, and wisely decided to stop the car. The reason for their trip, they said, was that they were going to Matera on court business; one of them was a lawyer and two of them were court employees, while the fourth man was their driver. It is a problematic tale, with this idea of crossing the front line to consign legal documents, and Schulze quite understandably concluded that they were some kind of

5. "The Positions Will Be Held; If Necessary, to the Last Man!"

spies. They were placed in the militia barracks (SIB 1944c: 21, 23, 45, 46, 49, 51). During the morning, arrests continued. Two more returning Italian soldiers—one with a five-day pass, one a deserter—were stopped while they were on the way home across the countryside, on foot, from northern Italy; they were taken by motorcycle and sidecar to the militia barracks. One of the soldiers, Natale Farina, managed to holler to a passing neighbor en route, "Go tell my dad that they're taking me away" (SIB 1944c: 60). The neighbor reached the Farina residence by around four o'clock and told Natale's parents what he had seen and heard. Francesco Farina fetched his savings—fifty thousand lire—and, after pausing before a portrait of Jesus Christ to make the sign of the cross, he rushed out in the direction of the militia barracks. Giuseppina Farina, distraught, followed her husband a few minutes later, but by the time she reached Via Cappuccini, her husband had been arrested and thrown inside the militia barracks alongside his son. As she and two or three other relatives stood wondering what to do, the air suddenly rang with the sound of explosions and gunfire coming from various corners of the town (SIB 1944c: 24–26, 63–64).

At around four o'clock on September 21, the people of Matera rose up against the Germans. Perhaps in anticipation of the insurrection and the imminent Allied attack, the occupiers' behavior had certainly worsened, with daily theft, bullying, and intimidation stoking enormous resentment among the populace; events were finally coming to a head. On that very afternoon, two of Wolf-Werner's men had sauntered into a jewelry store and, according to some accounts, held it up, waving a submachine gun at the lady proprietor. Someone alerted an officer and two men of the Carabinieri (Italian state paramilitary police) who intervened and tried to persuade the Germans to leave. They were joined by two Guardia di Finanza (Customs police) officers and three local police officers. The two Germans not only stood their ground but turned their weapons on the officers, who acted fast, brought the thieves to the ground, and killed them; in the process, the Carabinieri captain suffered a wound to his little finger. Meanwhile, at a barber shop in the town square, another of Wolf-Werner's men was issuing various threats, only to be cut and knocked to the ground by a local war veteran. If these actions were originally intended as provocation, they worked; as more Germans descended on the town in response, the civilians and police fought back ferociously. The Germans raced to seize the Palazzo del Governo—the town hall—but the mayor's staff acted quickly, barricading the entrances and calling on the Carabinieri and state police to defend it. Street fighting broke out everywhere, lasting for around two hours, with citizens producing knives, hand grenades, and firearms;

Divided Over Hitler

Stefano Fontana, the communal dog catcher, was later commended for supplying ammunition to the insurrectionists and for coordinating much of the action (SIB 1944a: Exhibit U).

At some point the Germans arrested a teenager, a messenger boy for the local antiaircraft unit, and added him to the prisoners in the militia barracks, along with several others who fell into their hands during the turmoil, bringing the number of prisoners to either fourteen or sixteen. At around five o'clock the Germans turned their attention to the electric company headquarters, a short distance from the town center, with the intention of attacking it. The exact reasoning behind this remains unclear, but there would appear to be two main possibilities; either they intended to cut off the town's power supply to impede the insurrection, or they were acting on intelligence that identified the electric company offices, or its staff, as having some kind of role in the resistance to the Germans, such as facilitating radio communication with the Allies. It is similarly not known whether such activity, if real, was connected to the mysterious arrival of the car from Allied-held Taranto the night before, whose occupants were detained at the militia barracks. Around sixty of Wolf-Werner's men surrounded the electric company building; two went inside, with hand grenades, and ordered the staff to get out. As the staff exited the building they were machine-gunned without warning; three were killed outright and two were wounded, one of whom died five months later from his injuries. As the wounded lay in the street, groaning in agony, they heard one of the hand grenades explode inside the building, the other one apparently failed to detonate. It does not appear that the grenades had been positioned in such a way as to interrupt the electric supply to the town, if that was indeed the intention, and it remains unclear what else they may have been hoping to destroy (SIB 1944c: 72–75).

The confused attack and massacre at the electric light company lasted no more than ten minutes, and it was becoming clear from the Germans' erratic behavior that this was almost their curtain call in Matera. The insurrection only showed signs of gaining momentum, and the insurrectionists, who, it was now clear, had somehow managed to arm themselves right under the Germans' noses all along, were not about to give up. With the Fallschirmjäger busy dealing with the revolt, they would be in no position to fend off the Allies, should they decide to attack in force to liberate Matera. Probing units, armored cars of the Canadian army, had already been seen approaching the outskirts of town; the German sentries had dissuaded them with bursts of light machinegun fire, but that would be unlikely to hold them off for a second time (Ambrico 2003: 51).

5. "The Positions Will Be Held; If Necessary, to the Last Man!"

Wolf-Werner weighed up the situation and gave the order to abandon Matera. At around half past five, the Germans climbed into their vehicles and prepared to leave, but not before Wolf-Werner's men carried out one final order in Matera; blow up the militia barracks, with the prisoners locked inside. The prisoners, it will be recalled, included Natale Farina and his father, Francesco, who had grabbed his savings and tried to buy his son's freedom, only to end up sharing his fate. The records suggest that fourteen people were trapped in the building, but the only survivor, soldier Giuseppe Calderaro, later swore that there were sixteen, including himself. What is certain is that this time, unlike the electric company attack, the explosion was more than sufficient to destroy the building and kill nearly everyone inside, by which time the Germans had sped off, abandoning Matera. Local residents, initially petrified by the massive explosion, started to creep towards the smoking ruins of the militia barracks. Groaning and wheezing could be heard from under the rubble; residents removed debris from on top of several victims, only to watch them breathe their last breath. One local noticed the top of a man's head poking out from the rubble and started to dig, tugging bricks aside to allow the man to breathe; his skull was almost entirely stripped of flesh, but he was alive, just for a few seconds. Helpless, dazed, horrified, and sick from breathing smoke and dust, the locals gave up their rescue efforts and returned home (SIB 1944c: 27–28, 30–32).

Thirteen bodies were recovered from the ruins of the militia barracks, of which two, almost certainly belonging to demobilized soldiers, were never identified. In addition to the thirteen corpses, firefighters collected two boxes of completely unidentifiable human remains—essentially pieces of flesh and bone—which may or may not lend weight to the theory that there were indeed fifteen victims in total. At first light on the following morning, Wednesday, September 22, 1943, units of the IV Canadian Reconnaissance Regiment (IV Princess Louise's Dragoon Guards) entered Matera, officially ending the German occupation (Ambrico 2003: 33–40, 51–52). The following month, October 1943, seventeen Allied nations founded the United Nations War Crimes Commission (UNWCC), which held its first meeting in January 1944. Section 67 of the Special Investigation Branch, of the British Military Police, was duly tasked with investigating war crimes in Italy, with the first cases on their desk being the two massacres in Matera. Captain William James Hutchins, DAPM (Deputy Assistant Provost Marshal) of 67 Section, arrived in Matera one year after the events. His eventual report, numbered WO310/102, would end up being officially catalogued under "German reprisals against civilians" because,

Divided Over Hitler

as the perpetrators were never apprehended and indicted, no war crimes charges were ever brought. Hutchins' conclusion, however, was unequivocal; the massacres at the electric company and the militia barracks could undoubtedly be classified as war crimes, the first ones to be investigated by the Allies in the Second World War (SIB 1944c: 1). This case constitutes another historical "first" as well; Matera was the first southern Italian city to rise up against the Germans, successfully expelling them. The city was awarded the Silver Medal for Military Valor (Medaglia d'Argento al Valore Militare) twenty years after the war, and the Gold Medal for Civil Valor (Medaglia d'Oro al Valore Civile) seventy years after the war, in addition to decorations awarded to individual insurrectionists.

Wolf-Werner and his men fled, joining the retreat taking place across southern Italy, with many German field commanders wondering when they would have a chance to fight back and change their fortunes. Kesselring's tactics continued to divide opinion. The OKW—Wehrmacht high command—doubted his ability, but Hitler was pleased with Kesselring's obsessive loyalty to him. Hitler trusted him and even became sympathetic to his idealism, while others saw Kesselring as overly optimistic, unrealistic, and gullible, with a too-high opinion of the Italians. Kesselring has continued to be an equivocal figure ever since, with historians unsure of how much blame to apportion to him, and his indecision, for the atrocities committed under his command, especially during the retreats. Hitler resolved to halt the ongoing retreat and impose a tough defensive line before winter set in; he ordered Kesselring to begin fighting a more tenacious rearguard against the Allies, who were advancing from the southeast after the Taranto landings and from the southwest after the Salerno landings. Kesselring interpreted these orders in his own confused way, once again. He gladly obeyed Hitler, convinced that all would be well; the prospect of abandoning Italy appalled him, and he was adamant that Italy south of the northern Apennines could easily be held for six to nine months. This assessment was based on his belief that the Allies would never conduct operations outside the range of their air cover, which could only reach as far as Salerno, but he ignored the fact that besides main cities and towns the Allies were capturing dozens of small and medium-sized airfields as they advanced. Kesselring had no difficulty, therefore, in espousing Hitler's ambitious goal of halting the Allied advance until the spring of 1944 (Sangster 2015: 93, 146, 147, 150).

The key part of the defensive "winter line" stretched continuously from the Tyrrhenian coast, near the mouth of the Garigliano river, to the Adriatic, near Ortona, just north of the Sangro river. This was named the

5. "The Positions Will Be Held; If Necessary, to the Last Man!"

Gustav line; it spanned the strategically vital Apennine mountain range and four rivers; the Garigliano, the Aventino, the Volturno and the Sangro. On November 15, 1943, Wolf-Werner was ordered to stand in as commander of the entire I (first) Fallschirmjäger regiment (Kommandant i. V.—"in Vertretung"—as a replacement or stand-in), an appointment that would last until he was himself replaced temporarily in January 1944 (Scherzer 2007: 688). The regiment was ordered to the Gustav line, arriving on November 18 (Andrae 1995: 109). Wolf-Werner was apparently still personally leading the III (third) battalion, I (first) regiment, as well as temporarily leading the whole regiment (Schreiber 1996: 153). On the highlands overlooking the Sangro valley was the small town of Roccaraso, with the village of Pietransieri beside it and a poor adjoining hamlet called Limmari. Both locations were tiny, with a just few hundred inhabitants. Limmari was no more than a collection of small farms, preserving centuries-old ways of life. Because of the war, the vast majority of the local population consisted of women, children, and the elderly (Mercuri 2020: 14).

The absence of men in the area perturbed the Germans. With the Armistice of September 8, 1943, the partisans' war had begun—known to the Italians as the war of national liberation—involving a wide range of anti-fascist volunteers, male and female, young and old, from Catholic activists to Communist militants, from Italian deserters to escaped Allied prisoners of war. It was a clandestine war fought by an invisible guerrilla army, using the mountains and forests to spring attacks on the German invaders. The Germans vowed "scorched earth" to weed out the partisans. On October 30, with Hitler's prompting, a printed announcement by Kesselring began to circulate, telling the local population around Roccaraso to evacuate from what was now the front line. This was indicative of a new "harder line" being tried by Kesselring. Anyone remaining in the scattered hamlets, farms, or mountain forests was to be considered a partisan, Kesselring proclaimed, and they would be subject to German wartime justice; execution on the spot. Few complied with the order and it is far from certain that everyone read it. The order seemed to have little relevance for isolated hamlets at four thousand six hundred feet (one thousand four hundred meters) above sea level, whose inhabitants had nowhere else to go. Their only livelihood—livestock—was there, and in any case normality was just around the corner; the Allies had landed, and the south was being liberated. They could not have known that there were another seventeen months of war to go, and the Allies had not quite reached Pietransieri yet. Most local people surmised that if they stayed out of sight in their remote mountain farms, rather than making themselves overly visible in the town, the Germans would have no reason to harm them and might not even notice them (Lingen 2009: 48). The German armed forces in general and the Fallschirmjäger in particular were extremely jittery, however. Before Russia they had never experienced guerrilla warfare; they were shaken by the partisans' capacity for sudden attack and sabotage, and as a result they resolved to respond uncompromisingly (Sangster 2015: 134–36). The ferocity and spontaneity of the uprising in Matera, and the fact that Matera's ostensibly placid citizenry, at the given moment, turned out to be well-armed and determined, had only made the Fallschirmjäger more fretful (SIB 1944c: 13).

Just over two weeks after Kesselring's warning was circulated, the III (third) battalion Fallschirmjäger arrived in Pietransieri, probably expecting to find the evacuation order obeyed and the village abandoned, which it was, but not completely, and the atmosphere was hostile; a local woman had been murdered by the previous German occupiers (Schreiber 1996: 153). Three days after their arrival, in the early morning of Sunday, November 21, while on patrol in the outlying farms of Limmari hamlet, Captain Schulze and his men were startled to realize that some of the farm buildings, cottages, and shacks were occupied. The German soldiers began to shout frantically, summarizing the contents of the Kesselring warning, which had either been not read or perhaps not understood by the largely illiterate population of Limmari. The Germans' gestures with submachine guns were clear, however, but it was too late to comply. In pairs, the soldiers were ordered to burst into each cottage and machine-gun whoever happened to be inside; there were only women, children, and the elderly. The victims did not even have time to comprehend what was happening; many were sat around the table having breakfast, and some were later discovered with their faces plunged into their bowls of barley coffee and black bread. As panic spread, a change of tactic was suddenly ordered; the cottages were barricaded shut from the outside and hand grenades were thrown through the windows. Finally, the remaining inhabitants were forced out into a clearing and machine-gunned where they stood. One hundred and twenty-eight people were killed, including sixty women and thirty-four children aged under ten. The oldest victim was eighty and the youngest was one month old. It was the worst atrocity committed in Italy up to that moment. Most sources indicate that only one person survived the breakfast-table shootings, and that one person survived the mass machine-gunning; she was a seven-year-old girl, Virginia Macerelli, who was shielded from the bullets by her mother's

5. "The Positions Will Be Held; If Necessary, to the Last Man!"

falling body and then hidden beneath it. In her mother's arms was Virginia's baby sister, and at their side was her little brother. Virginia was discovered alive on the evening of the following day, by her grandmother. Shortly after the massacre, the heavens saw fit to hide the appalling scene from view, covering the entire area in dense snow for months to come (Mercuri 2020: 14).

Kesselring's "winter line" achieved its goal of slowing down the Allied advance, but not for his ridiculously optimistic six to nine months, and at a considerable cost to both sides. The first defenses soon fell to the British Eighth Army, and on November 23, just two days after the massacre at Limmari, the Sangro was crossed. The following month, the Canadian First Infantry Division prepared to launch an assault on Ortona, facing Wolf-Werner's I (first) Fallschirmjäger. The Battle of Ortona, lasting from December 20 to 28, would be ominously renamed the Italian Stalingrad. It has been argued that Ortona was of considerable strategic importance, as it was one of Italy's few usable deep water ports on the east coast; Allied ships would be able to dock there, shortening the Eighth Army's supply lines, which stretched back to Bari and Taranto. Some historians, on the other hand, assign less importance to Ortona itself. Allied forces were ordered to maintain the offensive against the Gustav Line, and going through the built-up areas in and around Ortona seemed to be the only feasible option; the Allies may have anticipated a minor urban battle, but the Germans had constructed a series of interlocking defensive positions in the town. In the context of Hitler and Kesselring's exhortations to their forces to hold their ground at all costs, Ortona turned into a formidable obstacle (Atkinson 2013: 306).

The Battle of Ortona would end up accounting for a quarter of all Canadian deaths in the Italian campaign. On the eve of battle, we find an exceptionally rare record of a quote from Wolf-Werner von der Schulenburg, addressing his men, "You are the best unit in this sector, and I expect that the positions will be held; if necessary, to the last man!" (Ihr seid die beste Truppe in diesem sektor, und ich ervarter, das die Stellungen gehalten werden: falls notwendig, bis zum letzten Mann!) (Wilhelmsmeyer 1995: 220). The British Field Marshal Harold Alexander agreed, incidentally, that the first Fallschirmjäger division were the best German troops in Italy (Atkinson 2013: 303). Nevertheless, 1943 ended with the Germans withdrawing from Ortona, though the Allies could capitalize little on their victory. The Gustav line held through much of the winter, initially unbroken by new Allied landings at Anzio and the assault on Monte Cassino in January and February of 1944, but by March the line was cracking. Wolf-Werner himself was again placed in command of the I (first) Fallschirmjäger regiment in February, when he and his unit were ordered to leave Roccaraso and head straight to Monte Cassino (Andrae 1995: 268; Ambrico 2003: 12). As the Fallschirmjäger hurriedly departed from Pietransieri, spring was on its way, and the one hundred and twenty-eight corpses in Limmari, still lying where they fell, finally began to thaw.

Considering the events at Matera in September and at Pietransieri exactly two months later, it is impossible to be certain about what Wolf-Werner was really feeling when he spoke of leading "the best unit in the sector," but even to his warped mind those words must have sounded hollow. The embittered Fallschirmjäger could not have felt much like the best troops; they were a highly trained elite, but they were assigned to patrolling villages and guarding the countryside; they were crack paratroops, but they were reduced to common infantry, fighting hand-to-hand in half-deserted and inconsequential towns. It surely would not have escaped their attention, at some level of consciousness, that Germany was losing the war. The same was true of their commanders, but Kesselring refused to accept responsibility, claiming that his own plans for holding southern Italy would have worked, had they not been written-off at an early stage (Shirer 1960: 1001). Italy—once Germany's "Steel Pact" ally—was now an uncooperative occupied country, and the Germans poured their troops in. The Allies gave Italy the awkward status of "co-belligerent" rather than "ally," allowing Kesselring to blame Allied ambiguity for the tragedy that unfolded. He claimed that Hitler would have permitted Italy to quietly withdraw from the war unharmed, had the Allies agreed to respect its neutrality and not use it as a base for operations against Germany (Sangster 2015: 48, 53).

This petulant and fanciful postwar appraisal was typical of Kesselring's evasiveness and lack of realism. His assessment ignored the fact that Italians did not envisage, for themselves, a passive role in the ensuing defeat of Nazi-fascism; Matera was an early demonstration of their refusal to "quietly withdraw" and there would be many more such demonstrations. The Fallschirmjäger were suddenly faced with a partisan guerrilla war again, and the experience was destabilizing. Their shock at being outsmarted by these "peasant" partisan bands, mere untrained brigands, first in Greece, then in Russia, and now in Italy, quickened their transition into a shameless death squad, capable of shooting babies held in their mothers' arms. No-one, the Fallschirmjäger seemed to have declared, would be giving them lessons in fighting dirty; the unconventional nature of partisan

5. "The Positions Will Be Held; If Necessary, to the Last Man!"

warfare was used as a justification for adopting indiscriminately barbaric and inhumane tactics (Shirer 1960: 941). For all their anxiety over the partisans, frustration with Italian soldiers, and loathing of the Allied forces, however, the Fallschirmjägers' victims were overwhelmingly the unarmed and defenseless; women, children, and the elderly, and, apart from those few hapless Italian conscripts, they were overwhelmingly civilians; innocent people who never asked for their village to become the front line in the Second World War.

It has been pointed out that isolated units like Wolf-Werner's, freed from accountability and suffering various privations, have tended to commit the worst atrocities in times of war, and that disorganized retreats have often tended to involve violent reprisals (Lingen 2009: 48). These arguments have occasionally been advanced in an attempt to absolve such figures as Kesselring, whose "harder line" approach towards Italian civilians would seem to have provoked appalling war crimes. Kesselring's defenders have disputed that his orders led to such abhorrent violence, pointing to his order not to destroy Rome's bridges, making it an "open" city, and his actions to "save" many Italian art treasures. In reality, the first of these was ordered by Hitler, not Kesselring, and the motives behind the second order were highly questionable. The fact also remains that early atrocities, described above, were stepping stones to greater ones; Hitler went on to order even harsher reprisals in Italy, announcing that fifty civilians would be executed for every German killed by partisans. Kesselring's subordinates—and not Kesselring—took it upon themselves to mitigate this, ordering a ratio of ten civilians for every German instead, and this is what was carried out. It would take a massacre outside of Italy, and not against civilians, to alert the Allies to the extent of German war crimes in the Italian campaign, however; the foreign ministers of the Soviet Union, United Kingdom, and United States were meeting in Moscow when they learned that one hundred disbanded and disarmed Italian officers had been summarily executed in Greece. This led to the Moscow Declaration of October 31, 1943 (the day after Kesselring's fatal warning to civilians), which laid out the criteria for the punishment of war crimes committed by Germany and its allies. After the war, Kesselring was vague about his own role and claimed ignorance of his Führer's plans to exterminate "subhuman" peoples, but he also refused to criticize Hitler's actions upon "learning" about them. Kesselring's undignified pretense of ignorance was laughable, but his reputation as a simple soldier with an air of naiveté saved him from harsh punishment (Sangster 2015: 50–55, 68, 166, 177, 189). Those directly responsible for the war crimes at Matera and Pietransieri would not be charged at all; the exceptionally deadly Italian battles of Ortona and Monte Cassino claimed many of the lower-level culprits. Captain Georg Schulze is rumored to have died peacefully in bed, in old age, at home in Germany. Wolf-Werner would meet his fate and end his days in neither Italy nor Germany.

6

"We Want to Create Sacred, Inviolable Law Again"

The July Plot, 1944

"Whenever there are great virtues, it's a sure sign something's wrong."—Bertolt Brecht, *Mother Courage and Her Children,* 1939

"We took these actions to save Germany from unspeakable misery. I know I will be hanged for this, but I have no regrets."—Fritz-Dietlof Graf von der Schulenburg, at his show-trial in Berlin, quoted on a memorial plaque at the Klein Trebbow estate

There were at least a dozen serious attempts to assassinate Hitler, planned by a variety of individuals and groups broadly belonging to the German Resistance, which was a rather loose association of separate cells rather than an organized or regimented movement. Significant Resistance groups included the Abwehr plot (or the Oster conspiracy), the White Rose, and the Kreisau Circle, which, like many such groups, comprised an eclectic mix of young intellectuals and idealists, aristocrats, priests, trade unionists, landowners, and socialists (Shirer 1960: 1014–16). Not all of these Resistance groups planned to kill Hitler and not all of them were as diverse as the Kreisau Circle. Of the various assassination attempts, the one that has tended to capture people's imagination, and arguably the most complex, dramatic, and consequential attempt, has become known as the July plot. It is sometimes said that the work of the German Resistance "culminated" in the July plot, but this was more by accident than design; the scope and practicality of doing effective high-impact resistance rapidly diminished once the Allies had breached the Nazis' European stronghold. A number of senior figures in Nazi Germany, most notably in the military community, were involved in the July plot, though none of them remains as memorable for their part in it as the intended assassin himself, Colonel Claus Philipp Maria Justinian Schenk Graf von Stauffenberg.

Claus von Stauffenberg remains so strongly associated with the July plot that it is sometimes called the Stauffenberg plot; consider the title of the book by the late German historian Hans Mommsen, *Germans Against Hitler: The Stauffenberg Plot and Resistance Under the Third Reich* (the 2009 English translation is by Angus McGeoch). Meanwhile, the name of Fritz-Dietlof Graf von der Schulenburg, one of Stauffenberg's most trusted co-conspirators, is far from a household name, but, as Mommsen explained, "long before Von Stauffenberg took center stage, Schulenburg was the inner driving force of the conspiracy" (Mommsen 2009: 152). Remarkably, Fritz-Dietlof has even been excluded from many high-profile narratives recounting the July plot story; his character did not appear and was not even mentioned in the 2008 film *Valkyrie*, starring Tom Cruise as Stauffenberg; in reality, without Fritz-Dietlof, Cruise's character would never have been involved, and there would probably never have been a July plot. Notable authors have acknowledged Fritz-Dietlof's part in the plot, but they have sometimes relegated him to a minor support role rather than the driving force, the artful persuader, the master networker (Shirer 1960: 1047). It was Fritz-Dietlof who succeeded in recruiting Stauffenberg, who planted the briefcase-bomb in the meeting room, which detonated almost as planned, but which only succeeded in wounding Hitler.

Killing Hitler, though crucial to the July plot, was only intended to be phase one of the plan; the lethal bomb was to be immediately followed by an ingeniously orchestrated coup d'état, which would be triggered the moment the Führer's demise was confirmed. The operation is well-documented, and the mechanics of it are well-established, but that does not mean that there are no unanswered questions surrounding it. One of the most open areas of debate concerns what exactly the plotters would have done had the coup been successful; some of them, it is believed, envisaged a speedy armistice and peace conference with the Allies. They intended to present the Allies with a list of territorial demands, no less, as a condition for Germany's immediate surrender. This would have been very wishful thinking at best and sheer delusion at worst. Other areas of uncertainty concern the plotters' post-coup vision for German society; what kind of a Germany did they favor, to replace the Nazi regime they wanted to topple, and what were their specific motivations for that particular plot at that particular moment? Clues to a fuller understanding of events may be gleaned from the plot's timing, only about six weeks after the Normandy landings, though preparations had begun some time earlier

6. "We Want to Create Sacred, Inviolable Law Again"

of course, at Fritz-Dietlof's secluded temporary residence at the Klein Trebbow estate, managed by his sister Tisa.

Considering the situation in 1944, it is difficult to believe that any rational thinking Germans in the military could have realistically imagined a victory for the Third Reich, but this retrospective view fails to take into account the power of the Hitler myth, especially upon those closest to power and the Führer's orbit. Many civil servants, diplomats, and generals would remain quietly loyal to Hitler right up to the end, even when faced with clear, obvious, and imminent defeat (Sangster 2015: 132). The alternative, after all, was not just to accept political failure but to accept the total and fast-approaching destruction of Germany; some minds could cope with this reality and some minds could not, but this realization was still not enough to really fuse the disparate elements of opposition to Hitler. It was only late in the war that those who had always experienced a profound moral repugnance for Nazism, such as the religious wing of the Resistance, were united in sympathy with those whose patriotism and love of the Fatherland had only recently overruled their erstwhile approval of Hitler. Turning against the Führer was not easy to do; the army, like many national institutions, had traditionally abstained from aligning itself politically, even in the face of enormous pressure, and casting aside this military tradition was a major challenge, even for the sake of saving Germany. The July plotters have often been labeled "disaffected German Army officers" or similar, but it could be argued that their conversion to the Resistance required them to reach a point of desperation rather than disaffection, faced as they were with the very real prospect of the utter obliteration of Germany (Short 2013: 4, 11–12). "We took these actions," Fritz-Dietlof explained, "to save Germany from unspeakable misery. I know I will be hanged for this, but I have no regrets" (Steinau-Steinrück 2020). As Richard von Weizsäcker reflected, years later, "we could not possibly wait until this terrible war found its own end" (Kimmelman 2009). Their patriotism now had a new purpose.

The July plotters were indeed mostly military men, and they were mostly aristocratic, like Fritz-Dietlof. Weizsäcker recalled, however, that Fritz-Dietlof was always "down to earth … not typical high nobility" (Kimmelman 2009). Nobility, in any case, had never been a particular aid to success in the Nazi military, and especially not in wartime; Hitler increasingly saw the "old guard" of the generals' class as an obstacle to his military leadership. Nobles like Fritz-Dietlof were never ostracized by Hitler—the Führer had personally attended Fritz-Dietlof's father's funeral, after all—but there was no love lost between Hitler and the aristocracy.

The fact remained, however, that upper-class army officers were practically the only people who could get close enough to Hitler to kill him by 1944. Security around the Führer was extremely tight, and he was acutely aware of the danger of assassination. It is unsurprising that the July plot appealed to atypical high nobility like Stauffenberg and Schulenburg, who were deeply influenced by a mix of traditions, philosophies, and religious principles, with Nazism being only a recent addition. Fritz-Dietlof's attitude to Nazism still puzzles historians; his early membership of the Nazi party was both well-known and somewhat equivocal, but he was far from being the only mid- to high-level Nazi with a mixed agenda. The notion of "tactically" joining the Nazi party certainly existed and could have one of several ulterior objectives. Within Fritz-Dietlof's civil service profession there was a view that those who were socially open-minded and committed to the rule of law must do everything necessary to stay in their jobs, including joining the Nazi party, rather than be replaced by fanatical Hitlerites. One secretly democratic and fair-minded German diplomat confessed to his colleagues that joining the Nazi party, in his view, was the only viable way to influence national policy for the better (Herwarth 1981: 99).

The fact that such views circulated within the vast and complex German civil service says a lot, and it invites speculation as to how the war might have progressed, if only Hitler had been able to count on a genuinely loyal civil service. Despite the diversity of approaches to Nazi party membership, however, non-membership was ultimately not an option in most branches of the civil service, and this was finally written into law. Regarding his own stance, Fritz-Dietlof explained that he originally saw the Nazi movement as a potentially useful catalyst, a way to shake up the clunky party political system, break up the tired old alliances and dysfunctional pacts, and create openings for better parties to emerge (Malinowski 2020: 97, 270). Fritz-Dietlof's relentlessly optimistic nature did not go unnoticed; the role assigned to him in the Resistance was not so much that of planner—he was not regarded as having a strategic mind—but rather as the chief persuader, recruiter, and motivator. Fritz-Dietlof was regarded as the most significant intermediary during the plot's discussion stages, curating the huge task of networking required for the post-coup arrangements, when the ex-plotters would have a country—and a war—to run, with government posts to fill. His naiveté was perhaps a strength in this regard; he believed in personal authority and trusted that sincerity would always exert a certain power, as had always been his experience. Fritz-Dietlof was still sufficiently tied to Prussian tradition to believe in the higher orders

6. "We Want to Create Sacred, Inviolable Law Again"

setting an example, safe in the knowledge that subordinates would obediently follow (Mommsen 2009: 175, 177).

The extent of noble involvement in the July plot has led to suggestions that its true theme was aristocratic resentment. According to this interpretation, the July plot was the desperate cry of an elite who had totally lost influence under Hitler—whom they had mostly trusted—and who urgently wanted to regain that influence and preserve it for the postwar world (Evans 2015a: 198). The de facto leader of the plotters, Stauffenberg, was a complex aristocrat who seemed to embody the class resentment and distaste for Hitler experienced by many of his co-conspirators. In addition, he boasted two crucial qualities; an extraordinary level of physical courage and a very pronounced sense that German military honor was something worth rescuing from the ongoing chaos. This gives some clues as to his character make-up; he was a nobleman, a patriot, he had been very seriously wounded in North Africa, but he was also something of a poet, a mystic, and a cultist (Bullock 1962: 738). He had, like many of the July plotters, initially supported not only Hitler but also his racialist and expansionist policies. His opposition to Hitler was born amidst the stark reality of the front lines, where, for every thousand casualties, only three hundred replacements could be found; disaster for Germany seemed mathematically unavoidable. Coupled with this, Stauffenberg found himself increasingly repulsed by the brazen and lawless "special" units such as the SS, who, despite their use of ancient Teutonic symbols, had no precedent or foundation in German military history. He saw that the depraved behavior of these supposedly elite units had a corrupting influence on the traditionally honorable regular army. Furthermore, Stauffenberg was, and remained, a practicing Roman Catholic; soldier or not, the taking of life was no trivial matter to him, and he considered the indiscriminate killings of civilians and prisoners to be morally intolerable. In summary, the Germany that Stauffenberg idealized, the Germany of order, tradition, heroism, and values, was being systematically destroyed (Shirer 1960: 1028–30).

By various routes, therefore, middle- and upper-class Germans moved towards the Resistance, which, for the most part, consisted of small groups or cells with a fluctuating membership, each one only loosely connected to some of the others, if at all. There were monarchists, students, soldiers, Catholic priests, Evangelical pastors, businessmen, politicians, diplomats, artists, and mystical poets in the Resistance mix; it was an extraordinary combination (Bullock 1962: 735). Their only common trait was displeasure with Nazi regime, and even this varied in extent, depth, orientation, and motivation. Some of them, especially the

Divided Over Hitler

devoutly religious resisters, morally rejected Nazism in its entirety, while others, like Fritz-Dietlof, used to think that the Nazi movement could be reformed for the better. Some believed that once Hitler was dead, the priority would be to seize control of the state and run Germany to save it from ruin, while others thought that order could only be restored by the Allies. On the military side of the Resistance, the July plot leaders tended to be older and senior officers, while Fritz-Dietlof recruited from a younger generation of army officers, capitalizing on the growing awareness of Germany's impending moral and political vortex. In fact, dissenting talk among young army officers was commonplace, but the crucial step was to move from mere disillusionment to action, and it was Fritz-Dietlof's task to guide them through this step (Snyder 1991: 71, 74). Even Stauffenberg had needed help to make this transition; Fritz-Dietlof was a friend of Stauffenberg's uncle, Nikolaus Graf von Üxküll-Gyllenband, one of a small cohort of July plotters who were not active military. Together, they persuaded the young nobleman to join them in the Resistance; he was reluctant to make that leap, to begin with at least (Kramarz 1967: 72, 126). Richard von Weizsäcker, as a junior officer in the IR9, was similarly won over by the conviction of Fritz-Dietlof. "I saw him just four weeks before the twentieth of July," Weizsäcker later recalled, "and he told me that soon we would be where we want to go, that we would be called back to Berlin, that we would have jobs to do" (Kimmelman 2009). Fritz-Dietlof was confident about the July plot's success and was already making plans for staffing the post-coup emergency government.

At the Klein Trebbow estate, managed by Tisa, the secluded garden pavilion nicknamed the "teahouse" was the setting for preparatory discussions between July plotters. Once Stauffenburg had taken the fateful decision to join the Resistance, it became normal for Fritz-Dietlof to meet with him at the teahouse, but the July plot's real military planning stages required a larger gathering, and this greatly increased the risk. Bearing much of this risk were the Schulenburg siblings, Tisa and Fritz-Dietlof, and they were not even the only members of their family to be involved in the July plot. Friedrich-Werner Graf von der Schulenburg, the near-namesake of their late father, at times mistakenly referred to as their uncle but in fact their father's first cousin, was also a fully committed plotter. Friedrich-Werner, it will be recalled, held the singularly critical post of German ambassador to the USSR from 1934 to 1941; he brought no fanatical Nazi ideals at all to that role, but rather a conservative sense of duty to country that steered his diplomatic and military career, in peace and war, for forty years. His attempts to avoid war had not only been confounded

6. "We Want to Create Sacred, Inviolable Law Again"

and abused; they had led to his personal fall from grace, in Hitler's eyes, and relegation to an inconsequential role. On his return to Germany from Moscow he had been assigned to lead the "Russia committee," a department of the foreign office with "consultor" status and no political influence, which effectively neutralized Friedrich-Werner. Disgusted by news of Nazi atrocities in the east, he attempted to use his position, such as it was, to appeal for the humane treatment of the populations of the USSR, which only led to his Russia committee being officially ignored; he was accused of trying to undermine Nazi operating procedures, which in effect he was. He was drawn to the idea of a plot to overthrow Hitler in the hope of reaching a speedy armistice in the east, and he was ready and willing to go negotiate with Stalin, whom he knew, on behalf of the plotters. In the meantime, he used his extensive diplomatic connections and considerable personal popularity to aid the plot, broker post-coup arrangements, and persuade people to join, much like Fritz-Dietlof did. Had the plot been successful in overthrowing Hitler, Friedrich-Werner was slated to become a high-ranking official in the foreign office, probably foreign minister, though he was never a careerist or climber (Shirer 1960: 1072, Heinemann 1994: 167; Herwarth 1981: 92, 213–14, 251–52).

Previous plans to kill Hitler had always encountered major obstacles, and there was already a catalog of failed, thwarted, or aborted attempts. These precedents were now brushed aside as pure bad luck; Resistance members were disappointed but determined to try again (Snyder 1991: 73). The ideal way to carry out the assassination eluded them, until the right factors and the right people combined to produce the July plot. The July plan itself was an ingenious combination of providential timing, insider knowledge, brazen opportunism, and phenomenal courage. Providential timing ordained that on Saturday, July 1, 1944, Stauffenberg was given a new appointment as chief of staff to General Friedrich Fromm (1888–1945), the head of the Reserve Army, which was based in Berlin. By a stroke of good fortune, Fromm was not only aware of the Resistance's goal of assassinating Hitler but actively sympathetic to it, possibly in the hope of receiving a high government position in the aftermath of the coup (Shirer 1960: 1035). Crucially, Stauffenberg's new role involved attending some of Hitler's military conferences, either at the Wolfsschanze—"Wolf's Lair"—in East Prussia, or at Berchtesgaden, and it would thus give him an opportunity to kill Hitler by carrying a briefcase bomb right up to him. It was now a question of identifying the right day to do it, but the huge matter of what to do immediately after the assassination was where the insider knowledge and opportunistic cunning came in.

Divided Over Hitler

The plan was to hijack an already-existing procedure intended for the defense of Berlin in case of an unprecedented emergency situation. According to this emergency plan, codename Valkyrie, the Reserve Army, under Fromm, would be empowered to seize key strategic points in Berlin and elsewhere; the aim was to maintain order in case of an extreme event, such as an uprising by the millions of imported foreign laborers, or a catastrophe such as a high-level assassination. Hitler's approval of the Valkyrie plan owed more to his personal paranoia than to any real possibility of a slave-laborers' revolt or similar event (Shirer 1960: 1033–34). Upon confirmation of the Führer's death, therefore, Operation Valkyrie was to be put into action by the very people who had orchestrated the assassination; the Reich's own emergency counterinsurgency plan would thus be subverted into a coup d'état. In Norse-Teutonic mythology, the Valkyrie were awe-inspiringly beautiful maidens who surveyed the battlefield from above, selecting who was to be killed. The symbolism, for the plotters, was clear; the Valkyrie had chosen, and Adolf Hitler's moment to die had finally arrived (Snyder 1991: 75).

On the morning of July 20, Stauffenberg flew to the Wolf's Lair for one of Hitler's military conferences, carrying two English-made bombs in his briefcase. It was not his first trip to the Wolf's Lair, and it was not even his first trip there with a briefcase bomb; yet another previous attempt had already been aborted. At around half past twelve, just as the conference was about to begin, Stauffenberg asked to use the restroom adjoining Field Marshal Wilhelm Keitel's office; he explained that he had to change his shirt, which was damp with sweat, as it was a very hot summer's day. In the restroom, assisted by his aide-de-camp and fellow plotter Lieutenant Werner von Haeften, Stauffenberg used pliers to crush the end of a pencil detonator, which was inserted into a two-point-two pound (one kilogram) block of plastic explosive, wrapped in brown paper. The detonator consisted of a thin copper tube containing cupric chloride; the chemical would take about ten minutes to silently eat through a wire that was holding back the firing pin from the percussion cap. The task of arming the bomb was slow going, partly due to the war wounds that had cost Stauffenberg an eye, his right hand, and two fingers on his left hand; he sometimes joked that he had never needed all those fingers anyway. To make matters worse, he was interrupted by a guard knocking on the door, advising him that the meeting was about to begin. He was not able to prime the second bomb, which he gave to Werner von Haeften.

Stauffenberg placed the single primed bomb inside his briefcase and entered the conference room, where Hitler and twenty officers were now

6. "We Want to Create Sacred, Inviolable Law Again"

gathered. He positioned the briefcase under the large oak table, near to where Hitler was seated. After a few minutes, Stauffenberg received a pre-arranged telephone call and left the room. At this point, it is believed that Colonel Heinz Brandt, who was standing, felt his feet come into contact with the briefcase under the table and tried to push it aside with his foot. Unable to do so, he reached down for it and moved it to the other side of one of the thick table supports, which ran the full width of the table, unlike individual table legs. Brandt was standing next to Hitler, and by putting the briefcase at the other side of the table support, he unwittingly shielded Hitler from the bomb's blast, saving the Führer's life and losing his own. When the bomb detonated at forty-two minutes past twelve, Brandt's leg was blown off and he later died. The conference room was demolished and a stenographer was killed instantly. More than twenty people were injured and three officers later died. Hitler survived, as did everyone else who was shielded from the blast by the conference table. His trousers were singed and tattered, and he suffered from a perforated eardrum, as did most of the other twenty-four people in the room (Shirer 1960: 1051–53).

Before anyone could make sense of what happened, Stauffenberg had already talked his way past the guards and exited the grounds, heading towards the airfield. By the time his aircraft reached Berlin, shortly before four o'clock, General Erich Fellgiebel, an officer at the Wolf's Lair who was part of the plot, had managed to phone through to the Berlin plotters with the news that Hitler had survived the explosion; activating Operation Valkyrie would have no chance of succeeding once the ordinary officers of the Reserve Army knew that the Führer was alive. Confusion was added to the plotters' disappointment a few minutes later, however, when Stauffenberg's aircraft landed; he telephoned from the airport to confirm that Hitler was dead. The plotters did not know whom to believe. At four o'clock they decided to make their move; orders were issued to activate Operation Valkyrie. The vacillating General Fromm, however, phoned Field Marshal Wilhelm Keitel at the Wolf's Lair and was assured that Hitler was shaken and singed but alive. Then, Keitel demanded to know Stauffenberg's whereabouts. This alerted Fromm to the fact that the plot had been traced to his own headquarters, and that he himself was now in mortal danger. Fromm decided to employ a bluff, replying that he thought Stauffenberg was still at the Wolf's Lair. Fromm had effectively opted to switch sides, and he gave an order to have Stauffenberg arrested on sight. By this time, however, Himmler had grasped what was happening and took charge of the situation, issuing orders to countermand the mobilization of Operation Valkyrie. In many places the coup was already going ahead, however, led

Divided Over Hitler

by non-plotting officers who sincerely believed that Hitler was dead. Wilhelmstrasse, home of the Reich chancellery, the foreign office, and the propaganda ministry, was about to be seized, and Goebbels' arrest had been ordered. Similarly, in Vienna, Prague, and many other places, army troops occupied Nazi party offices and arrested Gauleiters and SS leaders.

Once the activation of the Valkyrie procedures was exposed as a failed coup, retribution began immediately. That very night, Stauffenberg was shot in the courtyard of army headquarters in Berlin, on the orders of fellow plotter General Fromm, who thus hoped—in vain, as it turned out—to save himself. Around two-hundred other suspects were quickly rounded up and executed in the immediate aftermath, as a prelude to a vast cull of the Resistance and opposition (Snyder 1991: 83). Within a few weeks, eighty senior plotters were given show-trials, presided over by the notorious Nazi Judge Freisler in his so-called people's court, all with the foregone conclusion of sadistic execution at Plötzensee prison. After being individually subjected to a lengthy, hysterical, whining harangue in Freisler's nasal, high-pitched, bleating voice, they were killed by slow, painful strangulation, hanging by piano wire from meat-hooks. The estimated final tally is bewildering; in all, between three and five thousand were executed (Bullock 1962: 750–51). Thousands more were sent to concentration camps, and many children, including Stauffenberg's, were taken from their families and placed in orphanages. Numerous plotters chose suicide rather than wait for their arrest and show-trial. General Carl-Heinrich von Stülpnagel fired a gun into his temple but did not die, instead shooting out one eyeball and wounding the other, which then had to be surgically removed. Eyeless and bandaged, Stülpnagel was carried into the people's court on a stretcher, tried, and hanged with the others (Shirer 1960: 1068–76). Many of those executed, like Stauffenberg, were from Germany's most distinguished families. Among them, of course, was Fritz-Dietlof, who was executed on August 10, and his late father's cousin, Friedrich-Werner, who was executed exactly three months later on November 10. The former ambassador, who had never been driven by personal ambition, did not ask for much in his will; only for his sword from the First Guards Field Artillery Regiment to be placed at his right hand, his officer's spurs to be placed on his boots, and for his corpse to be wrapped in an old Caucasian rug. It was not to be; his ashes would be tipped unceremoniously onto the prison yard and scattered by the Berlin fall wind (Herwarth 1981: 92, 95).

The complete liquidation of the plotters has obviously deprived history of large segments of the July plot story, including a fuller understanding of their scope and goals, and what exactly they would have

6. "We Want to Create Sacred, Inviolable Law Again"

done next, had the Valkyrie coup succeeded. From the evidence available, however, it seems that few of the July plotters desired the complete collapse of the existing apparatus of state and society, with most preferring to reform it. They refused to have anything to do with the communist Resistance, for example, finding the prospect of a future communist Germany as distasteful as a continuation of the Nazi one. The Resistance as a whole was divided over the question of communism and the Soviet Union. Friedrich-Werner believed that continuing the war with the USSR, without a change of tack, would ultimately be a disaster, while the idea of secretly inciting and arming a Russian revolt against Stalin and communism was more realistic. Fritz-Dietlof initially disagreed with his father's cousin, and he followed Stauffenberg's aggressive eastern outlook instead, but over time Stauffenberg himself came to agree with Friedrich-Werner (Herwarth 1981: 222; Heinemann 1994: 167). All three of them were "easterners"—pro-Russian but anti-Bolshevik—and they believed that some form of armed campaign might still be needed to resolve the Russia issue, even if it meant agreeing a separate armistice with the West. Most of the plotters, in fact, initially envisaged some kind of continuation of the war in the east, post-coup. On the other hand, Friedrich-Werner was also confident in his ability to broker an armistice with Stalin, but all of these hopes were dashed by the Allies' 1943 Casablanca declaration; there would be no separate peace deals with individual Allies, and only unconditional surrender would be accepted across the board. After Casablanca, and then Normandy, the plotters' post-coup deliberations were mostly delusional (Shirer 1960: 1032–33, 1043–47, 1068–76).

Fritz-Dietlof sympathized with the plight of the Russian people, but it would be a mistake to imagine that his liberal tendencies somehow made him tolerant of communism. Early in his civil service career, in Recklinghausen, he had been nicknamed the "Red Count" and he had certainly tended towards Strasser's left wing of the Nazi party, but Fritz-Dietlof was no socialist revolutionary. For all his open-mindedness and libertarian thinking, he remained true to aristocratic Prussian principles, deeply ingrained with the Protestant ethic; his socialism, if it can be called that, was the so-called "Prussian socialism" of moderate-conservative intellectuals. He was perhaps, more accurately, a "conservative revolutionary" or a "conservative radical," in favor of a small business economy of trades and crafts, and the repopulation of rural areas; he rejected modern metropolitan lifestyles as invasive manifestations of Western capitalism, consumerist materialism, and selfish individualism. He aspired to a Germany free of social classes and political parties, though one that retained its aristocracy to sustain moral order. This last hope betrayed both his aristocratic convictions and, once again, his naiveté; Fritz-Dietlof still envisaged, emerging out of the chaos of the war, the plot, and the coup, that the higher orders would still be there to lead morally, even in an ideal future classless society. It was not so much the class system that aristocrats like Fritz-Dietlof objected to, but class conflict, which was an economic phenomenon, not a moral one. Class conflict, apart from sounding synonymous with disorder and discord, was outside of the aristocracy's sphere of understanding, having emerged in the nineteenth and twentieth centuries with the mass society, which, from Marx's day to Hitler's, European nobility had completely failed to assert control over (Mommsen 2009: 33, 53–58, 175).

The class dimensions of the July plot have usually been presented in terms of a head-on clash of values and ideals. This interpretation has its roots in the methods of study of the Third Reich that prevailed in the first two decades after the war, which tended to focus on the political and military phenomenon of Nazism rather than seeking to understand its insidious, creeping cultural and psychological impact. The earlier approach encouraged the image of a standalone German society upon which something artificial called the Third Reich had been superimposed or grafted. It was presented as a dualist conflict in which this put-upon but persistent society stubbornly resisted, as best it could, the Nazis' various moves. The key to understanding the Third Reich, it was thought, lay in identifying the limits Germany placed on Hitler's power, rather than identifying—and admitting—the extent of Nazism's pervasive influence at every level of society. Furthermore, the uncomfortable fact that the events of the 1940s, not the 1930s, provide the clearest demonstration of the nature of Nazism, took time to be acknowledged. Classic—and cinematic—renditions of the July plot story have sought to spotlight the ultimate irreconcilability of true German nobility and Nazism, which is again presented as something wholly alien and foisted upon German society. In so doing, other, more elusive and less savory dimensions of the Resistance—such as class prejudice—may have been overlooked. The true traitors, in aristocratic eyes and Nazi eyes alike, were the spineless and ambitious middle class, the low-ranking commanders born to shopkeepers and schoolteachers, and the pen-pushing bureaucrats who administrated the horror. Ironically, it was this common loathing of the middle class, with its significant Jewish component, that had united nobility and Nazis in the first place (Malinowski 2020: 1–2). The eventual realization that class allegiance was not a straightforward and reliable key to understanding the dynamics

6. "We Want to Create Sacred, Inviolable Law Again"

of the Third Reich had another positive byproduct; it helped to establish racialism—or so-called race—as the major influencing ideological factor. This allowed the genocide of the Jews to finally take its place within the centerground of German historiography.

The emergence of a dedicated military caucus of resistance, in 1940 and 1941, had definitively shaken things up, partly because the army was so representative of the aristocracy—though not, it must be said, exclusively so—and also because the German military was regarded almost as a separate class in itself. The military cell of the German Resistance did not cut across class divides as such; rather, it opened up different perspectives on the Resistance's cause, taking the focus away from class aspirations and putting the focus on a search for shared patriotic values. Initially formed around General Henning von Tresckow of the IR9, the army branch of the Resistance also provided military minds for finding military solutions, planned in a military way; civilian Resistance branches were therefore free to prepare for the turnaround of German society, after the coup. Fritz-Dietlof had a foot in each camp; he was an IR9 lieutenant, charged with recruiting the younger officers, and he was also a civil servant, who had used his position to push for moderating reforms. His prewar reform ideas, however, were full of troubling items; surprisingly for a trained lawyer, Fritz-Dietlof did not seem to prioritize good legislation as society's safeguard, and for someone who called out corruption frequently, he did not propose any particular checks and balances to stifle it. Instead, he seemed to believe that underlying moral righteousness, the Prussian aristocratic influence, would assert itself and make everything good, just as soon as it could be released from the shackles imposed by the Nazis. Furthermore, even though Fritz-Dietlof—very bravely—criticized Nazi party mismanagement, eschewed nepotism, and refused to lick boots, his reform proposals were rather cosmetic; they did not radically challenge the Nazi institutional structure, and he offered nothing concrete to replace it. This all adds to a worrying sense that Fritz-Dietlof's real cause was not to rescue Germany from National Socialism, but to rescue National Socialist principles from National Socialist practice, the former of which were easily corruptible and the latter of which was abhorrent (Mommsen 1992: S118–21; 2009: 173–74).

It has been said that Fritz-Dietlof's most unique attribute was his tenacity in maintaining his dignity and independence in a regime where everything depended on intrigue, grift, and favoritism. He was a Nazi party member who never really conformed to the Nazi way. His early, voluntary adherence to the Nazi party still poses something of a mystery, and although he was not alone among the social elite in pinning hopes on Hitler, Fritz-Dietlof's case remains highly unusual. Some nobles joined the Nazi party but never joined in, they never played a serious part in it; Fritz-Dietlof did want to play his part in the arena of politics generally, and the Nazi party presented the best opportunity to do it, being the most active and dynamic entity on the political scene. He hoped that the Nazi party would address social problems, circumvent class strife, neutralize extremism, and do so in the name of national community spirit. He saw the Nazi party as the only thing that had a chance of renewing Germany; a genuine "people's movement" set to shed the characteristics of a political party and work to reshape society. The Nazis were, of course, democratically elected, but it is worth pointing out that the July plotters did not idealize democracy. Many plotters, including Stauffenberg and Schulenburg, supported German expansionism and even anti-Semitism; Fritz-Dietlof may have genuinely abhorred the ill-treatment of the Jews, but he did not repudiate his former anti-Semitic views. Joining the Resistance was not so much about abandoning earlier convictions, which in Fritz-Dietlof's mind were ultimately aimed at overcoming social problems and strife; rather, the Resistance was about finding a way to maintain that unshakeable belief in a coming greater Germany, which Nazism had initially appeared to offer a route to (Mommsen 2009: 153–55, 164–67, 176).

It is of course impossible to imagine, from the July plotters' perspective, the catastrophic moral and political vortex into which Germany was spiraling, in order to fully empathize with them and the solutions they mooted. Stauffenberg sought a solution in the tradition of Dichter und Helden—poets and heroes—of German philosophy and mythology. In this sense, and in others, he was an appropriate leader for the plot, unmistakably wearing the mantle of an almost mystical German past; a warrior Germany, a noble Germany, a poetic Germany, a Germany of legend and longing. In practical terms, however, we are still left to speculate as to what kind of Germany Stauffenberg really had in mind, had the July plot succeeded, but we do have a few clues to work with. In keeping with the complexity of the man, Stauffenberg's dying words were unfortunately ambiguous, and they remain the subject of debate; he said either "Long live our sacred Germany" or perhaps, as some heard, "Long live our secret Germany." In German, there is even less of a discernible difference between the words "sacred" and "secret" than there is in English. It is not completely clear what this secret Germany, or however the July plotters termed it, represented, but it was almost certainly no progressive, democratic utopia (Cartwright 2009).

6. "We Want to Create Sacred, Inviolable Law Again"

The idea of a better, nobler Germany, uncorrupted by alien philosophies, moral degeneracy, even by supposed racial inferiors, and led by a powerful world figure, was not invented by Hitler. This secret vision of Germany was the long-standing ideal of the conservative, aristocratic opposition, but the phrase itself was borrowed from, and paid homage to, Stefan George (1868–1933), a poet, mystic, and self-styled aristocrat. George conjured up the notion of a "secret Germany" as a great alliance between the wise, the noble, and the good. How all this wisdom and greatness would have played out in reality remains unknown (Malinowski 2020: 2). Stauffenberg may have had in mind a kind of "hybrid" society that satisfied his initial enthusiasm for Nazism, his Prussian noble patriotism, his mystical heroic leanings, and his Catholic values; a new state combining ethical socialism with aristocratic traditions (Snyder 1991: 71). This was harmonious with "Prussian socialist" ideas that had been circulating in the radical-conservative camp since the nineteen-twenties (Mommsen 2009: 158). Stauffenberg, in fact, did also envisage space in the new order for socialist and trade-unionist friends of his (Shirer 1960: 1028–30).

In contrast to the heroic and mystical allusions of this secret Germany, postwar German historians were eager to detach all the events of the Nazi years, good and bad, from German history and culture; they were especially anxious to refute any suggestion that those events were somehow derived from or inspired by German tradition. The same old elites, to a large extent, still had control of the debate, however, and their time-honored values, which had not been eradicated by the collapse of Nazi Germany, remained influential. This, among other things, continued to prevent them from acknowledging the extent of the communist role in the German Resistance to Hitler, which suddenly became one of the most contentious issues in divided postwar Germany's politics. Over time, however, old enmities and suspicions crumbled and dissolved, allowing a fuller appreciation of the Resistance's political diversity to emerge. A new, more generous and more realistic perspective on the Resistance also prompted a recognition that its chances of success, and especially its chances of successfully guiding Germany to an agreeable peace deal, were quite small, whichever point on the political spectrum individual Resistance members came from. It is important to remember that Fritz-Dietlof's aristocratic and military cell of the Resistance was just one of many disparate cells, and there was no unified movement; had the fractious Resistance managed to breach those divides of class and politics and unify, who can say what would have happened (Mommsen 1992: S112–14).

"We want to create sacred, inviolable law again," Fritz-Dietlof had stated, but the July plotters overestimated the options available to Germany, even after a Führer-eliminating coup. As part of the inner circle of the July plot, one of Fritz-Dietlof's greatest fears was not that Nazism would continue, barring some kind of intervention, but that a catastrophic social revolution would erupt from below, sweeping away the best of German society and culture along with the worst. The aristocracy's basic anti–Bolshevik fears were still very strong, and the prospect of a mass insurrection could not be separated from chilling images of the 1917 revolution; the nobility, who were, after all, somewhere between just one and two per cent of the German population, did not like their chances of survival in that scenario. Some of Fritz-Dietlof's fellow plotters, as an illustration of how different views coexisted within the Resistance, believed just the opposite, that without a mass popular uprising, a purely military coup would never succeed. Both opinions may have missed the point; most of the July plotters counted on receiving considerable leniency from the Allies, and on being given the chance to surrender conditionally, rather than unconditionally, as a reward for dispatching Hitler. They expected to be in a position to remodel Germany themselves, or at least to reform those aspects of it that they disapproved of, with minimal Allied interference. This was not a realistic expectation, especially considering that the nearest Ally, geographically, was the Soviet Union. No part of the Nazi experience had diluted the aristocracy's hostility to communism, a factor that played no small part in their comparatively mild anti–Semitism as well; the Nazis frequently highlighted the supposed correlation between Judaism and Bolshevism, and Fritz-Dietlof himself never stopped believing that the "excessive influence" of Jews must be curtailed (Mommsen 1992: S119–20; 2009: 179, 256, 260).

There may have been some questionable or contradictory aspects to Fritz-Dietlof von der Schulenburg's thinking—he was admittedly no systematic thinker—but it is easy to see how these aspects of his character were outweighed by his immense courage and dedication. Even his interrogators at Gestapo headquarters, following his arrest, were impressed by the depth of his convictions, his calm, and his composure. The same was noted during the farce trial; he was the most steadfast and eloquent of the July plotters in the dock, and his measured responses left the revolting Judge Fiedler speechless and befuddled (Mommsen 2009: 175–80). Tisa von der Schulenburg and her sister-in-law Charlotte bravely travelled to Berlin for the trial, but they were refused entry to the courthouse. They would never see Fritz-Dietlof again. Still calm and composed, he went to his hanging at Plötzensee prison on August 10, 1944. As if it were necessary,

6. "We Want to Create Sacred, Inviolable Law Again"

Charlotte was officially notified of the execution one month later, and in a carefully crafted final insult, she was asked to reimburse the state for the cost of the hanging, as well as being billed for the drafting of the invoice itself, plus postage (Seymour 2013: 421–22). Charlotte and her children endured a lenient form of house arrest for the remainder of the war. It was not to be until the 1950s that she received a war widow's pension. Pensions in Germany were traditionally denied in the case of high treason, and German bureaucrats decided to apply that rule to the executed July plotters, even after the war. When Charlotte protested, authorities frostily pointed out that Fritzi had joined the Nazi party in 1932 and was therefore hardly an innocent victim. This was emblematic of the contradictions Germany faced, and the widowed Countess's life became a metaphor for the post-war era. Tisa, studying the courtroom photos of her brother, was struck but not surprised by his absolute self-assuredness. Fritzi had been a quiet boy, she noted in her an unpublished memoir, but "During these years of war he had become more serious, a man of immense willpower and self-control, with a look intense and determined. His wit and his quickness sharpened, like the good fencer he was" (Kimmelman 2009). Fritz-Dietlof rose to the challenge of the age without ever seeking, whether in the Nazi party or in the Resistance, power or advantage for himself. Without Fritz-Dietlof there would have been no July plot, which came so close to changing the course of history, but the alternative he strove for was an illusion (Mommsen 2009: 180).

7

"Demanding a Better Future"
Survivors and Surviving, 1945 and Beyond

"She saw from the family's failures that you can go through life and make yourself blind ... and she saw what it meant to forgive."—Elisabeth Ruge, Tisa's great-niece, quoted in Kimmelman, "High-Born Prussians Who Defied Their Origin," 2009

"Human beings, vegetables, or cosmic dust, we all dance to a mysterious tune, intoned in the distance by an invisible piper."—Albert Einstein, interview with M.K. Wisehart for *American Magazine*, 1930

There was surely no greater contrast between two brothers' experiences of and involvement in the Third Reich than the second and fourth of the Schulenburg brothers, Wolf-Werner and Fritz-Dietlof. Wolf-Werner rose to prominence within the Nazi regime in peacetime and wartime, a Nazi party member, Reich sports director, SA brigade leader, and officer in the Luftwaffe's elite parachute branch. Chief among the accolades he received were the award of the Knight's Cross of the Iron Cross in June 1943, and, later that year, being appointed to the command of the I (first) Fallschirmjäger regiment, first as a stand-in and then as commander in his own right, though only briefly. His rank upon taking command of the regiment was still only major; promotion to lieutenant colonel was on its way, though not in the circumstances Wolf-Werner would have liked to anticipate. In March 1944, a fifth Fallschirmjäger division was formed in France, commanded by Lieutenant General Gustav Wilke. This would be the last Fallschirmjäger division to receive a semblance of full training, though actual parachute operations were out of the question at that stage of Germany's war. The division contained the XIII, XIV, and XV Fallschirmjäger regiments, and it had its own complement of artillery, anti-aircraft, anti-tank, engineering, and signals units. After the Battle of Monte

7. "Demanding a Better Future"

Cassino, Wolf-Werner was transferred from command of the I (first) regiment to command of the XIII (thirteenth) regiment, in the new fifth division, whose demand for experienced officers was insatiable. The agony of anticipation, doubt, and uncertainty over the imminent Allied invasion of northern Europe—where, when, how, or even whether it would be executed at all—wore down the nerves of the German army in France. With the exception of many soldiers who were still nursing wounds from Russia, they were physically ready to fight, but in spirit they were already crushed (Shirer 1960: 1036–37). Two months after Wolf-Werner's new appointment, in June 1944, when news arrived that the Allies had landed in Normandy, only the new XV (fifteenth) Fallschirmjäger regiment was ready for combat; it was hastily attached to the XVII (seventeenth) SS Panzergrenadier division and sent to Normandy. The rest of the new division would gradually be assigned to combat slightly later, in July (Götzel and Student 1980: 449).

In mid-July, Wolf-Werner and his XIII regiment were moved up to the front line to face the advancing U.S. Army at Saint-Lô, in the Manche district of Normandy. The ensuing Battle of Saint-Lô was one of three conflicts making up the "battle of the hedgerows," which took place between July 7 and 19, 1944. Saint-Lô had fallen to the Germans in 1940, and, after the Normandy landings, the Americans targeted the city because it sat at a strategic crossroads, part of the Allies' chosen route westwards. American bombardments caused enormous damage to the city, destroying more than ninety per cent of it and causing a high number of casualties; this resulted in Saint-Lô earning the tragic sobriquet "the Capital of Ruins," popularized by Samuel Beckett. The task of taking control of Saint-Lô was entrusted to the XIX (nineteenth) Corps of the U.S. First Army, under General Charles H. Corlett. In July 1944 the corps included the 29th Infantry Division, located on the Bayeux road from La Luzerne to Saint-André-de-l'Épine, the 30th Infantry Division, located on the road to Périers to the west of Saint-Lô, and the 35th Infantry Division, located on the Isigny road and fighting south to Saint-Lô. A new and largely inexperienced German infantry division, the 352nd, faced the Americans, alongside the fifth Fallschirmjäger division. The fifth division was still understrength and short of vehicles and weapons, but although it comprised both inexperienced, experienced, and exhausted soldiers—including many veterans of Russia, forced back into the front line—the officers were nevertheless mostly capable and battle-hardened. This was the case with Wolf-Werner in command of the XIII regiment, and his brother officers Major Herbert Noster in command of the XIV regiment, and Major Kurt Gröschke in command of the XV regiment.

Divided Over Hitler

The American 29th Infantry Division attacked through the hedgerows to the northeast of Saint-Lô, near the Madeleine quarter, taking heavy casualties. On the evening of July 14, some American units unwittingly began to advance ahead of other divisional elements. They were to find themselves cut-off and isolated about a thousand yards (nine hundred meters) east of Saint-Lô for an entire day, running low on both ammunition and food. The Fallschirmjäger surrounded them and called in their artillery. The Americans took twenty-five wounded and had only three medics to treat them; they had to call in planes to urgently drop plasma, but they were far from beaten. They returned fire consistently against the XIII and XIV Fallschirmjäger and shocked the Germans with their resilience and the intensity of their defensive fire. Wolf-Werner was hit numerous times, and was then killed almost instantly, a rifle bullet piercing his Knight's Cross of the Iron Cross, worn around his neck, and passing through the center of his sternum (Scherzer 2007: 688). Several bullets hit him, but the upper chest wound was undoubtedly the fatal one. His Knight's Cross, with the fatal bullet hole, is today kept at the German Historical Museum (Deutsches Historisches Museum) on Unter den Linden, Berlin, along with some of his other awards. Modern analysis of the bullet hole reveals, unsurprisingly, that the weapon used was almost certainly the standard .30 M1 Garand semi-automatic rifle of the American infantryman. With Wolf-Werner lying dead, the battle through dense vegetation continued, but the Germans' fortunes did not change. Major Noster of the XIV regiment was seriously wounded, not for the first time in his Fallschirmjäger career. The inexperienced 352nd division, fighting alongside the Fallschirmjäger, would never recover from its losses. By July 17 the Germans were retreating west towards Rampan (Götzel and Student 1980: 449).

Wolf-Werner was posthumously promoted to lieutenant colonel (Oberstleutnant) in the reserve, on July 23, 1944 (Fellgiebel 2006: 318). On July 19, at the Klein Trebbow estate, a telegram arrived; Tisa approached her sister-in-law Charlotte and said "Wolf has fallen." It was almost exactly forty years since the death in battle, in German South West Africa (modern day Namibia), of their maternal uncle, Wolf-Werner Graf von Arnim, after whom the younger Wolf-Werner was named. The timing felt like a chilling omen. Charlotte, in fact, had just returned from seeing her husband Fritz-Dietlof off at the station for the last time; he was on his way back to Berlin for the execution of the Valkyrie plot. "You know," he said to Charlotte on the horse-drawn cart-ride to the station, "the chances are fifty-fifty." It was the last time they ever spoke. Charlotte turned

7. "Demanding a Better Future"

thirty-five the following day, July 20; they had celebrated her birthday in advance of the fateful date (Meding 1997: 118–19). Having been killed in action five days before the July plot was carried out, it is unlikely that Wolf-Werner ever knew about the extent of Fritz-Dietlof's involvement in the Resistance against Hitler, though he may have suspected it. It is not clear, either, whether Fritz-Dietlof, at that time busy preparing for the July plot and the expected seizure of power, ever learnt that his older brother had died in battle for the Reich, though it is possible that word reached him through contacts in Berlin on the evening of July 19 or the morning of July 20. The plot coincided, in fact, with the beginning of the military collapse in east and west, though no-one would argue that this made the plotters' timing ideal (Shirer 1960: 1047, 1085). Some would even conclude that after Normandy any plot to remove Hitler could only be of negligible relevance, because the Allies would never discuss favorable conditions for surrender (Herwarth 1981: 286).

As the Normandy campaign progressed, the late Wolf-Werner's fifth Fallschirmjäger division continued to suffer heavy losses, and it was subsequently withdrawn to the Netherlands to rebuild and refit. The division then took part in the Battle of the Bulge, and, after retreating through Germany, the division would surrender in batches near the Nürburgring stadium in the Rhineland and in the Ruhr Pocket. Wolf-Werner's brother officer, Major Noster of the XIV regiment, committed suicide in Berlin shortly before the war's end. Once the last hope of the Battle of the Bulge had faded, Germany's doom was clear to all but the most deluded hardcore deniers. The Nazis had looted grain stocks, foodstuffs, crops, cattle, machinery, and every other commodity from all over Europe, but with their opportunities for thieving now gone, the country faced the direst poverty. Goebbels ordered "total mobilization" including the military draft for boys aged fifteen to eighteen and men aged fifty to sixty. Schools, universities, offices, and factories were combed for potential recruits, thus crippling what remained of German industry. From the existing armed forces, desertions increased, leading to a declaration by Himmler that the families of deserters would henceforth be shot. Such was the greater Germany that Wolf-Werner had just died for (Shirer 1960: 943–45, 1087–88).

On January 13, 1945, the eldest of the Schulenburg siblings, and the last remaining brother, Johann-Albrecht Werner Adolf Hermann-Moritz von der Schulenburg, was also killed. He was forty-six. As with so many events in the chaotic closing months of the war in Germany, uncertainty surrounds the cause of his death. With the widespread destruction, deliberate or otherwise, of many documents and archives, it may not have been

Divided Over Hitler

difficult to keep the circumstances of his death a secret, if that indeed has been the intention. For a prominent member of Third Reich society, an officer and a Nazi, there were, to put it crudely, plenty of ways to die as the war drew to a close, whether by enemy action, opportunism, reprisal, robbery, or the settling of old scores, as well as, in many cases, suicide. Jutta, the widow of another Schulenburg brother, the late Adolf-Heinrich, was also reported dead several weeks later, aged forty-one, through cause or causes unrecorded. Johann-Albrecht's death was said to have taken place in combat; this is not impossible, but it seems unlikely. The Allies were not far away, and advancing steadily, but on January 13 they had not yet reached the area of Tressow Castle, which is listed as Johann-Albrecht's place of death. Death by aerial bombardment is technically possible, though the castle beside a lake would hardly be a target. That was probably the last time, though, that Germany's borders retained some semblance of integrity; two days after Johann-Albrecht's death, Hitler visited the western front for the last time. By April, as the country disintegrated, even the most committed deniers finally began to admit that Germany was defeated, while vowing that a future Germany, with no Hitler, would not be worth living in for a "true" German. Hitler's inner circle turned to infighting at the last hurdle, amidst revelations of defection and betrayal by Himmler, Göring, and nearly all the leaders of the armed forces. Nineteen eighteen was strikingly different to all this; at the end of the First World War, the monarchy collapsed, the army was defeated, but the main institutions of German daily life continued. In 1945, the state dissolved with a totality and a suddenness that were unparalleled in history. No source of authority or basis of governance remained. Judiciary, industry, transport, even the remotest town hall, village council, and insignificant civil defense unit was left leaderless and directionless, except for the rule of the occupying Allies. Any German armed forces members instantly became prisoners of war in their own land (Shirer 1960: 1111–126, 1139–140).

In the space of just six months, the three remaining Schulenburg brothers had all been killed, leaving just one surviving sibling, Tisa. In the first year of the war, both her parents and one of her brothers had died, and her younger brother, the baby of the family, had already been killed in a car accident. The descendant of, among others, Bismarcks and Arnims, great-grandniece many times removed of an English Queen, daughter of the commander of the elite Garde du Corps cavalry regiment and chief of staff to the Crown Prince, Tisa had been born exactly one-hundred and seventy-five years to the very day that her family's noble title had been

7. "Demanding a Better Future"

created, and now she alone would live to see her family's land confiscated and the world she had known crumble and vanish. Her earliest memories were still colored by the Anglophilia of her parents; a bilingual upbringing, with English nurses and governesses, and a home filled with books, artifacts, and mementoes from England—chintz furniture covers, carpets from London's East India Docks, tweed coats, bone china—and then their father's despair upon the outbreak of war—a war that he had foreseen clearly—between the two countries he loved. Tisa recalled the family's first prewar days as the happiest years of their lives (Seymour 2013: 142, 203).

Tisa's impressionable pre-teen years coincided with the First World War, when the physical distance from her father was replicated in emotional distance: "When [our father] went to war in 1914, Fritzi was eleven, I was ten. We had probably never exchanged a personal word with [our father, just] 'stand to attention,' 'yes and no,' 'good morning.' ... Throughout the war we had father for one day here and half a day there. ... So in the spring of 1919 we met our father [almost for the first time]. We were far removed from him in our interests" (Heinemann 1994: 2). A lasting bond between Tisa and Fritzi was formed in that common experience. For Tisa, as for many Germans, the postwar sense of desperation after 1918 never fully dissipated. She helped Fritzi with his English and they mooted the idea of him claiming British citizenship (he was born in London) in order to escape the drudgery (Seymour 2013: 252). Tisa developed into a magnetic and charming individual, always winning praise, fair-haired and attractive, and, in the words of Richard von Weizsäcker, Fritzi's army comrade, she had a "peculiar and outstanding personality" (Kimmelman 2009). Tisa was, in summary, both a notorious black sheep and a prodigal daughter, destined to be one of several prominent artists of Prussian noble origins who actively opposed Hitler (Malinowksi 2020: 49, 253).

Tisa's artistic credentials were significant. At the age of just sixteen, she introduced herself to the artist Max Liebermann (1847–1935) of the Prussian Academy of Arts in Berlin, presenting him with some of her artwork, with which she had already been experimenting for a number of years. Liebermann recognized Tisa's talent, but her father said that he would not give her permission to attend the academy until she was twenty-one. When she did eventually get there, she studied under the sculptors Otto Hitzberger (1878–1964), Fritz Klimsch (1870–1960), and Edwin Scharff (1887–1955). During a semester abroad in Paris in 1927 she met the sculptor Charles Despiau (1874–1946), who also praised and encouraged her work. Whether in Berlin or Paris, Tisa led a life in the true spirit of the rebellious 1920s, unrestrained and intoxicating. As previously mentioned, she was a regular visitor to the Berlin home of Jewish banker and art collector Hugo Simon, the (second) owner—at that time—of Edvard Munch's *The Scream*. Simon was a founder member—with Albert Einstein—of the pacifist New Fatherland League (Bund Neues Vaterland) in 1914, which later gave rise to the German League for Human Rights (Deutsche Liga für Menschenrechte). At Simon's house, Tisa mixed with theater practitioner Bertolt Brecht (1898-1956), the caricaturist and painter George Grosz (1893-1959), former Communist Party leader and Social Democrat (SDP) politician Paul Levi (1883-1930), Nobel laureate Thomas Mann (1875-1955) and his brother the novelist Heinrich Mann (1871-1950), artist Max Pechstein (1881-1955), authors Erich Maria Remarque (1898-1970) and Stefan Zweig (1881-1942), and even Albert Einstein himself, as well as other Berlin personalities (Escher 2010: 435-36; Seymour 2013: 264). Tisa discussed politics, art, philosophy, and science with them all, acquiring an incomparably privileged and comprehensive education in twentieth-century thought. At the age of twenty-four, Tisa met the charming, wealthy Jewish entrepreneur and art collector Fritz Hesse, whom she married in 1928, to the considerable displeasure of her father and older brothers. In later years she would recall, however, that her father, despite his anti-Semitism, always treated his son-in-law with courtesy. The love of a father for a daughter could transcend prejudice, Tisa realized (Seymour 2014).

After the so-called seizure of power by the Nazis, Tisa belatedly but wisely decided to read Hitler's *Mein Kampf*. The systematic persecution of Jews, progressives, conservatives, and moderates was quickly becoming apparent, but the book confirmed it. Artist friends of Tisa began to be followed, searched, and pushed into exile, and her own studio was searched. Rumors of violence, disappearances, and concentration camps began to circulate. Tisa later expressed the uncompromising view that anyone who really wanted to know the truth about what was going on could have known it at an early stage (Seymour 2013: 284-94). The prophecy of *Mein Kampf* was, arguably, well on the way to being consummated by the time Tisa actually read the book, and Fritz and Tisa Hesse wasted no time in leaving Germany. In 1933, it is fair to say that Tisa was the only member of her family to unequivocally stand against Nazism; her younger brother, Wilhelm, aged nineteen, was not a party member like his father and brothers, but his disinterest in Nazism did not amount to opposition. It could be argued that the Nazi convictions of Tisa's father and older brothers were not entirely vehement either, in 1933, but the political situation was genuinely confusing; the crisis of employment, economics, order,

7. "Demanding a Better Future"

and leadership was authentic, not a propaganda fabrication, and Nazism seemed to provide a port in the storm. Hitler, meanwhile, whose continued leadership was not a foregone conclusion, was still molding the movement as he went along, and it did not offer consistency or clarity at that point. The status and future of the SA, and of leftwing Nazi party members, were also still uncertain, as was the Nazis' long-term hold on power, at least as far as the outside world was concerned. For good or ill, Germans' decisions were made in the absence of all the facts.

The Hesses settled in England, where, in 1935, Tisa met the sculptor and painter Henry Moore (1898–1986), who inspired her to try her hand at bronze sculpture. Meeting Moore also provided Tisa with an introduction to the hitherto unknown north of England, Moore's home region, which would soon become a second home for Tisa. With a Suffolk-coast house in Walberswick (a favorite among exiled and refugee artists) and a home in Highgate, London, most of Tisa's large group of sophisticated friends were distinctly southern-based. In 1936, Tisa gave an exhibition of her art in London; she titled it "Degenerate Art" in mocking reference to the Nazis' own phrase to condemn their artistic opponents, and Tisa intended it as a public and direct critique of the Nazis. As a result she was elected to the board of the British anti-fascist artists' group, an affiliate of the Artists International Association (AIA). This was a fondly remembered period of her life, but in that same year, Tisa was distressed to be unable to attend the funeral of her youngest brother, Wilhelm, who had been killed in a car accident; her passport had expired, and she had understandably been unwilling to approach the Nazified German embassy in London to renew it. This incident served as a stark reminder of the paradox at the heart of her existence; the Schulenburg family was truly united by pain but divided by politics, as Tisa commented (Seymour 2014).

One of the Artists International Association (AIA)'s objectives was to close the social gap between workers and artists. One of the initiatives emerging from this goal would see Tisa begin a lifelong connection to the miners of County Durham, with her first visits there to give lectures on art and to deliver woodcarving courses, much in the spirit of contemporary creative initiatives aimed at benefiting the workers, such as the Ashington Group. In the coalmines and surrounding communities Tisa witnessed the misery of Depression-era working-class Britain; an incredible two-hundred thousand miners were unemployed at the time, and those who were still employed in the mines worked in appalling conditions. This was the type of environment described vividly, from within, in George Orwell's *The Road to Wigan Pier,* written at exactly the same time as Tisa's first expeditions "up north." Coincidentally, Orwell's home at the time was in genteel Southwold, a little over a mile (less than two kilometers) from Walberswick, where Tisa lived. No doubt fully aware of the impoverished situation highlighted by Orwell, Tisa was deeply impressed by the welcome and openness she experienced in County Durham and she passionately reciprocated, demonstrating solidarity and commitment to the region and its plight. She traveled to the area several times more each year until 1939, delivering lectures, workshops, and courses, lodging unpretentiously in the Spennymoor miners' "pit village." Like Orwell, Tisa was one of few outsiders to be given the honor of actually going down the mines to see the miners' job firsthand, and, like Orwell, her statuesque height proved inconvenient for underground workplaces. Back at ground level, as well as discovering and nurturing new talents, Tisa produced new drawings and carvings based on her mining community experiences (Seymour 2013: 358–60).

Tisa's ideological maturation, her ongoing development into a socialist, was less dramatic and less life-threatening than the political transformation of her brother Fritzi, gradually becoming an opponent of Hitler. "I had never really met a worker [before]," Tisa later admitted, which was merely in keeping with her background and class (Seymour 2013: 359). In order to make the transition from privileged to socialist, Orwell suggested, "you have got to decide whether things at present are tolerable or not tolerable, and you have got to take up a definite attitude on the terribly difficult issue of class" (Orwell 1958: 153). The class gap was much greater for Tisa, who was connected to royalty, than for Orwell, who was upper-middle-class, and the physical incongruity was also greater; Tisa made her first appearance up north dressed in fine clothes, pearls, and furs, ingenuously talking to the miners about international workers' equality (Seymour 2013: 454). She would forever recall being initially met with bafflement, when she presented her thirty-strong class of working men with the prints of destitute families that Van Gogh had used for inspiration during his stay in England, followed by her announcement that she wanted them to produce something much better. The reaction of the Durham miners, it was said, evolved from astonishment to amusement and then to enthusiasm and ultimately gratitude, but not every radical appreciated these initiatives. Orwell came away from his mining community experiences with considerable skepticism about what he called the "class-breaking activities" of the privileged, such as Tisa's art lessons. He felt that these initiatives risked intensifying class prejudice rather than combatting it, by accidentally emphasizing the width and insuperability

7. "Demanding a Better Future"

of the class gap (Orwell 1958: 194). From Tisa's perspective, her commitment was very real, as was her fascination for the industry that she would continue to revisit throughout her life. She would continue to accept those invitations to go down the mines—still considered an unusual privilege for an outsider and a lady—well into her sixties, which in Tisa's case was a mark of appreciation, affection, and respect. She passed on lasting skills to those she encountered, teaching countless unemployed miners how to carve, and in the process she got to know them and became their friend. Reflecting on her years in England, Tisa ultimately felt that County Durham had been more of a home to her than London or Suffolk (Gowrie and Rea 2001).

In 1938, after ten years of marriage, Tisa and Fritz Hesse divorced. Nineteen thirty-nine brought a whirlwind of loss and disappointment for Tisa, culminating of course in the protracted tragedy of the war. Her parents died within a few months of each other that year, at ages that would not nowadays necessarily be considered greatly advanced; seventy-three and sixty-five. Not long afterwards, the third-born of the Schulenburg brothers, Adolf-Heinrich—Heini—died of colon cancer. This was also the period in which Tisa learned of Fritz-Dietlof's early involvement in the Resistance, and that he was using his somewhat nominal senior role in the administration of Silesia as a kind of cover. During her brief widowhood, their mother stayed in the elegant Baltic seaside resort of Travemünde, where she had relatives, and it was not very far from Tressow Castle. Tisa also spent some time there, and it was in Travemünde that she met up with her childhood friend and former lover Carl Ulrich von Barner (1899–1978), an open-minded and well-liked Prussian landowner, and began a relationship with him. With war certain to break out, Barner was recalled from the reserve of officers to serve in the army, and on the evening of the day that he received his mobilization, August 27, he and Tisa were civilly married (Seymour 2013: 420–22).

Tisa went to oversee the Barner family's estate, Klein Trebbow, soon to be joined there by Fritz-Dietlof and his wife Charlotte, with their children. Klein Trebbow became a rural refuge and meeting place for opponents of Nazism, where the two sisters-in-law received visits from Claus von Stauffenberg and other Resistance members. After the failed coup of July 1944, Tisa went to Berlin with her devastated sister-in-law, on the day of Fritz-Dietlof's execution. Afterwards, Tisa created a memorial plaque with the inscription "I acted according to my conscience and now I have no regrets." The quote was taken from the German scholar and Protestant reformist Ulrich von Hutten (1488–1523). The plaque was placed in the park of the Klein Trebbow estate, and this act led to Tisa being denounced to the local Nazi party branch sometime in early 1945. Perhaps due to sympathy, apathy, or just the general feeling of hopelessness taking hold in Germany, no action was taken against her. Tisa's sister-in-law and the six children stayed out of sight for the remainder of the war, under virtual house arrest. Tisa decided to lodge nearby in Travemünde, at the seaside, in order to lower her profile, while also ensuring that she would find herself in the Western zone of Germany as the war drew to an end (Meding 1997: 116–19; Seymour 2013: 420–22).

At the war's end, Johann-Albrecht's widow, Angela, took her children and fled westwards, abandoning Tressow Castle before the region became part of Soviet zone of occupation. In the fall of 1945, the surviving Schulenburgs were formally expropriated. A school for children with learning difficulties was set up at the castle, named after the communist Resistance fighter Katja Niederkirchner (1909–1944); many years later it would be renamed in honor of Fritz-Dietlof von der Schulenburg. Tisa managed to find work as a secretary for the British Military Administration's Industry Office. Her husband, Carl Ulrich, who had ended up in a prisoner-of-war camp in Italy, was released and transported home, but their hurried wartime marriage had no future and they divorced in 1946 (Seymour 2013: 422). Tisa then moved to Glinde, near Hamburg, and worked on the welfare staff of the Allied military base there. She initiated a workers' council for the locals employed on the base and was able to arrange subsidies in the form of basic food supplies for them. To help her own postwar recovery, she was selling the highly prized cigarettes sent to her by friends in England, and saving the money in the hope of being able to work as a freelance artist. From 1947 she worked as a freelancer for Hamburg's *Die Welt* newspaper, before going to spend six months reporting on life in the Ruhr in 1948. She opted to live in a miners' village in Recklinghausen; it was a return to the immersive experience of a struggling and socially troubled mining community, the environment echoing Tisa's years among the miners of the north of England. It was a doubly evocative and emotional experience, in fact; Recklinghausen was Fritz-Dietlof's first major posting as a civil servant. Tisa visited numerous mines in the Ruhr, including the Carolinenglück, Hanover-Hannibal, and President mines in Bochum, the Unser Fritz (Our Fritz) mine in Wanne-Eickel (today merged with the city of Herne), and the General Blumenthal mine in Recklinghausen, where pit horses still drew the coal carts to the surface. The Ruhr was a spiritual and social choice—"I chose the Ruhr," Tisa explained to a friend, "wanting to live where others had to live. No more roar of the sea, nor the smell

7. "Demanding a Better Future"

of bracken and gorse. I have delighted in that to the full." Whether this was a kind of penance or a way of atoning for survivor's guilt, the last of her generation of Schulenburgs began her Ruhr pilgrimage and re-found her inspiration; Tisa finally began to draw and carve again (Seymour 2013: 420–22).

These years in Tisa's life seemed to be characterized by two factors; a longed-for return to creating art among the industrial poor, and solitude; a novel experience for her. It was the first time in her life that she was without family, or husband, or social whirl around her. In some senses, Tisa clearly embraced this solitude—it appears to have been part of allowing her artistic calling to resurge—but from another perspective, something seemed to be missing from her life. It was against this background that Tisa converted to Roman Catholicism on her return to Hamburg, after her lonely six-month stay in the Ruhr. In nearby Münster, Tisa had learned much about the case of the recently deceased Roman Catholic Cardinal Clemens August Graf von Galen (1878–1946) and the extent of the Catholic Resistance to the Nazi regime. It is reasonable to speculate that this new understanding nourished not only her new-found spirituality but also her hunger for reconciling the recent past (Seymour 2013: 422). It is no wonder, also, that the story of Cardinal Galen, a nobleman by birth, resonated with Tisa. As a priest and then a bishop, Galen was a political conservative whose opinion of the Nazis vacillated between acceptance and repugnance. Before 1933, he argued for Hitler to be given a chance, but after the Nazis seized power he was scathing of their racial policies. Galen backed the invasions of Poland and the Soviet Union, but as stories of euthanasia programs, revenge murders, and attacks on churches started to circulate, Galen's opposition to Hitler became crystalized. In 1941, a series of sermons by Galen were printed and distributed illegally, and they were even dropped among German troops by the British Royal Air Force; the sermons criticized the Nazis' tactics, the climate of fear, the desecration of churches, and the concentration camps. Germany, Galen said, was being destroyed not by the Allied bombing from outside but by Nazi forces from within. Predictably, some senior Nazis wanted Galen removed, arrested, or executed, but Goebbels felt that a hasty or extreme response would be counterproductive, especially for the morale of German Catholics in the armed forces and generally. Galen's sermons were reaching millions of Germans who were now hanging on his words, and they were horrified by the revelations of the semi-secret euthanasia program. The resulting protests led to the truth surrounded the program being exposed; the program continued, but in much greater secrecy (Gill 1994: 60).

Divided Over Hitler

The Nazis' solution was to place Galen under virtual house arrest from 1941 to 1945, and it appears that they intended to hang him at the end of the war, but he was spared severe punishment in the short term. Exposing the euthanasia program, however, served as a watershed, and readers of Galen's sermons were already drawing wider conclusions about Nazism. Galen's outspoken courage energized the broader German Resistance, not just Catholic groups, and his actions inspired the rest of the German Catholic episcopate to oppose the Nazi regime (Evans 2009: 529–60). Although Galen opposed Nazism almost in its entirety, he did not give up his belief in Germany as a bulwark against atheistic communism, much like other conservative dissenters. He wished, in fact, that Hitler could see the great potential for fully including German Catholics in a national anticommunist crusade, whereby Catholics could, Galen believed, act as a moderating force upon Nazism, gently but firmly curtailing its excesses (Gill 1994: 60, 188). Galen's views read very much like a Catholic version of the liberal-conservative Fritz-Dietlof's outlook, and they are not very different to the devout Catholic Stauffenberg's positions. Galen was criticized for being slow to condemn the persecution of the Jews in comparable measure to his attacks on the Nazis' euthanasia program and other crimes, but he did personally denounce Nazi racialist policies, including specifically anti–Semitic measures, on multiple occasions. Nevertheless, the conservative opposition in general struggled to renounce its own anti–Semitism and recognize the persecution and genocide of the Jews as the central and gravest crime of the Nazi regime.

It was not until after the end of the war, and after the passing of then-Cardinal Galen, that Tisa took time to evaluate the Catholic Resistance's contribution and perspective. Resistance, art, and a deeper sense of purpose seemed to coincide, for Tisa, in Roman Catholicism. In late 1948 she became acquainted, through friends in Recklinghausen, with the Ursuline convent in bomb-shattered Dorsten, a small town in the same area. There, Tisa began to combine her new-found faith with her art, producing crucifixes, figures of the Virgin Mary, Stations of the Cross—the Via Crucis—and other sacred sculptures; this contributed enormously to replacing artworks that had been lost, looted, or destroyed in Dorsten, including at the convent itself, during or immediately after the war. At the age of forty-six, in 1950, Tisa began convented religious life as Sister Paula. One of her fellow sisters in the convent, and later superior of the community, was Johanna Eichmann (1926–2019). Eichmann was the daughter of a so-called "mixed" Jewish-Catholic marriage and would later be the founder of the Westphalia Jewish Museum. Though they were completely

7. "Demanding a Better Future"

different in background, age, and culture, Tisa and Eichmann were equals in representing a generation of German religious and clergy who were profoundly committed to reconciliation and memory. Sister Paula began teaching drawing and art history at the schools run by the Ursuline order, first at the secondary school and later at St Ursula's grammar school. After thirteen years of teaching, she would again be able to devote herself entirely to her art.

The Ursuline order, still present and active in Dorsten today, was a strict order until the liberalizing reforms of the Second Vatican Council (1962–65), usually referred to as Vatican II. Tisa saw Vatican II as the latest of several liberations in her life; while remaining a nun, she could wear colorful "civilian" clothes again and travel outside of the convent and outside of Germany. She paid regular visits to Fritz-Dietlof's children, some of whom lived in the British Isles. She was able to keep alive the old Schulenburg ties to England, and she was also able to encourage the next generation of Schulenburgs to do the same. She finally had the time to transform old wartime sketches into ink drawings and to turn scenes captured in her memory into wooden sculptures. Besides religious topics, she focused on themes of war, the plight of refugees, and the persecution of minorities. She mustered the energy to develop new techniques, exploring bronze and aluminum casting methods for her reliefs. She exhibited regularly and also accepted commissions for fountains, cenotaphs, columns, and window and wall designs. Tisa also happily returned to the mining environment, being invited to visit the Fürst Leopold mine in Dorsten. New challenges were never lacking; from 1968 to 1969, now in her mid-sixties, Tisa worked in Ethiopia, at a leprosy community, broadening her existing solidarity and commitment for the workers and unemployed into an active concern for all those who suffer. All of her experiences were translated into drawings or sculptures, as well as the iconic tragedies of the era that Tisa did not personally witness; the Vietnam War, the famine in Biafra, and the political persecution in Chile. In a rare instance of Tisa receiving an award for her endeavors, she was granted honorary citizenship of the city of Dorsten in 1972 (Gowrie and Rea 2001; Seymour 2013: 142).

In 1974, Tisa made a return trip to County Durham, England, and in particular to visit what had become the Bede Gallery in Jarrow, an initiative launched by photo-chronicler Vince Rea several years earlier, housed in a former Cold War bunker. The Bede Gallery had evolved from plans to host exhibitions promoting working-class history and soon became a rallying point for young artists and writers to meet, talk, swap ideas, and share their enthusiasm. Rea recalled Tisa's interest in archive material

Divided Over Hitler

about the Jarrow Crusade, wanting to see the place—Jarrow Slake—where William Jobling, the Jarrow miner, was hanged during the miners' strike of 1832. Tisa's visit came against the backdrop of the 1972 and 1974 miners' strikes, the latest of several similar disputes in recent years. This visit led to a very successful exhibition of Tisa's work at the Bede Gallery in 1975. Miners and their families came from Durham and the surrounding mining villages of Spennymoor, Easington, Westoe and Horden. Tisa encouraged the miners to bring their paintings, drawings and carvings for discussion and feedback, transforming the event into an interactive exhibition—years ahead of its time—rather than a mere display of pictures. The exhibition was seen to break down widely perceived barriers that plagued the world of art and art galleries for ordinary working people (Gowrie and Rea 2001).

In 1979 Tisa traveled to Israel, meeting with Holocaust survivors who were living in Dorsten's twin town of Hod HaSharon, and also in Jerusalem. In 1984, aged eighty, she designed a set of reliefs to mark the expansion of the General Blumenthal mine, including the Haltern mines, in Recklinghausen, which she had first visited in the 1940s. At the unveiling ceremony for these sculptures, Tisa met the then-West German president, Richard von Weizsäcker, who had been Fritz-Dietlof's friend, Resistance recruit, and fellow junior officer of the IR9 in Potsdam. In 1994, the then-Minister for Women and Youth, Angela Merkel, decorated Tisa with the Member of the Federal Cross of Merit (Verdienstkreuz am Bande), in a simple ceremony held at the wages hall of the Fürst Leopold colliery, in recognition of her life's work and for her conspicuous social commitment. In 1997, the planned closure of that mine, at the height of its productive output, led to protests in which Sister Paula, already dubbed "Saint Barbara of the Ruhr" gladly took part. She demonstrated alongside the miners and created a bronze and stone sculpture to mark the event.

Until the end of her long life, Tisa was praised for being a passionate, unpretentious, empathic, and inclusive artist with a profound understanding of the twentieth century, so many pivotal events of which she had lived firsthand; her work had the strength and individuality to effectively communicate these experiences. Tisa had come a long way from a privileged and idyllic childhood at the ancestral home, timelessly Prussian yet infused with a passion for England; in accordance with her parents' wishes, the infant Tisa's world had been populated by English-speaking nurses, governesses, and domestic servants, and surrounded by English books, ornaments, and artifacts. She emerged from this aristocratic realm only to find her preconceptions about national identity and social class

7. "Demanding a Better Future"

being challenged—philosophically, ideologically—in her meetings with Brecht, Zweig, and Mann; it was symbolic of her confusion that when she finally mixed with the real working class, she did so adorned with pearls and dressed in furs. Even decades later, when Tisa had adopted very simple habits and mannerisms, people always somehow intuited that Tisa was a German countess. She was amused to hear about one Durham miner's comment, on discovering her roots, "Man, she's been decked out in diamonds from the day she wuz born; wi'd have t' win the football pools fifty times just t' get back t' where she started from." In reality, the later-life Tisa had no money, pearls, or diamonds, but she did have her personality, her passion, and her art, and she shared these freely. She showed an intelligence and a compassion for the lives of all those she encountered (Gowrie and Rea 2001; Seymour 2013: 142, 203, 264, 454).

The Jarrow community that Tisa had supported and encouraged appreciated Tisa for her lifelong commitment as an artist and humanitarian. Her art struck them as "a committed art, demanding a better future. She would like her art to be for the workers mainly, an art to be understood by all" (Gowrie and Rea 2001). When the Jarrow gallery was revived, this time based in the middle of a Jarrow shopping center, Tisa was overjoyed. At ninety-six, she seemed vivacious and in good spirits. Vince Rea and the other Jarrow gallery organizers planned a new one-woman show for Tisa's work, but when they wrote to her to begin making the arrangements, the reply they received was a barely legible scrawl; an accompanying note explained that Tisa was lapsing in and out of consciousness. Instead of writing to invite her to the gallery, therefore, Rea decided to have a video recording made, in the form of a private viewing followed by film of the open visits to the exhibition, so that Tisa could see her works on display one last time. Elisabeth Ruge, Fritz-Dietlof's granddaughter and Tisa's great-niece, commented that "Tisa saw human nature in all its complexity…. Again and again she started something new, finding another place for herself in the world. She loved her family, she was loyal to it despite her differences … because she was tolerant and saw from the family's failures that you can go through life and make yourself blind. But [Tisa] knew that to criticize the weaknesses of others you've got to understand your own weaknesses," her great-niece added, "and she saw what it meant to forgive" (Kimmelman 2009). Tisa died on Thursday, February 8, 2001.

8

"A Grave Legacy"

Recriminations, Restitution, and Reconciliation

"Anyone who closes their eyes to the past is blind to the present. Whoever refuses to remember the inhumanity is prone to new risks of infection."—Richard von Weizsäcker, in the plenary hall of the German Parliament, May 8, 1985

"To forget is the secret of eternal youth. One grows old only through memory. There is much too little forgetting."
—Erich Maria Remarque in *Three Comrades*, 1936

The story of the Schulenburg family is extraordinary from every perspective. Political divisions cut right through the entire family, but the individuals themselves were also full of contradictions (Mommsen 2009: 33); a member of the Prussian old guard who rose to the second-highest rank in the SS, while still longing to see the monarchy restored, somehow; his devoted daughter, a socialist who married a Jew and later became a twice-divorced Roman Catholic nun; her lawyer brother with a half-American wife, orchestrator of Olympics and war crimes, until he was shot by an American soldier; their other brother, the idealistic "Red Count" who ended up rejecting all ideologies except, perhaps, aristocracy; and their ambassador cousin, rising above politics, committed to law and order, but ultimately committed to assassinating his head of state; this, in crude terms, summarizes the paradoxical state of the Schulenburg family. Friedrich's remarkable fifty-year career spanned an extraordinary period in German history and witnessed incredible changes. He became an officer cadet (Fahrenjunker) on June 1, 1888, before Adolf Hitler was even conceived; he would receive his final promotion, as a three-star general in the SS (Obergruppenführer) as part of Hitler's fiftieth birthday celebrations. In vastly different epochs, in peace and war, under monarchs, republics, and dictators, Friedrich can be seen doing his duty for the Fatherland,

8. "A Grave Legacy"

unflustered and almost indifferent—through dissociation, dissonance, or denial, perhaps—to the form of government; his patriotism sought to look beyond the immediate objectives of state. But is this attitude consistent or contradictory; is it to be commended or decried?

Tisa believed that she saw, in her father's ability to set aside his anti-Semitism and receive her Jewish first husband in a cordial manner, vestiges of the timeless grace appertaining to the ancient nobility, but it is easy to make too much of this. The fact that Tisa never lost her affection for her father is surely to her credit, and the fact that she managed to defend him, while never denying his anti-Semitism, may be admirable, but the implication that noble values could conquer Nazi prejudices does not ring true. Friedrich's SS—and it certainly was "his" SS, as he helped to conceptualize it—took a dimmer view of Jews married to Christian women than Friedrich himself did, and the "half-breed" children of such unions were not treated to olde-worlde courtesy and respect. Many, many people, of course, Germans and non-Germans, completely misjudged Nazism and were totally taken in by Hitler's sleight-of-hand, but Friedrich and his sons were no duped outsiders, no clueless foreign observers, and by 1933 the nature of the regime was clear. Some Schulenburgs saw it and some Schulenburgs refused to see it. History has sometimes contrived to give the nobility a free pass; in many contexts, movies and history books included, a noble title can still work wonders. Embarking on the Schulenburg story, we are first faced with the family patriarch's impressive list of credentials; he was a Count, a knight, a swordsman, a cavalry general, a great-great-great-great-nephew of the Queen of England; but Friedrich Bernhard Graf von der Schulenburg finished his days as a Nazi, an anti-Semite, a hierarch of Himmler's thuggish SS, an enabler and legitimizer of a genocidal regime, and an accomplice in phenomenal evil.

Friedrich's beloved army and the Nazis were not natural or immediate bedfellows, and Hitler had to work for years to win over the military. Hitler rejoiced in the conversion of veteran imperial generals like Friedrich; he was eager for the legitimacy and continuity their endorsement could confer upon the Nazi movement. In 1927, overt Nazis were actually banned from joining the army or even from working as civilians on military bases, but although the Nazis denied it they were busy infiltrating the army anyway, and the tide steadily turned in Hitler's favor. The surprise election results of September 1930 convinced many skeptics in the army that eventual Nazi government was inevitable (Shirer 1960: 139–142). The idea of the army and the Nazis having common enemies did a lot to change military minds as well (Malinowski 2020: 271). Fear—of impending chaos, of a communist revolution, of a takeover by swarthy hordes—pushed people to act irrationally; for fear of violence and lawlessness, Wolf-Werner von der Schulenburg and his brothers joined the paramilitary SA when it was at its most violent and lawless. Hitler himself realized that the SA mob was out of control; it served to transport the Nazis into power, but it was a stone around Hitler's neck beyond 1933. The SA also threatened Nazi-army relations, which had cost so much time and effort to build, by giving a bad name to the German uniform; the SA comprised the most anarchic, unruly, shameless, and alcohol-fueled elements of the Nazi party, usually clamoring for an all-out revolt in the streets. In 1934, Hitler still faced a crisis of internal instability; Hindenburg—still a focus of unity for most Germans—was fading fast, and what was left of the political opposition called for the restoration of the monarchy or democracy. Hitler prepared to maneuver himself into the coming power vacuum. He decided to eliminate the SA's leaders and other rivals, debilitate the SA, and supplant it with his super-loyal SS. The army did not shed a tear (Shirer 1960: 206–207, 213–14).

Fritz-Dietlof did not join the SA like his brothers, but his commitment to the Nazi movement was initially heartfelt, if somewhat unconventional. For Fritz-Dietlof, it was not the Nazi party's activism that alerted him to the need for political change, it was the exact reverse; he believed that German society needed a complete overhaul, a root-and-branch reform, to pull it out of its malaise, and he was on the lookout for the right movement to do it. The imperfect Nazi party, he felt, at least had the potential to circumvent petty class squabbles and focus on real social problems, inspired by a traditional moral order and a spirit of national community; it was radical conservatism, a moral revolution. The social and political situation was genuinely desperate and only the Nazi party appeared to have the necessary drive to renew broken Germany. It was a truly popular movement that eschewed the tropes and trappings of the professional political elites and their flawed party system. Within the Nazi party, Fritz-Dietlof was a critical and discontented member, and when he finally turned against Nazism entirely he did not renounce or abandon his earlier aspirations for German society, he only revised his strategy for realizing them. With the national situation even more desperate than before, Fritz-Dietlof found a new movement to put his faith in, while still clinging to his belief in a coming greater Germany (Mommsen 2009: 154, 155, 176). As with much of this story, Fritz-Dietlof's Nazi career was peppered with contradictions and paradoxes. Consider his dealings with Berlin police president Wolf Heinrich Graf von Helldorff; the police chief grumbled

8. "A Grave Legacy"

over having the vaguely disreputable Schulenburg assigned to him, only for the two of them to get on brilliantly. Then, however, Helldorff masterminded Kristallnacht and the persecution of Berlin's Jews, Fritz-Dietlof's criticism of which saw him excluded from the Nazi party. The two men met again as co-conspirators, standing before Judge Freisler in the "people's court" after July 20, 1944 (Gregory 2018: 88). Legend has it that Hitler was so infuriated by Helldorff's participation in the July plot that he gave orders for Helldorff to be forced to watch his fellow conspirators hang prior to his own execution.

It is evident from these pages that we know much less about some Schulenburg siblings than others, and there are predictable reasons for this. To say that one person's life has been less remarkable than another's cannot avoid sounding uncharitable, perhaps, but compared to the extraordinary careers of Tisa, Fritz-Dietlof, and Wolf-Werner von der Schulenburg, and their father Friedrich and his cousin Friedrich-Werner, there is obviously no shame in being less famous, or less infamous, than any of them. Another influential factor is of course children, especially surviving children, whose prerogative it may be to curate the memory of their loved one and, to the extent that they are free and able to do so, maintain the family's privacy. Some lives, of course, create too lengthy a public record or "paper trail" to really be kept secret, while others leave a longer list of unanswered questions. Wolf-Werner had no children and nor did Tisa, while Johann-Albrecht had seven and Adolf-Heinrich had two; their descendants live in Europe and North America. The circumstances of Johann-Albrecht's wartime demise remain unclear, and the same is true of Adolf-Heinrich's wife Jutta, while we know that Adolf-Heinrich himself died of cancer. Wilhelm, the baby of the family who did not involve himself in politics, died young as the result of a car accident. The widowed Charlotte von der Schulenburg, who did much to preserve the memory of Fritz-Dietlof, was left with six children; Fredeke, born in 1934, Christiane, born in 1936, and then the couple's namesakes Fritz-Dietlof, born in 1938, and Charlotte, born in 1940, followed by Angela and Adelheid, born in 1942 and 1943 respectively (Meding 1997: 116). They grew up in stark awareness of their father's sacrifice for the cause of justice, raised as they were in an informal confraternity of July plot survivors and plotters' children. This became a sort of caste, a new mark of nobility; they understood each other, and in some cases they intermarried. Charlotte (junior) married Nick Bielenberg, son of Kreisau circle member and July plotter Peter Bielenberg, with whom she settled in Ireland and raised a family. In the 1970s she became involved in leftwing politics through the Marxist-Leninist group called Official Sinn Féin (Myers 2004).

Historically, the nobility have been regarded as masters of self-reinvention and self-portrayal, exercising enviable control over how their image, myth, and legend are established and transmitted throughout the ages. This talent may have helped to popularize the perception of nobility and Nazism as being fundamentally irreconcilable, and to promote the identification of Nazism's "real" co-conspirators as being the spineless and ambitious middle class. It was the middle class, some would argue, that produced most of the careerist officers, the unscrupulous pen-pushers, and the opportunistic businesspeople looking to make a buck at any cost; they were the ones who really carried out, facilitated, and administrated the Nazi horror. It is too hard a sell however, and though the nobility may be seen as an insignificantly small proportion of Third Reich society—only one to two per cent of the population—the fact of its significant acquiescence in the Nazi regime is undeniable. So how did it come about that the nobility, steeped in centuries-old traditions, could switch its allegiance from the Kaiser to the Führer? How could a class that valued heredity, innate superiority, and moral leadership fall into step with the lower-middle and working-class rabble-rousers and mountebanks of the chaotic radical Right? Were they saving their class or betraying it? (Malinowski 2020: 1–10).

The German aristocracy had taken a huge hit with the defeat of 1918. All of their centuries-old traditions and conservative values did not seem to have served them overly well, and that values system looked set to collapse, like the nobility itself. This was a radicalizing experience, in which any movement promising to restore or restructure the flow of power in society could seem attractive. Hitler was no Kaiser, to be sure, but the age of Kaisers, after all, was gone. The existence of the resulting void was not debatable, but the question of what should fill the void was an open and lively discussion. The nobility in Germany and in much of Europe was shaken not just by the events of 1918 but also by the flurry of revolutions and insurrections that followed it. Nobles in stable, victorious countries could not fully relate to this profound sense of destabilization, though in many cases German nobles' complaints of near-impoverishment were gross exaggerations. Such claims by aristocrats were often intended to distance themselves ideologically from the feverish money-making of the rising middle class, whom they generally despised, as did the Nazis; it was more dignified to be seen as poor than ambitious. Germany's aristocrats were unsettled, but they did not disappear; they still had their influence,

8. "A Grave Legacy"

their connections, their property, and their savoir faire, making them important and capable players in Weimar politics. This combination of weaknesses and strengths further fueled the mutual attraction with the Nazi party (Malinowski 2020: 1–4, 9–10).

Northern, Prussian nobility—the Protestant aristocracies—like the Schulenburgs were generally more susceptible to Hitler's courtship of the elites than their southern, Bavarian counterparts, who experienced a much less severe existential crisis. The Bavarian, Catholic nobility still had their sources of higher authority to look to—the pope and their crown prince—and they were more likely to have successfully preserved their sources of wealth as well. They were better connected—spiritually and economically—with the rest of Europe and its royal houses, and this self-assurance led many Bavarian nobles to resist or stand up to the Nazis (Malinowski 2020: 6–7) For southern Germans of all classes, the combination of Catholicism, monarchism, and Bavarian traditions often combined to inspire hostility and resistance to Nazism (Herwarth 1981: 104). This applied to the Bavarian Royal House of Wittelsbach as well; the heir apparent, Crown Prince Rupprecht, was vocally anti–Hitler. Friedrich von der Schulenburg had briefly served as Crown Prince Rupprecht's Chief of Staff during the First World War (Heinemann 1994: 2); both men were passionate about restoring the monarchy, but Friedrich felt that the Nazi revolution might actually lead, perhaps indirectly, to achieving their goal. This view, which even at the time must have appeared quite unlikely, was more popular among northern, Prussian aristocrats like Friedrich, and it suggests that their support for Nazism was calculated and opportunistic, rather than passionate and ideological (Sangster 2015: 26; Shirer 1960: 6). Aristocratic acceptance of this gambit—support the Nazi revolution but pray for a restoration of the monarchy—recalls the paradoxical phrase from Lampedusa's *The Leopard*: "For things to remain the same, everything must change" (Malinowski 2020: 9). Friedrich had also been Chief of Staff to the other crown prince, Wilhelm of Germany, who supported Hitler until he realized that it would never lead to a return of the monarchy. Hitler then banned former royals from serving in the armed forces, after the death of Wilhelm's son during the invasion of France unleashed a torrent of ordinary Germans' support for the abolished monarchy.

Clearly, a range of opinions circulated among the aristocracy. There was not one type or level of aristocrat, and the nobility was not one homogenous group. Aristocrats spanned several social and economic strata, including the stereotypes of affluent and impoverished, but also different religions and different self-understandings of their class and role. The paradoxical convergence of aspirations between nobles and Nazism was not a forgone conclusion, but a gradual and conflict-ridden rapprochement between two antithetical groups. The various views and positions of individual members of the Schulenburg family were not in themselves unusual for the aristocracy; all of their views were represented amongst nobles, almost making the Schulenburg family a microcosm of German nobility and its responses to Nazism, but for such polar views to be so dramatically demonstrated within the same family unit is bizarre. The nobility provided some of the key promoters and facilitators of Hitler's rise, though history has not always apportioned much blame to the upper class, often preferring the traditional scapegoat of that supposedly lame and resentful lower-middle class (Malinowski 2020: 4, 5).

Class was still an influential factor in people's contrasting visions for society, and involvement with the supposedly classless Nazi party did not soften prejudices. The idealized "secret Germany" aspired to by the July plotters and the conservative, aristocratic opposition was envisaged as an alliance between the wise, the noble, and the good; in practice this would have meant restoring the traditional class-based moral order of aristocratic Germany. This vision inspired the Resistance oath "We want a New Order that makes all Germans supporters of the state and guarantees them law and justice, but we scorn the lie of equality and bow before the hierarchies established by nature." This oath reflects the social order that was lost in 1918 and which nobles initially saw, in Nazism, the potential to regain, but the Nazis let them down, first with their classlessness rhetoric and then with their apparent dedication to democracy, elections, and referendums. Real democracy, had it actually emerged, would have been only a step away from Bolshevism, in aristocratic eyes, and, as in Russia, power would have passed to minor intellectuals and the middle class, loathed by nobles and Nazis alike. It was common targets of hatred such as the middle class, more than patriotism or shared values, which drew nobles and Nazis together. Both nobles and Nazis, generally speaking, hated Weimar, communists, modern art, nightclubs, and, of course, Jews, who were the common thread running through all of these disliked categories. Aristocrats could overlook the shamelessly proletarian rabble behavior of organizations like the SA, which was a grotesque parody of German uniformed tradition, because the Nazis' enormous rearmament programs really seemed to be restoring Germany's former military greatness. Rearmament had direct implications for aristocrats who owned land in the east, and also for those who had been ruined and dispossessed; Hitler's foreign expansion

8. "A Grave Legacy"

ambitions hinted at the possibility of being granted land and cheap labor in the conquered territories. Another important incentive was jobs; the simultaneous expansion and purging of the judiciary, the civil service, and the diplomatic corps created openings for aristocrats to return to some of their traditional occupations, and the launch of new government departments, such as the Reich sports directorate, created new opportunities for loyal Nazi aristocrats (Malinowski 2020: 8–14).

Historian Stephan Malinowski has described the convergence of aspirations between nobles and Nazis as a "misalliance"—borrowing the nobles' own term for a marriage beneath one's rank and status, for emotional reasons or for personal gain—and these same motivations might explain the German nobility's otherwise inconsistent commitment to the Nazi cause (Malinowski 2020: 2–3). This idea of a noble-Nazi misalliance sits within broader analyses of political alliances between the "elite" and the "mob." These terms may be very crude, but the theory of misalliance as the modern way of doing politics continues to gain traction in studies of movements with a broad but inconsistent appeal, from the Brexit campaign in the UK to MAGA in the U.S. These alliances or misalliances are not purely the creation of media-savvy political fixers and kingmakers, however, and nor do they spring from a void. The German aristocracy already had a strong culture of leadership and obedience, but they had lost their leader; it was never beyond the realm of possibility that they might switch their allegiance to another capable individual. Hitler was, in some very real senses, a leader of certain talent and credibility; he learned how to court and flatter the military and the aristocracy, while sweet-talking and incentivizing the working class and the industrialists. The concept of an all-powerful ruler sat well with conceptions of leadership in Prussian tradition, which were easily shown to be compatible with the Führerprinzip—leader principle—touted by the Nazis, as they both had the same philosophical basis. Both visions of leadership owed much to Social Darwinism and the idea that certain special individuals were born to rule; it would be ideologically difficult and quite contradictory to uphold aristocracy on the one hand and yet not accept the Führerprinzip on the other. Transferring their obedience also gave the nobility a get-out clause; they could claim that they were endorsing Hitler's model of authority in principle, rather than pledging personal allegiance to him. Whatever the merits or demerits of this exercise in tautology, there was also no shortage of aristocrats who preferred the clarity and unambiguity of obsessive, fanatical, and personal loyalty to Hitler (Sangster 2015: 42–43, 131, 146, 152).

Divided Over Hitler

The Schulenburg family certainly had its share of fully committed Nazis, most notably the father and son team of Friedrich and Wolf-Werner, and their noble rank and station did not make them unusual. The Schulenburgs' ties to England, the English royals, and the English-speaking world, however, which had deeper roots than their Nazi connections, were a more unusual trait. The question of how Germans managed (or indeed failed to manage) such multiple and mismatched loyalties provides a fascinating area of study. After 1945, the only Schulenburg who was left to contribute to postwar reconciliation between Germany and Great Britain was of course Tisa, and her contribution, mostly through her art, was not insignificant. Tisa was one of several notable Germans who used a wide variety of skills in the cause of rebuilding relations, with little reward, exemplified by the case of Herbert Sulzbach (1894–1985). It is worth considering Sulzbach's remarkable story. He was born in Frankfurt am Main, a German of Jewish descent who became devoted to reconciling what he regarded as "his" two countries, Britain and Germany. He was the son a Frankfurt banker and composer, Emil Sulzbach; his grandfather Rudolf co-founded the private bank Gebrüder Sulzbach (Sulzbach Brothers). The young Herbert was homeschooled and later attended the Goethe Gymnasium, and from 1906 to 1908 attended Dr. Hoch's Conservatory. During the First World War, Sulzbach served as a frontline artillery officer for four years, and was awarded the Iron Cross first and second class. He was deeply patriotic, believing until the end that a German victory was possible; this was a hopeful theme he often recorded in his diary, which he published as a memoir in 1935. Its 1973 English translation, titled *With the German Guns* earned praise for its clear, accessible prose and arresting imagery. After the war Sulzbach was married briefly and then divorced. In 1923 he married for a second time, to Beate Scherk, the niece of orchestral conductor and composer Otto Klemperer. Beate was a theater actress who also worked in film (*The Secret of the Green Mask*, 1916; *My Leopold*, 1924). Sulzbach's background, therefore, was thoroughly German, steeped in tradition, music, and culture; the Sulzbachs were patriotic, artistic, and well-off, though firmly upper-middle class rather than upper class, and by no means aristocrats.

Sulzbach's 1935 memoir sold well for the time, even sitting on bookshop shelves alongside gushing hagiographies of Hitler and Mussolini. This success was surprising for two reasons; Sulzbach had become a vocal critic of the Nazi party, and he was also Jewish. In 1938, he fled to England with Beate, her sister, and his daughter from his first marriage. In their absence, Germany stripped them of their citizenship and seized their

8. "A Grave Legacy"

assets. Some of Sulzbach's other family members also managed to flee, and others later perished in the camps. With the outbreak of war, the British authorities designated the stateless Sulzbachs "enemy aliens" along with other German immigrants, and shipped them off to a temporary internment camp on the Isle of Man. Sulzbach endured this patiently, and as soon as he could he enlisted in the British Army's Pioneer Corps, spending the next four years constructing air and sea defenses against German invasion or attack. Sulzbach's superiors were impressed with his attitude and loyalty and promoted him to staff sergeant. From Normandy onwards, large numbers of German prisoners-of-war arrived in Britain, and Sulzbach was sent to work as an interpreter at a POW camp near Comrie in the Scottish Highlands, where four thousand Germans were being held. There, on a daily basis, he spoke to men who openly considered him subhuman; Sulzbach decided to respond by displaying relentless humanity. He helped them, joked with them, taught them, and befriended them; even hardened SS members eventually lowered their defenses and warmed to him. He encouraged the POWs to look ahead, he took them seriously, he listened to their personal problems, and he helped them to reflect on human values. The effect of Sulzbach's efforts was that tension and resentment among the POWs were gradually defused, paving the way for the first steps towards reconciliation.

Sulzbach decided to dedicate the rest of his life to the mission of reconciliation that he had begun in the POW camps. From January 1946 to May 1948 Sulzbach worked as translator and cultural affairs officer at the POW camp at Featherstone Park, near Haltwhistle in Northumberland. The camp, based inside Featherstone Castle, was established in 1944 and lasted until 1948. Originally holding Italian POWs, from 1945 it served as a camp for German officers. Thanks to the efforts of people like Sulzbach, postwar POW camp policy began to stress reconciliation rather than punishment; Sulzbach was asked to provide not just political reeducation for the POWs but also a wide range of cultural and sporting activities. They were also given the opportunity to study, earn qualifications, or learn a trade; a camp university was set up, helping the POWs to prepare for civilian life. Teachers at the camp university included Norman Bentwich, chair of international relations at the Hebrew University of Jerusalem, Benjamin Britten, Victor Gollancz, Yehudi Menuhin, Basil Liddell Hart, Ivone Kirkpatrick, and Harold Nicolson. Sulzbach also called upon Gerhard Leibholz, Pastor Martin Niemöller, and Hugh Trevor-Roper to give guest lectures. The success of these initiatives was immense; the POWs showed enthusiasm for reconciliation and commitment to democratic and internationalist ideals. Former POWs later cited Sulzbach as having the greatest influence on them; despite his traumatic personal relationship with Germany, he worked tirelessly for his people and supported them without prejudice.

Sulzbach retired from the British Army with the rank of captain. In 1951, West Germany appointed him cultural attaché at its embassy in London. After Featherstone Park camp closed, former staff and prisoners organized reunions, resulting in the foundation, in 1960, of their own German-British friendship society, the Featherstone Park Association, of which Sulzbach became honorary chairman. Based at the embassy, he continued to work with various projects aimed at promoting German-British reconciliation for thirty years, until his retirement at the age of eighty-seven. He provided information about Germany to the British public, he supported town-twinning programs between British and German communities, and he promoted numerous international conferences and exchange programs. He corresponded with thousands of ex-POWs and founded a group to promote Anglo-German friendship. He was appointed Officer of the Order of the British Empire (OBE) and was awarded the Great Federal Cross of Merit of West Germany. When the great peacemaker died in 1985, he was buried alongside his wife Beate at Hampstead Cemetery in London (Taylor King 2019).

People like Herbert Sulzbach, Gerhard Leibholz, and Martin Niemöller managed, to a modest extent and in their unassuming way, to revitalize the centuries-old bond between the British and German people, of which the Schulenburgs had considered themselves to be an integral part. That bond was almost systematically broken, not in 1939 but in 1914. War ended a tradition of friendship between the two countries that reached its peak in the time of the German-born George I, the first British (by adoption) king of the House of Hanover, and his Queen, Melusine von der Schulenburg. King George never renounced his Germanness, and Germany never rejected him. The fact that he was German posed no barrier to him being the British king and it encouraged the vital Anglo-German bond. The bond itself predated George I and led back to his maternal grandparents, Friedrich V (1596–1632), Elector Palatine of the Rhine in the Holy Roman Empire from 1610 to 1623, and briefly King of Bohemia from 1619 to 1620 (earning him the derisive sobriquet of The Winter King) and Elizabeth Stuart (1596–1662), second child and eldest daughter of James VI and I, King of Scotland, England, and Ireland. Friedrich and Elizabeth were born just seven days apart, and they were married on St Valentine's Day in 1613, when they were sixteen years old. The union was popular and

8. "A Grave Legacy"

greatly celebrated, and the happy couple was beloved of the people, but this marriage of the two major powers was more than symbolic; it was hoped that the alliance would ensure peace in Europe, or at least peace between two of Europe's greatest nations.

This peaceful bond remained safe in the hands of royals and aristocrats for three hundred years, but times had changed. By 1945, Europe's royal and aristocratic houses were in no position to promote peace and reconciliation; many of them were deposed, disgraced, impoverished, or implicated in the recent tyrannies. The new breed of reconcilers—Sulzbach, Leibholz, Niemöller—were not only no aristocrats, they were from sectors of German society that found themselves despised rather than beloved of the people; the grasping middle class, the preaching moralists, and, in Sulzbach's case, the Jews. Sulzbach, Leibholz, and Niemöller, like George I, never renounced their Germanness, but in its madness Germany rejected them. Some reconcilers, like Tisa von der Schulenburg, were technically still aristocrats, but that did not save them from being rejected and despised in their time as well. Better remembered than all of them, perhaps, is Bert Trautmann from Bremen, the son of a desperately poor port worker, who possibly did more than anyone to heal Anglo-German relations. As a teenager Bernhard—"Bert"—Trautmann (1923–2013) joined, coincidentally, the Fallschirmjäger, and served in Russia. By 1944, Trautmann was one of the exhausted Fallschirmjäger veterans being corralled into new units to fight in Normandy; he allowed himself to be taken prisoner and was sent to England. There, Trautmann revealed a gift that was sure to endear him to the British people; he was a fantastic goalkeeper. In 1948, no longer a POW, he opted to remain in England to play football. Manchester City wanted to sign him, but with Manchester still partly in ruins from the Blitz, the decision was controversial. Twenty thousand fans marched in protest against Trautmann's signing, but he persevered and won their hearts, breaking down walls of mutual distrust and wariness. He played more than five hundred matches for Manchester City between 1949 and 1964, winning Footballer of the Year in 1956. Trautmann was welcomed into the Football Hall of Fame in both England and Germany, and he was decorated by both countries for helping to repair Anglo-German relations, like Herbert Sulzbach; both men, ironically, received the Officer of the Order of the British Empire (OBE) to add to their Iron Crosses. Examples of Germans articulately repudiating Nazism are plentiful enough to challenge the perception of Germany "following blindly" as though entranced by Hitler, but postwar reconciliation has so often been in the hands—or gloves—of humble individuals carried along by the tide of history, like Trautmann, rather than ideologues and aristocrats (Shirer 1960: 5–6).

The encouraging case of Bert Trautmann, winner of Germany's Iron Cross and England's beloved F.A. Cup, was a remarkable and surprising feature of postwar reconciliation efforts. One of the infinitely more difficult legacies of the Nazi years, however, and of the wounds it left upon individuals and communities, was the task of understanding the roles of blame and responsibility. Oppression, persecution, and mass killings changed people's lives, not only those of victims and survivors, but crucially those of perpetrators and bystanders too. The quest for justice began with the Nuremberg tribunal, starting in November 1945, and other trials, whose goal, beginning at the top, was to hold leading Nazis accountable for their crimes. While the trials were no doubt a necessary part of the search for justice, they tended to leave many questions unresolved. This was partly because, with the events still being very fresh in November 1945, Germans' responses and reactions could only be transitional; they were, at most, halfway between closure of their old life and acceptance of the new reality, and there was so much to digest. It was long enough, however, for a few individuals to recant; Hans Frank, former Nazi governor of Poland, uttered his famous phrase—"A thousand years will pass and the guilt of Germany will not be erased"—before being hanged at Nuremberg (the phrase serves as the epigraph to Shirer's *The Rise and Fall of the Third Reich*). While Frank's last words still have an air of ambivalence, it is generally acknowledged that he was among the very few Nuremberg defendants to show remorse. His gallows curse names Germany, rather than Germans, inviting questions as to whether a whole nation can be held responsible for crimes against humanity, and whether it is even possible to achieve meaningful justice for crimes like genocide. Talk of restitution and reparation can seem conclusive, but the terms alone do not set out what is actually owed to the victims and survivors. Talk of restoring peace between different groups and repairing society can also sound encouraging, but this may be unsatisfactory or offensive to individuals, or at odds with their individual aspirations and perspectives.

These questions make up the challenge of doing "transitional justice," the term used by scholars to describe the steps a society can take after it emerges from a period of war, injustice, and mass violence, as it strives to move towards a better future. As part of Germany's transition, moving away from the gallows of Nuremberg, more nuanced voices began to speak of Germans' responsibility rather than Germany's guilt. "Germans must bear responsibility," wrote Willy Brandt in *Verbrecher und andere*

8. "A Grave Legacy"

Deutsche (Criminals and Other Germans) in 1946, "but responsibility is not the same as guilt." The distinction is recognized by legal scholars as a crucial one, but transitional justice also includes the challenge of societies having to discern how much responsibility they must accept and how. Societies must decide whether or not to punish individuals and certain entities, such as companies, and how this moving forward will be affected by the ongoing presence of perpetrators, victims, survivors, and bystanders. These are interconnected problems that tend to provoke the European philosophical mindset into employing binary analyses, seeing "pairs" of dangers such as doing too much memorializing or not enough, wallowing in the past or forgetting it, giving too much acknowledgment of victimhood or too little recognition of survivors. These dilemmas have haunted many societies emerging from experiences of violence, war, and terrorism, as well as affecting the progress of individuals recovering from these traumatic events (Minow 1998: 2).

In the decades since the Second World War and the Holocaust, Germany has had to face all of the difficult questions mentioned above. Immediately after the war, the Allies demanded that all property seized by the Nazis or signed over to them under duress be returned to the rightful owners. If the rightful owner had died and left no heir, the property would be sold and the proceeds donated to organizations aiding survivors of Nazi persecution. People were slow to comply with the policy and it was not widely enforced. Germany was then split into two countries, with the eastern half—the German Democratic Republic—allied to the Soviet Union, and the new Federal Republic of Germany (West Germany) adopted new policies of restitution for Nazi-era crimes. The West German government declared that "unspeakable crimes had been committed in the name of the German people which entail an obligation to make moral and material amends." This took the form of a compensation scheme for those who had suffered injury or discrimination "because of the opposition to National Socialism or because of their race, creed, or ideology." This program is known in German as Wiedergutmachung, which translates as "to make good again" (Pross 1998: 22).

This financial reparations scheme was, predictably, controversial, complicated, and flawed. Qualifying for compensation required an individual to prove that they had been persecuted for racial, religious, or ideological reasons and had suffered injuries that were not only disabling but also the direct result of the persecution. Many survivors found it difficult to meet the heavy burden of proof, while others were excluded from the scheme altogether, such as slave laborers, victims of forced sterilization,

Divided Over Hitler

homosexuals, ethnic Roma and Sinti, and families of the victims of euthanasia. Even with these exclusions, however, the Wiedergutmachung program has paid out more than sixty billion U.S. dollars in reparations. Some of this money went directly to the State of Israel, to support Holocaust survivors who had settled there and also as investment in the country's economy. Some money went to programs that assisted survivors, provided Holocaust education, and enforced the return of Jewish property. In addition, pensions were provided for individual survivors throughout the world. When the Wiedergutmachung program began in the early 1950s, it was not strongly supported by the German public; a survey found that just five per cent of Germans felt any guilt towards Jews, and only twenty-nine per cent agreed that Germany owed restitution to the Jewish people (Judt 2005: 271).

This apparent lack of sensitivity has been described as a "moral anesthesia" that affected ordinary Germans in the years immediately after the war, numbed by defeat and unwilling to face their memories. Some engaged in revisionism of their own pasts; Johnnie von Herwarth, former secretary to Ambassador Schulenburg in Moscow, lamented the fact that indifferent bystanders of the Nazi years later claimed to have sided with the Resistance. Herwarth admitted that the Resistance was ultimately a failure, but if the number of people who later claimed to have joined it really had taken part, it might not have failed (Herwarth 1981: 7). By the mid-1960s, a new generation of Germans was more willing to face the past honestly and even condemn the actions and inactions of their parents' generation. Victims and their relatives continued to demand justice, and as knowledge of Nazi crimes increased over the years, so did efforts to carry out restitution and remembrance. Companies that used slave labor finally agreed to pay compensation, litigation in pursuit of stolen Jewish property, including works of art, continued into the twenty-first century, and history classes about Nazism and the Holocaust were mandated in all public schools. In recent years, Germany has also been assiduous in extraditing and prosecuting accomplices in murder at concentration camps, sparking debate over the usefulness of jailing men and women in their late nineties. Individual German towns and cities launched their own remembrance initiatives, including programs to bring former Jewish residents on an all-expenses-paid trip to revisit their city and meet its dignitaries (Buruma 1994: 24). Latterly, the worthiness of these costly return visits was questioned, with some arguing that these visitors nearly all left Germany at a very young age, and they have no recollections of the city they are visiting (Kulish 2008).

8. "A Grave Legacy"

A lasting and constructive strategy for coming to terms with its past may be Germany's extensive creation of museums and memorials, including those dubbed "sites of memory" such as concentration camps and Gestapo headquarters that have been preserved and turned into visitor centers. Hundreds of memorials and exhibitions have been launched across the country in large cities and small towns, especially over the last two decades. History is boldly, publicly, and enthusiastically acknowledged, and visitors have the opportunity to confront the country's past in tangible ways. Nevertheless, Germany's relationship with its Nazi past still regularly generates controversy. Most countries seek to celebrate the best features of their pasts, while Germany risks appearing to relentlessly promote its worst side. This has been met with both cynicism and praise. At a 2008 event commemorating the Holocaust and the liberation of Auschwitz, former Israeli ambassador to Germany Avi Primor asked, "Where in the world has one ever seen a nation that erects memorials to immortalize its own shame? Only the Germans had the bravery and the humility" (Kulish 2008). Today, the building of monuments to the Nazi disgrace continues unabated, with special care being given to remedying previous omissions; a memorial near the Reichstag now honors Sinti and Roma victims of the Nazis, and another one, not far from the Brandenburg Gate, pays tribute to gays and lesbians killed in the Holocaust.

The question of making amends has long been recognized as a difficult balancing act. Indeed, Germany's leaders have consistently worked to connect their nation's history with a sense of identity and responsibility, in the sense of taking responsibility for the future rather than breast-beating over the past. At a commemoration ceremony in 1985, then-Chancellor Richard von Weizäcker pointed out that the vast majority of Germany's population, at that time, had either been children during the Nazi years or had not been born yet. "They cannot profess a guilt of their own for crimes that they did not commit," he said, "but their forefathers have left them a grave legacy. All of us, whether guilty or not, whether old or young, must accept the past ... it is vital to keep alive the memories.... [A]nyone who closes his eyes to the past is blind to the present. Whoever refuses to remember the inhumanity is prone to new risks of infection" (Weizsäcker [1985] in Perry et al 2010: 400). For Germany, managing that "grave legacy" has clearly meant many things, including passing laws, paying reparations, building memorials, and mandating education. These German efforts to put things right, educate, and memorialize are, like previous programs, neither perfect nor complete. Not every German, even today, repudiates the crimes of the Nazis with equal conviction, and not every

Divided Over Hitler

German repudiates them at all; neo–Nazi groups and Nazi-apologist think-tanks, political parties, and authors still operate, even as the majority of people in Germany today are clearly committed to democracy and human rights.

Germany's grave legacy creeps into contemporary debates over subjects as varied as troop commitments overseas, the nation's low birthrate, and its dealings with foreigners. Some see Germany as having an excessive preoccupation with its Nazi past, blaming this on Germans' philosophical temperament, or continued awe at the unprecedented combination of organization and brutality, or the sense that the crime was so great that it has permanently infected the German psyche. It is not solely a preoccupation of the old, hardly any of whom now remember the Nazi years anyway; young Germans, who are required to study the Nazi era and the Holocaust intensively, show no particular signs of wanting to let the matter drop, despite the distance from the events. The younger generation seems to have built upon Richard von Weizäcker's proposal to study the past not as a source of guilt but as a source of motivation, to take responsibility on the world stage for peace and social justice (Kulish 2008). These are of course not just German concerns. Wherever and whenever a leader pushes the boundaries of a fragile democracy in a quest for increased power, and their followers are given license to cheat, lie, and bully others, with good reason people sense the reawakening of the specter of Nazism. Unbridled power tends to lead to barbarity, whether in individuals, armies, businesses, mobs, or any other human institution. Today's Germany is no exemplar of this, however, and nor is Japan; few countries, in fact, have enjoyed such protracted periods of peace and stability as the defeated former Axis powers. Human nature has not changed, but politics has, through determined and deliberate effort. Both countries worked to install and maintain efficient democracies, meaning that those who would abuse that democracy are kept out with the ballot box. Democracy itself is not infallible, of course, but it has worked so far. Those who would deny Germany the credit for their achievements, and choose instead to see them as unredeemed children of the Nazis, are arguably the ones who have learned nothing from the past (Buruma 1994: 307).

Not all Germans feel that their country has handled the Nazi legacy successfully. Some feel that schools, senates, and councils have dealt with Nazism only in a superficial way, and that the young will soon tire of hearing about it. They fear that building monuments and opening exhibitions has mutated into ritualized behavior and that it will eventually dissipate unnoticed (Kulish 2008). How far Germany still needs to go with the task

8. "A Grave Legacy"

of honoring, memorializing, educating, and atoning is, of course, a decision for the German people to make. Many of the oversights of the past have been put right—certain "forgotten" victims of Nazi atrocities have now been recognized at long last—but memorializing is surely not just about making sure that everyone gets their own memorial. This does not even seem viable; there will always be forgotten victims, forgotten perpetrators, and forgotten heroes, as the story of the Schulenburg family seems to attest. The efforts of key members of the Schulenburg family—Friedrich-Werner, Fritz-Dietlof, and Tisa—in opposing Hitler and Nazism, will perhaps always be somewhat difficult to categorize, given their family's complex, ambiguous, and intertwining ties with nobility, nationalism, and the military. In a family so bound up with Germany's fortunes, no resistance or rebellion would be total enough to extricate the individual members from some degree of complicity; they were, like many, caught up in a web that was not of their making. It seemed inevitable that the younger, male Schulenburgs, like Wolf-Werner and Fritz-Dietlof, would be drawn to high-profile positions in the regime—they had the necessary education, confidence, and ability—but their positions demanded clear ideological choices, which not only divided the brothers but also led to their doom. Not all German families' dilemmas were so consequential, even in families that, like the Schulenburgs, were divided over Hitler. There were many divided families, but not all of them were so conspicuous and visible, with onerous national roles, and so vocally and vehemently militant for their chosen faction, up to the bitter end. For a family with such strong ties to England, the Schulenburgs' fates are perhaps fittingly Shakespearean, with no winners or losers at the finale, only tragedy.

Appendix I
Schulenburg Family Tree

THE HOUSE OF SCHULENBURG~TRESSOW

Title created in 1728 by Charles VI, Habsburg, Holy Roman Emperor, for

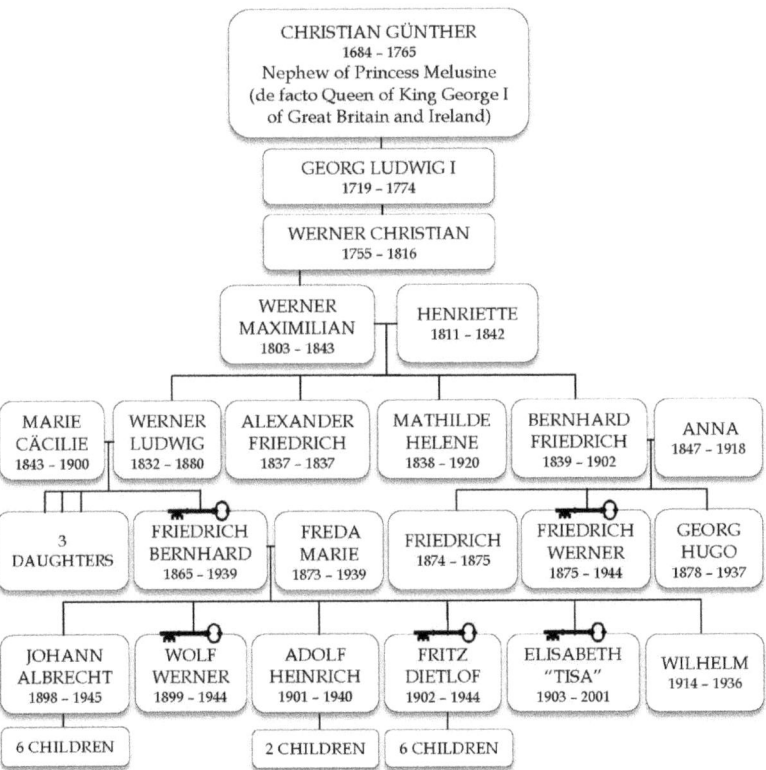

Appendix II

Biographical Notes

(a) COUNT FRIEDRICH

Friedrich Bernhard Karl Gustav Ulrich Erich Graf von der Schulenburg
November 21, 1865–May 19, 1939

Friedrich Bernhard Karl Gustav Ulrich Erich Graf von der Schulenburg of Tressow Castle was born on November 21, 1865. He was the second child and first son of Werner Ludwig Ernst Karl Heinrich Achat Graf (Count) von der Schulenburg (1832–1880) and his wife Marie Cäcilie Hedwig Sophie Pauline, nee Freiin von Maltzahn (1843–1900). Friedrich's birthplace was officially registered as Bobitz, Mecklenburg; he was almost certainly born at the ancestral home of Tressow Castle. He succeeded to the Schulenburg title on April 18, 1880, becoming the sixth Graf von der Schulenburg rather unexpectedly, aged only fourteen, upon the untimely death of his father. After briefly attending the University of Heidelberg he joined the Second Guards Uhlan Regiment of the cavalry in 1888, garrisoned in Berlin. He transferred to the more prestigious Gardes du Corps cavalry regiment, the Kaiser's own special life guards, in 1890. In 1894 he was appointed regimental adjutant of the Gardes du Corps and, in 1897, personal adjutant or aide-de-camp to Duke Johann Albrecht (1857–1920) who had just become regent of the Grand Duchy of Mecklenburg-Schwerin, the Schulenburgs' home state in the German Empire (Ruvigny 1914: 1332, 1333).

On July 21, 1897, First Lieutenant Friedrich married Freda Marie Gräfin (Countess) von Arnim. She was the daughter of Georg Werner Graf von Arnim of Boitzenburg Castle, part of the ancient Arnim family, one of the oldest extant Prussian noble families, and she was eight years Friedrich's junior. On September 14, 1900, Friedrich was promoted to Captain (Rittmeister, in the historic rank system of the Prussian cavalry) and assigned to assist the Higher General Staff in Berlin. The following

Appendix II

spring, Friedrich was posted overseas with his young family, to take up the prestigious appointment of military attaché to the German Embassy in London. There, Friedrich perceived the danger of a breakdown in Anglo-German relations, and he felt that Britain would side with France in a future war (Singapore Free Press 1930: 8). In March 1907, Friedrich was promoted to major, and he returned to his work with the Higher General Staff in Berlin. In 1913, he was appointed to the command of the Gardes du Corps regiment. At the same time, Kaiser Wilhelm II appointed him his aide-de-camp, with promotion to lieutenant-colonel (Ruvigny 1914: 1333).

In 1915 Friedrich was promoted to colonel, and in August 1916 he was appointed Chief of Staff of the Sixth Army, under Crown Prince Rupprecht of Bavaria (Heinemann 1994: 2). After only three months in this role, however, he was appointed Chief of Staff to Crown Prince Wilhelm of Germany and his eponymous Army Group German Crown Prince, which from February 1917 was engaged in intense defensive battles on the Aisne and in Champagne (Malaya Tribune 1923: 2). Despite repelling a large-scale French breakthrough attempt in April 1917, Friedrich and the Crown Prince concluded that a German victory was impossible, and that they should use their recent success to broker for peace. It is worth recalling that April 1917 saw the entry of the United States into the war (Dellmensingen 1930: 192). Friedrich was promoted to major-general in June 1918 (Heinemann 1994: 2). On November 9, 1918, at the Germans' final war council at Spa, Friedrich was the only one present to advise the Kaiser not to abdicate, or at least to step aside temporarily but not flee (Singapore Free Press 1939: 12). Several hardline advisors felt that the Kaiser should seek an honorable and heroic death, leading the final charge, but only Friedrich dared to suggest it out loud (Hull 2004: 290).

Friedrich was transferred to the army reserve of officers on December 28, 1918, and released from active service on March 29, 1920, keeping his rank of major-general. Friedrich was privately scathing of the Kaiser and Crown Prince Wilhelm's perceived defeatism; nevertheless, when a fellow aristocrat publicly called the Kaiser a coward, Friedrich challenged him to a duel. Postwar, Friedrich contemplated going into the tobacco business (Singapore Free Press 1930: 18). He became involved with the conservative DNVP—the German National People's Party—and in December 1924 he was elected to the Reichstag to represent them, serving for a term of nearly three and a half years (Klee 2005: 565). He later joined the short-lived offshoot of the DNVP, the more monarchist KVP, the Conservative People's Party. Still an ardent royalist who hoped for the restoration of the

Appendix II

monarchy, Friedrich considered the Weimar republic a disaster and communism a clear and present evil. He felt that both of these threats urgently needed to be quashed, even if it took an unpleasant, anti-monarchist opportunist like Hitler to do it; "only a Titan can master the situation" Friedrich wrote (Malinowski 2020: 86, 87). Like his sons, Friedrich joined the Nazi party and the SA, cutting his ties to the DNVP. He would return to the Reichstag for a term, this time as a Nazi party deputy.

Friedrich's most significant single contribution to the Nazi cause was probably his suggestion to create an elite corps under the direct command of the Reich chancellor, just as Friedrich's old regiment, the Gardes du Corps, had sworn personal allegiance to the Kaiser. The unit Friedrich ideated would come to fruition in the reformed and reoriented version of the Schutzstaffel (Protection squadron) or SS, which Friedrich himself then joined, in 1936 (Haupt 2001: 111). On April 1, 1938, on the occasion of the fiftieth anniversary of his joining the army, Friedrich was made an honorary full four-star general of the cavalry (Seymour 2013: 418). He was seriously ill by that time, suffering symptoms of tuberculosis. On April 20, 1939, Hitler turned fifty years old, and a wave of honors and appointments were bestowed upon the faithful. Friedrich became one of only a handful of people ever promoted to the three-star general rank of Obergruppenführer in the SS, second only to the Reichsführer-SS, Heinrich Himmler. The appointment was backdated to take effect from January 30, presumably because of Friedrich's poor state of health. Just over a month later, on May 19, 1939, Friedrich died of old-age tuberculosis, aged seventy-three. Hitler ordered a state funeral for May 24, with the military cortege first passing through the traditional army citadel of Potsdam. Hitler, Himmler, and von Brauchitsch, the army commander-in-chief, attended (Singapore Free Press 1939: 12). Himmler insisted on a holding a second funeral procession at Tressow Castle, as a strictly SS event.

Friedrich's Awards

    Order of the Crown, third class
    Knight of Honor of the Order of St. John
    Prussian Service Cross
    Bavarian Military Order of Merit, third class
    Knight's Cross, second class, of the Order of Henry the Lion
    Knight's Cross of the Order of the Wendish Crown
    Knight's Cross of the Griffon Order

Appendix II

Knight's Cross of Honor, second class, of the Oldenburg Order of Merit of Duke Peter Friedrich Ludwig, with silver crown
Knight's Cross, first class, of the Albrecht Order
Knight's Cross, second class, of the House Order of the White Falcon
Commander, first class, of the Ducal Saxe-Ernestine House Order
Iron Cross (1914) second and first class
Royal House Order of Hohenzollern
    Knight's Cross with Swords (1915)
    Commander's Cross with Swords (1917)
Pour le Mérite with oak leaves
    Pour le Mérite (1917)
    Oak Leaves added (1918)
Order of the Red Eagle, second class, with swords, oak leaves and crown
Honor Cross of the World War 1914–1918 (Ehrenkreuz des Weltkrieges) with swords
Golden party badge of the NSDAP (Nazi party) awarded April 1, 1938
Wehrmacht Long Service Medal (Wehrmacht-Dienstauszeichnung)
Commander of the Order of Leopold II (Belgium)
Knight's Cross of the Order of the Dannebrog (Denmark)
Officer of the Legion of Honor (France)
Commander of the Order of the Redeemer (Greece)
Commander of the Royal Victorian Order (Britain)
Officer of the Knightly Order of Saints Mauritius and Lazarus (Italy)
Knight of the Order of the Crown (Romania)
Commander, second class, of the Order of the Sword (Sweden)
Officer of the Order of the White Elephant (Siam [Thailand])

(b) COUNT FRIEDRICH-WERNER

Friedrich-Werner Graf von der Schulenburg
November 20, 1875–November 10, 1944

Friedrich-Werner Erdmann Matthias Johann Bernhard Erich Graf von der Schulenburg was born in Kemberg, Wittenberg district, in Saxony (today Saxony-Anhalt) ten years after his cousin Friedrich, on November 20, 1875. Friedrich-Werner was the second son of Bernhard Friedrich

Appendix II

Wilhelm Graf von der Schulenburg (1839–1902), who was the younger brother of Werner Ludwig Ernst Karl Heinrich Achat Graf von der Schulenburg, Friedrich's father. Friedrich-Werner's branch of the family was apparently less wealthy than Friedrich's, and when he took the first steps towards a diplomatic career he opted for the less glamorous consular service, rather than the prestigious diplomatic corps itself, which required a more costly degree of social mobility, education, and ease of travel (Herwarth 1981: 91). Friedrich-Werner did his compulsory year of military service with the First Guards Field Artillery Regiment, remaining in the officers' reserve of his regiment after his discharge. He then studied law in Lausanne, Munich, and Berlin, and entered the consular service in 1901, which sadly coincided with his father's illness and then death the following year. His consular career took him to Barcelona, Lemberg (Lviv, Ukraine), Prague, Warsaw, and Tiflis (Tbilisi, Georgia). His years in Warsaw left a particularly strong impression, and he would retain a lifelong affection for the Polish people. On May 12, 1908, Friedrich-Werner married Elisabeth von Sobbe (1875–1955), who gave birth to their daughter, Christa, on December 29 of the same year, but the marriage was short-lived; they divorced in 1910 (Ruvigny 1914: 1333).

When the First World War broke out, Friedrich-Werner returned to the First Guards Field Artillery Regiment, serving at the First Battle of the Marne. In October 1914 he was promoted to captain in command of an artillery battery. In 1915 he was appointed liaison officer to the Third Army of the Ottoman Empire, Germany's ally, on the Armenian front. By October 1915 he had effectively returned to a diplomatic role, first in Turkey and then in Georgia. He was instrumental in launching the Georgian Legion, dedicated to destabilizing Russian imperial rule and fighting for Georgian independence. Friedrich-Werner's wartime service earned him the Iron Cross and several honors from the Ottoman Empire. After the defeat of both the German and Ottoman Empires in 1918, he was interned by the British on the island of Prinkipo (Büyükada), near Istanbul. At this time he learned that his mother had died. After returning to Germany in 1919, he was appointed German consul in Beirut. In 1922, Friedrich-Werner was a driving force behind the Treaty of Rapallo, which established good relations between Germany and the new Soviet Union, as a defense against the somewhat overbearing victors of the First World War (Bullock 1962: 515). Then, having risen up through the consular service for twenty years, he was named German ambassador to Iran, where he served for nine years. He was transferred to Romania in 1931, after which he was assigned to Moscow (Stackelberg 2007: 1964).

Appendix II

Friedrich-Werner arrived in Moscow in the autumn of 1934, when he was nearly fifty-nine years old, bringing with him an air of reassurance at a time of growing uncertainty. Initial impressions confirmed his reputation as a true diplomat; one who accepts the status quo that he or she finds and aims to work within it as well as possible. Sensitive, tactful, and guided by Christian values, he came to the rescue of German Jewish refugees stranded in the USSR without valid papers. He provided them with passports, in violation of standing orders from Berlin. Friedrich-Werner was not influenced by ideology or party politics; the simple realization that people were suffering would gradually transform him into an opponent of Nazism. The embassy secretary, Johnnie von Herwarth, described this as the transformation of "a skilled observer and diplomat [into] a statesman bent upon action" (Herwarth 1981: 66–68, 88, 95–96). When relations between Germany and the USSR worsened, Friedrich-Werner became committed to the idea of a non-aggression treaty in order to avoid war. He approached Stalin's foreign minister to propose that they arrange a "truce" in their respective countries' press, persuading them to cease attacking Stalin and Hitler. This "gentlemen's agreement" vastly improved everyday relations between the two countries. In negotiating the non-aggression pact, and in shepherding German-Soviet relations generally, Friedrich-Werner emphasized trade, as this was a more vital and less controversial basis for dialogue than arms or ideology. During 1939, Hitler, fixated on a late-summer invasion of Poland, pressured Friedrich-Werner to land the non-aggression deal quickly. He complied, with such an enthusiasm for peace that Hitler wondered where his loyalties really lay. Disparity in the two men's objectives was not a secret, but the mounting pressure increased the risk of Schulenburg being exposed as anti–Nazi (Herwarth 1981: 108, 142–45; Shirer 1960: 492–94; Kershaw 2008: 488, 489).

As negotiations reached their peak, both sides sought to excuse their erstwhile hostility, and German delegates echoed Friedrich-Werner's long-held theory of a "convergence" between German and Soviet interests. Hitler considered the ambassador to be his top expert on Soviet affairs, but once the German-Soviet pact was signed, Friedrich-Werner rapidly lost his usefulness to the Nazi regime, as well as losing Hitler's favor. He was not even informed about Hitler's invasion plans, and he only knew for certain that the invasion was going ahead a few hours before it was launched, on June 22, 1941. Friedrich-Werner was interned for a few weeks before being escorted by the NKVD to the Soviet-Turkish border for repatriation. On his return to Germany, he was placed in charge of

Appendix II

the Russia desk at the foreign office; an ineffectual role that was intended to neutralize him but keep him busy. In fact, his work brought the Nazis' atrocious conduct in the East to his attention, and, appalled to his core, he took the fateful step of contacting members of the conservative Resistance (Herwarth 1981: 81, 115–18, 187, 191; Bullock 1962: 646–48; Stackelberg 2007: 1964).

Friedrich-Werner's attempts to avoid war with the USSR had not only been confounded and abused; they had led to his personal fall from grace and relegation to an inconsequential role. He attempted to use his position, such as it was, to appeal for humane treatment of the populations of the Soviet Union, which led to his committee being sidelined; he was accused of trying to undermine Nazi operating procedures, which in effect he was. He supported the idea of a plot to overthrow Hitler in the hope of negotiating a speedy armistice in the east, for which he was willing to go and meet with Stalin again, on behalf of the plotters. Had the plot been successful, Friedrich-Werner would probably have taken the role of foreign minister. In the meantime, he used his experience and reputation to advise the Resistance, which was divided over the Soviet question. Friedrich-Werner believed that a mere continuation of the war with the USSR would lead to disaster, while inciting a Russian revolt against communism would be more effective. He was, naturally, an "easterner" in sympathies—pro-Russian but anti-Bolshevik—and he accepted the potential need for separate armistices with east and west; these hopes were dashed by the Allies' 1943 Casablanca declaration, which ruled-out separate peace deals among the Allies, stating that only unconditional surrender would be accepted. In the event, of course, the anti-Hitler plot was a failure anyway. Thousands were executed in retaliation, including Friedrich-Werner on November 10, 1944. He did not ask for much in his will; only for his sword of the First Guards Field Artillery Regiment to be placed at his right hand, his officer's spurs to be placed on his boots, and for his corpse to be wrapped in an old Caucasian rug. It was not to be; his ashes were tipped unceremoniously onto the prison yard and scattered by the Berlin fall wind (Herwarth 1981: 92, 95, 213–14, 222; 251–52; Heinemann 1994: 167; Shirer 1960: 1032–33, 1043–44, 1046–47, 1068–76).

Friedrich-Werner's Awards (partial list)

Iron Cross (1914) second and first class
Knight of Justice of the Order of St John
Orders of the Ottoman Empire

Appendix II

(c) COUNT WOLF-WERNER

Wolf-Werner Graf von der Schulenburg
September 14, 1899–July 14, 1944

Wolf-Werner Graf von der Schulenburg was born on September 14, 1899, at the historic military town of Muskau. Nicknamed "Wolfi," he was Friedrich and Freda's second-born son. Then-First Lieutenant Friedrich was serving in Muskau, in Saxony (today Bad Muskau), the ancestral home of the Arnims, Countess Freda's family. Eager to qualify as an officer in time to see action in the First World War, Wolf-Werner enlisted in the reserve in August 1917, while still at school, and was eventually appointed lieutenant in September 1918, just in time to see combat before the end of the war. It was long enough to be quite badly wounded, and sufficient to merit the award of the Iron Cross, second class (Heinemann 1994: 3–4; Hammerstein-Equord 1966: 110). In September 1919, Wolf-Werner, aged twenty, was part of the "Corps Saxonia" student volunteer unit of the Freikorps, a paramilitary force aiming to counter the various insurrections taking place across Germany. Wolf-Werner's unit fought against Polish separatists and their ultimately successful Silesian Uprisings of 1919–1921, in which the Freikorps became notorious for violent tactics, including assassinations of critics (Möller 2004: 152). Obtaining a degree in commercial law, Wolf-Werner went into the import-export business. On November 12, 1929, he married Gisela Elisabeth Louise Therese Freiin von Stralenheim (1902–1986). As the unmarried daughter of a German Freiherr (literally "Freeman" and roughly equivalent to an English Baron) she bore the title of Freiin, but Wolf-Werner's new mother-in-law was American, from Berkshire County, Massachusetts.

After the Nazis' surprise gain of one hundred and seven Reichstag seats, in the Federal elections of September 14, 1930, Wolf-Werner's thirty-first birthday, he became the first Schulenburg to unequivocally support Hitler. He joined the Nazi party six weeks later, on November 1, and the SA shortly after that, on February 1, 1931 (Teichler 1991: 111). When the Nazis came to power in 1933, Wolf-Werner was appointed Regional Head of Department in the German Reich Association for Physical Exercise (DRL), the Nazis' all-embracing national sports authority. On June 13, 1936, six weeks before the start of the Berlin Olympics, he was appointed Region Leader of the Overseas Region, and international advisor for the entire DRL. He was not without credentials for overseeing high-level international relations, in terms of bilingual upbringing, overseas business and family connections, and having a half–American wife. Similarly,

Appendix II

his credentials as a German patriot, decorated war veteran, and opponent of Weimar, were impeccable by Nazi standards. In March 1938, after the annexation of Austria, Wolf-Werner was sent to Vienna as special Reich commissioner for sport, to coordinate the integration of Austrian sports organizations into the Nazi system (Teichler 1991: 111, 134; Mengden 1980: 63, 73; Marschik 2020: 440).

By 1939, in terms of standing within the Nazi regime, the number one spot in the Schulenburg family was taken by Wolf-Werner; an influential figure in Reich sports organizing, now attached to the office of the Reichssportführer. He kept a relatively low profile in the vaguely disreputable SA, being still only a junior officer, but in August 1939, with the outbreak of war imminent, Wolf-Werner prepared to join his military unit full-time. The SA was reorganized as a network of military training units to supplement the regular armed forces. His service resumed in dramatic style when he was selected, at the age of thirty-nine, for parachute training, receiving the coveted Parachutists' badge. He was assigned as adjutant to I (first) Fallshirmjäger (paratroopers) regiment of the first Fallshirmjäger division (then called the seventh air division or Flieger division) with which he would take part in the first major campaigns of the war, starting with their arrival in Poland on September 14, his fortieth birthday, before being transferred to Denmark and then Norway (McNab 2000: 39).

The Fallschirmjäger faced their first real test on May 10, 1940, with the airborne invasion of the neutral Netherlands. Wolf-Werner had just been promoted to first lieutenant (Oberleutnant). These were some of the first ever mass parachute drops, signaling the start of a six-day battle; ultimately a success for the Germans, but at a cost of hundreds of casualties and prisoners. Wolf-Werner was given a double award of the Iron Cross, first and second class, and was then sent to Norway for a second time. Almost a year later, the Battle of Crete saw the Fallschirmjäger being used as the principal method of attack for the first time, rather than in support of a ground attack; it was the first mainly airborne invasion in history. Wolf-Werner had been promoted to captain, now with the III / I Fallschirmjäger (third battalion of the first Fallschirmjäger regiment), when they dropped into west Heraklion on May 20, 1941. On their descent, the regiment took severe anti-aircraft fire, and in some places Greek troops and armed civilians were waiting to attack them as soon as they landed. What ensued was more than a week of laborious house-to-house fighting, often by night and fraught with mishaps. The arrival of German reinforcements eventually forced the exhausted Allies to evacuate, but despite this success, Hitler lost faith in large-scale airborne assault, having now used it

Appendix II

in two key operations, both times with mixed results. The elite Fallschirmjäger would henceforth serve as ordinary ground troops. Wolf-Werner was placed in command of the first battalion, and from the end of September 1941 they joined the invasion of Russia, first tasked with anti-partisan warfare in the rear of the Smolensk sector, they were later involved in intense fighting around Orel, when the Soviet counterattack broke through near Kursk. On November 9, 1942, Wolf-Werner was promoted to Brigade Leader in the SA. His unit would remain on the eastern front until early 1943, when they were sent to Italy (Böhmler and Haupt 1971: 99; Beevor 1991: 229–30; Teichler 1991: 111; Kurowski 2010: 81, 111–113, 206; Schreiber 1996: 153; Ailsby 2000: 66).

There, on June 20, 1943, Wolf-Werner was awarded the Knight's Cross of the Iron Cross, symbol of the very elite of Nazi warriors, for his conduct in combat at Orel (Fellgiebel 2006: 318; Scherzer 2007: 688). Even his father, Friedrich, did not count the Knight's Cross among his two-dozen-plus orders and medals. Promotion to major was to follow. On September 7, Wolf-Werner's I (first) battalion, first division, first Fallschirmjäger regiment, were dispatched to Matera, in south-east Italy. On September 9, the Allies landed at Taranto, just forty-three miles (seventy kilometers) away. Just over a week later, seven of Wolf-Werner's soldiers were attacked and wounded by civilians. Sensing the start of a local insurrection in support of the Allied landings, Wolf-Werner had a number of local civilians arrested; then, a further clash with civilians left two Germans killed. Further arrests were made, more or less at random, until as many as seventeen people were detained at a disused fascist militia barracks. As fighting erupted in the town, Wolf-Werner's men attacked the power company, presumably to prevent communication with the advancing Allies; the staff were led outside and machine-gunned in the street. Wolf-Werner ordered his men to abandon the town; their parting gesture was to blow up the militia barracks with the detainees trapped inside. These would be the first German atrocities to be investigated as war crimes during the Second World War (Ambrico 2003: 11–16; Andrae 1995: 77).

From November 15, 1943, Wolf-Werner stood in as commander of the entire I (first) Fallschirmjäger regiment, while still personally leading the III (third) battalion as well, when the regiment was sent to the "Gustav line"—the Germans' coast-to-coast defensive line—on November 18. The Fallschirmjäger arrived in Roccaraso, with the village of Pietransieri beside it and a poor adjoining hamlet called Limmari, expecting to find the area deserted following an evacuation order. Three days later, in the early

Appendix II

morning of Sunday, November 21, a patrol in the outlying farms of the Limmari hamlet was startled to realize that some of the farm buildings, cottages, and shacks were occupied. In pairs, the Germans burst into each cottage and machine-gunned whoever happened to be inside; because of the war, the vast majority of the local population consisted of women, children, and the elderly. Some cottages were barricaded shut from the outside and hand grenades were thrown through the windows. The remaining inhabitants were forced out into a clearing and machine-gunned. One hundred and twenty-eight people were murdered, including sixty women and thirty-four children aged under ten. It was the worst atrocity committed in Italy up to that point (Scherzer 2007: 688; Andrae 1995: 109; Schreiber 1996: 153; Mercuri 2020: 14).

Following this, the Fallschirmjäger failed to stop the Allies taking the town of Ortona, in a ferocious battle dubbed "the Italian Stalingrad." Wolf-Werner, again in command of the I (first) Fallschirmjäger regiment, was ordered to abandon Roccaraso and join the battle at Monte Cassino. In March, Wolf-Werner was placed in command of the new XIII (thirteenth) regiment, part of the new fifth Fallschirmjäger division forming up in France; the division was understrength but led by capable and battle-hardened officers. In mid–July, Wolf-Werner and his new regiment faced the advancing U.S. Army at Saint-Lô, Normandy. On the evening of July 14, the Fallschirmjäger surrounded some isolated American units, who, despite taking casualties, surprised the Germans with the intensity of their defense. Wolf-Werner was killed almost instantly, a rifle bullet piercing his Knight's Cross of the Iron Cross, worn around his neck, and passing through the center of his sternum. He was posthumously promoted to lieutenant-colonel (Oberstleutnant) in the reserve on July 23, 1944 (Andrae 1995: 268; Ambrico 2003: 12; Götzel and Student 1980: 449; Scherzer 2007: 688; Fellgiebel 2006: 318).

Wolf-Werner's Awards

Iron Cross (1914) second class
Silesian Eagle (Schlesischer Adler) medal, first class
Honor Cross of the World War 1914–1918 (Ehrenkreuz des Weltkrieges) with swords
Parachutists' badge (Fallschirmschützenabzeichen)
Iron Cross (1939) second and first class
Wound Badge
Luftwaffe Ground Combat Badge

Appendix II

Cuff-band battle honor for Crete
Wehrmacht Long Service Medal (Wehrmacht Dienstauszeichnung)
Knights Cross of the Iron Cross (1939) in 1943

(d) COUNT FRITZ-DIETLOF

Fritz-Dietlof Graf von der Schulenburg
September 5, 1902–August 10, 1944

Fritz-Dietlof Graf von der Schulenburg was born in London, England, on September 5, 1902. He was the fourth son of Freda and Friedrich, who was serving as military attaché to the German Embassy. Fritz-Dietlof was the only one among his siblings to be born in England and the only one not born in Germany; how and to what extent this difference impacted upon his psychology is not known, but "Fritzi" was set to always do his own thing. As a child he was already considered a loner; a thin and tender boy with a brooding demeanor, absorbed in his books, indifferent to the military atmosphere of his upbringing. His personality developed as conservative, in his own way, but with a deep sense of individuality and freedom. While at school during the First World War, he resolved to reject the traditional family career path into the army, though his contemporaries longed to graduate in time to fight in the war. Finishing high school in 1920, Fritzi studied law at Göttingen and Marburg, where he dueled in the Corps Saxonia fraternity. After university he pursued a civil service career; an appropriate and acceptable alternative to the army, for a son of the aristocracy (Krebs 1964: 31).

Fritz-Dietlof began as a courthouse clerk in 1923 and rose steadily through the ranks of the civil service. His individualism made him a controversial figure in a context where convention and conformity were valued. His liberal views earned him the nickname the "Roter Graf" or the "Red Count." His views drew him towards the growing Nazi party—which was by no means strictly conservative or conventional either—and he veered towards the larger and more socialist wing of the party, under the Strasser brothers rather than Hitler. Fritz-Dietlof's civil service career progressed, despite clashing with some of his superiors, and, convinced that the then-diverse Nazi movement sufficiently resonated with his liberal political outlook, he formally joined the Nazi party in February 1932. This pleased his immediate family, at least three of whom were already Nazi party members. Fritz-Dietlof saw Nazism as an all-embracing and

Appendix II

all-inclusive national movement with the potential to unify Germans and shake up politics. He further satisfied his family's expectations by getting married, to twenty-three-year-old Charlotte Kotelmann, on March 11, 1933. By that time he was running the political office of the controversial Gauleiter of East Prussia, Erich Koch; the two men clashed, and each used their influence to avoid too much contact with the other (Mommsen 2009: 154–55; Meding 1997: 116; Gregory 2018: 88).

Fritz-Dietlof objected to some aspects of Nazism, but he believed that it could be reoriented or reformed for the better. Even this mildly critical stance was considered intolerably subversive after the Nazis came to power, and any kind of dissent in the civil service was due to be stamped-out (Kershaw 1993: 117). Fritz-Dietlof probably risked elimination when Hitler purged the Nazi movement of his opponents and critics on the so-called Night of the Long Knives. Conscious of the dangers facing high-profile leftwing Nazis, Fritz-Dietlof sought to decelerate his own rise in the civil service, feeling, also, that he could more effectively mitigate the extreme effects of the Nazi regime from an intermediate position. Still not a confirmed anti–Nazi, his commitment to law and order was increasingly offended by the Nazis' playbook of duplicity, deception, and nepotism. His slow maturation into an opponent of Nazism may be bewildering today. It was a process of gradual disillusionment for those, like Fritz-Dietlof, who longed for a genuine national renaissance and a cultural reawakening; aspirations that Nazi propaganda relentlessly exploited. By 1936, Fritz-Dietlof's capacity for giving the Nazi regime the benefit of the doubt, while trying to improve it from within, was becoming exhausted. He was appointed vice president of police in Berlin in 1937, by which time he was officially regarded as politically untrustworthy. He was one of the few Nazis to voice disapproval over Kristallnacht and other horrors, joining the handful of senior Nazis mockingly labeled "Jew lovers." His views were considered laughably unorthodox and naively liberal rather than seriously subversive, but he would be allowed to progress no further in the Nazi party. He was sent to Silesia as acting Oberpräsident or provincial governor, an ineffectual and largely symbolic office, stripped of any real power (Shirer 1960: 200; Bullock 1962: 272; Mommsen 2009: 152, 157, 159, 163; Gregory 2018: 88).

At their father's funeral in 1939, Fritz-Dietlof took his sister Tisa to one side, away from the others, and confided in her that he was already in contact with circles of opposition to the Nazi regime. Shortly after the outbreak of war, whether it was in order to avoid further criticism, to deflect suspicion from his dissenting views, or simply out of genuine patriotism,

Appendix II

Fritz-Dietlof joined the army. He still perceived a slim chance of curtailing the worst excesses of the Nazi regime, and he may have seen the war as an opportunity for Nazism to purify itself. He joined Infantry Regiment 9 (IR9), where his unusual personality and frequently brusque candor drew mixed responses from the young officers. He served for a time on the eastern front, an experience that reinforced his critical view of the Nazis' conduct in the war. Though he may still have been ignorant of the extent of Nazi atrocities in the east, he was appalled by the realization that obscene crimes were being committed against Jews, in widespread fashion. To what extent his army superiors were aware of his disaffection is unclear, as their handling of him was equivocal; he was decorated with the Iron Cross first class, but in early 1942 he was sent back to the reserve battalion at the IR9 in Potsdam, to sit out the war where he could do no harm, or so it was thought (Mommsen 2009: 153–62).

IR9 was rich in tradition, with a high quota of aristocrats in its ranks, many of whom shared Fritz-Dietlof's displeasure with Nazism. Nineteen officers and former officers of the IR9 were involved in conspiracies against Hitler, far more than in any other regiment. In this setting, Fritz-Dietlof's understanding and assessment of the Nazi problem was now radically transformed; his reservations about Nazism had intensified over the years, but he had tended to see the problem as a moral one of leadership and direction, with the hope that society's institutions—including the military—would ultimately steer Nazism onto the right path. The Russian front, however, had exposed Fritz-Dietlof to the reality. He saw that supply, logistics, manpower, strategy—everything, in fact—was in chaos, and that the chaos was being systematically covered up by deception, misreporting, and subterfuge; far from applying order to a chaotic situation, the Nazified institutions were collapsing into disorder as well. Fritz-Dietlof saw that the regime was fundamentally dysfunctional as well as morally wrong, and it could not be redeemed with a change of leadership. Nor did society's institutions—whether law, aristocracy, military, or intelligentsia—any longer enjoy sufficient confidence or influence to apolitically guide the nation back in the right direction (Meding 1997: 117).

Fritz-Dietlof became involved in what would be known as the July plot or the Valkyrie plot of 1944, to kill Hitler and take control of Germany. Killing Hitler, though crucial to the plan, was only intended to be phase one of the July plot; it was to be immediately followed by an ingeniously planned coup d'état, which would be triggered the moment the Führer's demise was confirmed. Unanswered questions still hang upon

Appendix II

this well-documented operation, especially with regard to what the plotters envisaged or hoped for, longer term. The swift execution of the plotters deprived history of any clarity on this question. Fritz-Dietlof's role in the plot was not so much that of planner—he was not regarded as having a strategic mind—but rather as a persuader, recruiter, and motivator. Fritz-Dietlof was regarded as the most significant figure in these aspects of the plot, curating the huge task of networking required for making post-coup personnel arrangements; the plotters fully expected to have a country—and a war—to run. The man who would become almost synonymous with the actual execution of the plot, Colonel Claus von Stauffenberg, came forward because Fritz-Dietlof was a friend of Stauffenberg's uncle, Nikolaus Graf von Üxküll-Gyllenband. Together, they worked hard to persuade the young officer to join the Resistance, a step Stauffenberg was initially reluctant to take (Kramarz 1967: 72, 126).

Eventually Stauffenberg agreed that a coalition of the clear-sighted and genuinely patriotic must replace the Nazi leadership root and branch, starting at the top; Hitler had to go immediately. Stauffenberg's continued position of trust within the military would allow him unique access to the Führer's inner circle, and the chance to plant a bomb. Fritz-Dietlof's name never went down in history like that of his recruit and most trusted co-conspirator, but Fritz-Dietlof was the driving force of the Resistance long before Stauffenberg took center stage (Mommsen 2009: 152). Fritz-Dietlof's wife Charlotte turned thirty-five on the day of the unsuccessful plot, July 20; the couple celebrated one day prior, on July 19. "You know," Fritz-Dietlof told her, on their way to the train station before he departed for Berlin, "the chances are fifty-fifty." It was the last time they spoke (Meding 1997: 118–19). He was executed by hanging on August 10, 1944.

Fritz-Dietlof's Awards

Iron Cross (1939) second and first class

(e) COUNTESS TISA

Elisabeth Karoline Marie Grafin von der Schulenburg
December 7, 1903–February 8, 2001

Elisabeth Karoline Mary Margarete Veronika Grafin von der Schulenburg—"Tisa"—was born on December 7, 1903, while the family

Appendix II

was living in London, though her mother Freda returned to Tressow Castle for Tisa's birth. She grew up recalling nothing of her childhood stay in London, but she was always aware of the family's Anglo-Saxon legacy, growing up bilingual in a home filled with mementoes of England and the empire, not to mention English nurses and governesses. Her impressionable pre-teen years coincided with the First World War, marked by physical and emotional distance from her strict father (Heinemann 1994: 2). Her closest bond was with her slightly older brother, Fritz-Dietlof. In the grim postwar days after 1918, she helped "Fritzi" with his English, and they mooted the idea of claiming British citizenship (he was born in London) in order to escape the drudgery. Childhood at Tressow Castle was mostly pleasant, however, and Tisa, the only girl, emerged as a unique character. Her distaste for convention was challenged when she was sent to a strict convent school for the daughters of the nobility, where Tisa and her classmates welcomed the announcement of the postwar republic, decorating their hair with red ribbons and refusing to curtsey to their teachers; they did not mourn the fall of the monarchy (Seymour 2013: 142, 203, 252).

Tisa's artistic vocation was already evident. She was attracted to the burgeoning leftwing Bauhaus movement, which her father did not approve of, but as a compromise he agreed in principle to let her study art and sculpture. Aged just sixteen, Tisa introduced herself to Max Liebermann of the Prussian Academy of Arts in Berlin and presented him with some of her artwork. Liebermann recognized her talent, but her father clarified that his permission to study art would take effect in 1925, when Tisa was twenty-one. Living in Berlin in the 1920s, Tisa's unconventional personality, striking looks, and bold artistic talent allowed her to integrate with the rebellious leftwing and liberal intelligentsia of the Weimar years. Influential figures like Hugh Simon operated a revolving door policy at their art-filled homes; a whirlwind of parties famed for free expression and free love. In this environment, Tisa would meet and begin a relationship with Fritz Hesse (1886–1976), a charming and wealthy Jewish art collector. Tisa's relationship with her father, surprisingly, would not only survive his learning the details of her new lifestyle, but also the shock of her marrying Hesse, who was, apart from being Jewish, nearly twenty years her senior and divorced. Tisa later recalled that in spite of his disappointment—and anti–Semitism—Friedrich treated his new son-in-law with great courtesy (Seymour 2013: 231–32, 263–64).

The couple lived an opulent lifestyle in Berlin, even though Tisa continued to identify as leftwing, but the years of free expression were drawing to a close; Fritz and Tisa, who had read *Mein Kampf,* interpreted the signs of the times accurately, and, like many others in their social circle, they abandoned Germany after 1933. The Hesses settled in England, allowing Tisa to rekindle the Schulenburg affection for the Anglo-Saxon world. She would later recall her years in 1930s England as being among her happiest. She made new friends, progressed with her art, and, as a result of giving art lessons to unemployed miners, she formed an unlikely but lifelong association with the Durham mining community. Tisa and Fritz Hesse divorced in 1938, but by that time she was well-established in her own right in English society, which she always associated with personal and political liberty. At the same time that her father and brothers were increasing their commitment to the Nazi cause, Tisa joined "Artists Against Fascism" in London. The family's deep divisions were clear, if still unspoken, by 1939. Her parents' illness compelled Tisa to return to Germany, just in time to say a final goodbye to her father. She observed her older brothers on one side, with their various positions and ranks in the Reich, and on the other side listened to Fritzi confiding his dissenting views, and even learning of their mother's disdain for Hitler. Tisa was refused reentry to England after her father's funeral, especially when the British officials found a newspaper report of Friedrich's funeral among her possessions, with photos of Hitler as a mourner. It was Tisa's belief, however, that she had made an enemy inside the British border authorities; not for reasons of politics or nationality, but because she had rebuffed an impromptu marriage proposal (Seymour 2013: 263–64, 357–60, 417–419).

Tisa was destined to spend the war years "exiled at home" in Germany. She briefly stayed with her widowed mother, who then died just three months after her husband. The family was quickly whittled down to just three brothers and Tisa. Days before the outbreak of war, Tisa married for the second time, to childhood friend Carl Ulrich von Barner, who then departed for the war. Tisa's artistic work, unlikely to find the required environment, stimulation, and outlets in wartime Germany, came to a standstill. By 1943 she was living at the Klein Trebbow estate, near Tressow Castle. Klein Trebbow belonged to the Barner family, who asked Tisa to manage it. Fritz-Dietlof, increasingly involved in the German Resistance, seized the opportunity to be based somewhere far from inquisitive eyes, and with his wife Charlotte they too went to live temporarily at Klein Trebbow, transforming it into a kind of haven for the anti–Hitler movement. Tisa herself was involved in the Resistance in small but significant ways, including hosting key visitors such as Colonel Claus von Stauffenberg, the central figure in the attempt on Hitler's life of July 1944. After the failure of the July plot and Fritz-Dietlof's arrest, Tisa and Charlotte bravely travelled to Berlin for the trial, but they were refused entry to the courthouse. They would never see Fritz-Dietlof again (Meding 1997: 119; Seymour 2014; 2013: 421–22).

For her comparatively minor involvement in the Resistance, and her unmistakable anti–Hitler opinions, Tisa was reported to the Nazi party in the final months of the war. For one reason or another, no action was taken. When the war was over, she worked as a secretary for the British Military Administration, moving to Glinde, near Hamburg. Her husband, whom she had hardly seen, returned from the war, but the relationship was not rekindled and they divorced in 1946. From 1947 she worked for Hamburg's *Die Welt* newspaper, and in 1948 she spent six months reporting on life in the Ruhr. She opted to live in a miners' village in Recklinghausen and visited numerous Ruhr mines; it was a spiritual and socially conscious choice. It was also a doubly evocative and emotional experience; it recalled her years among the unemployed miners of the north of England, and it also reminded her of Fritz-Dietlof, whose first major posting as a civil servant was in Recklinghausen. Whether this was a kind of penance or a way of atoning for survivor's guilt, the last of her generation of Schulenburgs began a Ruhr pilgrimage and re-found her inspiration; Tisa finally began to draw and carve again (Seymour 2013: 420–22).

Tisa converted to Roman Catholicism, and in late 1948 she made contact with the Ursuline convent in bomb-shattered Dorsten, a small town in the Recklinghausen area. She combined her new-found faith with her art, producing a number of religious-themed works to replace those that had been lost, looted, or destroyed during or immediately after the war. At the age of forty-six, in 1950, Tisa took her first vows and began religious life as Sister Paula. She taught art at school for thirteen years, before fully devoting herself to her own works again. The Ursulines were a strict order until the liberalizing reforms of the Second Vatican Council, which Tisa saw as the latest of several liberations in her life; she could wear colorful "civilian" clothes again and travel outside of the convent and outside of Germany. She often visited Fritz-Dietlof's children, some of whom lived in the British Isles, encouraging them to maintain the old Schulenburg ties to England. Besides religious topics, her art focused on war, refugees, and persecution. She exhibited regularly, accepted commissions, and developed new techniques. From 1968 to 1969, now in her mid-sixties, Tisa worked in Ethiopia, at a leprosy community (Gowrie and Rea 2001; Seymour 2013: 142).

Tisa was also able to continue her friendships with mining communities in Germany and England. In 1974, she returned to County Durham, England, at the time of nationwide strikes, which led to a very successful

Appendix II

exhibition of Tisa's work in Jarrow the following year. Tisa encouraged participants to bring their own artworks for feedback, thus breaking down barriers and transforming the event into an interactive exhibition, far ahead of its time. In 1979, Tisa traveled to Israel, meeting with Holocaust survivors in Dorsten's twin town. In 1984, at the unveiling ceremony of her new sculptures, Tisa met the then-West German president, Richard von Weizsäcker, who had been Fritz-Dietlof's friend, Resistance recruit, and fellow junior officer of the IR9 in Potsdam. In 1994, the then–Minister for Women and Youth, Angela Merkel, decorated Tisa with the Federal Cross of Merit in recognition of her life's work and social commitment. In 1997, ninety-three-year-old Sister Paula—dubbed "Saint Barbara of the Ruhr"—took part in protests against the local mine closure. For the rest of her long life, Tisa was hailed as a passionate, unpretentious, empathic, and inclusive artist with a profound understanding of the traumatic twentieth century, so many pivotal events of which she had lived firsthand; her artwork had the compassion and vigor to effectively communicate these experiences. She died on Thursday, February 8, 2001, aged ninety-seven (Gowrie and Rea 2001; Seymour 2013: 142, 203, 264, 454).

Tisa's Awards

Honorary Citizen of the city of Dorsten (1972)
Member of the Federal Cross of Merit (Verdienstkreuz am Bande) (1994)

Appendix III
Timeline

1865	Friedrich is born on November 21
1873	Freda is born on December 18
1875	Friedrich-Werner is born on November 20
1880	Friedrich inherits his title upon his father's death
1888	Friedrich joins the army
1897	Friedrich and Freda wed on July 21
1898	Johann-Albrecht is born on June 5
1899	Wolf-Werner is born on September 14
1901	Adolf-Heinrich is born on May 25
	Friedrich is appointed military attaché and moves the family to London
	Friedrich-Werner enters the consular service
1902	Fritz-Dietlof is born on September 5
1903	Tisa is born on December 7
1906	The family returns to Germany
1907	Friedrich is promoted to major
1913	Friedrich is promoted to lieutenant-colonel, aide-de-camp to the Kaiser
1914	Wilhelm is born on February 15
	Friedrich-Werner rejoins the army
1915	Friedrich-Werner is appointed liaison officer to the Ottoman Third Army
1917	Wolf-Werner joins the army
1918	Friedrich is promoted to major general
	Wolf-Werner is commissioned as a lieutenant and wounded in action
1919	Wolf-Werner serves in the Freikorps against the Silesian Uprising

Appendix III

1923	Fritz-Dietlof enters the civil service
	Adolf-Heinrich weds Jutta on June 29
1924	Friedrich enters the Reichstag in December for the DNVP (until May 1928)
1928	Tisa weds Fritz Hesse on September 15
1929	Wolf-Werner weds Gisela on November 12
1930	Friedrich briefly switches to the short-lived Conservative People's Party
	Wolf-Werner joins the Nazi party
1931	Wolf-Werner joins the SA
	Adolf-Heinrich joins the Nazi party and the SA
	Johann-Albrecht joins the Nazi party
1932	Fritz-Dietlof joins the Nazi party
	Friedrich joins the Nazi party
1933	Fritz-Dietlof weds Charlotte on March 11
	Wolf-Werner begins work in the Reich sports administration (DRL)
	Friedrich joins the SA
	Johann-Albrecht weds Angela on December 2
1934	Friedrich reenters the Reichstag for the Nazi party
	Tisa and Fritz Hesse begin their exile in England
	Friedrich-Werner is appointed ambassador to the Soviet Union
1935	Fritz-Dietlof is appointed to the East Prussian Gauleiter's office
1936	Wilhelm is killed in an automobile accident on July 23, aged twenty-two
	Wolf-Werner is promoted to head of international affairs in the DRL
	Friedrich resigns from the SA and joins the SS
1937	Fritz-Dietlof is appointed vice-president of police in Berlin
1938	Tisa and Fritz Hesse divorce
	Friedrich is promoted to honorary four-star general of the cavalry
1939	Friedrich is promoted to the second-highest rank in the SS
	Friedrich dies on May 19
	Freda dies on August 25
	Tisa returns to Germany and weds Carl Ulrich von Barner on August 27
	Friedrich-Werner concludes the Molotov-Ribbentrop Pact on August 27
	Wolf-Werner rejoins the army and serves in Poland
1940	Adolf-Heinrich dies of colon cancer on June 6

Appendix III

	Wolf-Werner serves in the Netherlands and Norway
	Fritz-Dietlof joins the army
1941	Wolf-Werner serves in Crete and is wounded
	Friedrich-Werner exits Russia and is placed in charge of the Russia committee
1941–43	Wolf-Werner serves in Russia
1941–42	Fritz-Dietlof serves in Russia
1943	Wolf-Werner is implicated in a series of war crimes against civilians in Italy
1944	Wolf-Werner fights at Monte Cassino and is transferred to France
	Wolf-Werner is killed in Normandy on July 14
	The Valkyrie plot fails on July 20
	Fritz-Dietlof is executed on August 10
	Friedrich-Werner is executed on November 10
1945	Johann-Albrecht is killed on January 13
	Jutta dies on March 12
	Tisa begins work for the Allied occupying forces
1946	Tisa and Carl Ulrich von Barner divorce
1948	Tisa converts to Roman Catholicism
	Tisa enters the Ursuline convent at Dorsten
1950–63	Tisa—as Sister Paula—teaches art
1963–97	Tisa travels, teaches, exhibits, and creates art extensively
2001	Tisa dies on February 8

Bibliography

Ailsby, Christopher. 2000. *Hitler's Sky Warriors: German Paratroopers in Action, 1939–1945*. Staplehurst: Spellmount.

Allen, William Sheridan. 1973. *The Nazi Seizure of Power: The Experience of a Single German Town, 1930–1935*. New York: Franklin Watts.

Ambrico, Francesco. 2003. *War Crimes at Matera [Le stragi tedesche del 21 settembre 1943 a Matera]*. Matera: Associazione Culturale, 21 Settembre 1943.

Andrae, Friedrich. 1995. *Auch gegen Frauen und Kinder: der Krieg der deutschen Wehrmacht gegen die Zivilbevölkerung in Italien 1943–1945 [Also Against Women and Children: The War of the German Armed Forces Against the Civilian Population in Italy]*. Munich: Piper.

Atkinson, Rick. 2013. *The Day of Battle*. Auckland: Abacus.

Bankier, David. 1992. *The Germans and the Final Solution: Public Opinion Under Nazism*. Oxford: Blackwell.

Beevor, Antony. 1991. *Crete: The Battle and the Resistance*. London: Penguin.

Böhmler, Rudolf, and Werner Haupt. 1971. *Fallschirmjäger: Bildband und Chronik [Paratrooper: A History in Words and Pictures]*. Dorheim: Hans-Henning Podzun.

Bullock, Alan. 1962. *Hitler: A Study in Tyranny*. New York: Konecky and Konecky.

Buruma, Ian. 1994. *The Wages of Guilt: Memories of War in Germany and Japan*. New York: Farrar, Straus and Giroux.

Cartwright, Justin. 2009. "Secret Germany." *The Guardian*. January 10. https://www.theguardian.com/film/2009/jan/10/valkrie-tom-cruise-hitler-plot [retrieved June 18, 2022].

Collier, Paul. 2014. *The Second World War (4): The Mediterranean 1940–1945*. Oxford: Osprey.

Day, Martyn. 2018. "The Monarch and the Maypole." St. Margaret's, London. July 30. https://stmargarets.london/archives/2010/07/the_monarch_and_the_maypole.html [retrieved November 27, 2021].

Dellmensingen, Konrad Krafft von. 1930. *Das Bayernbuch vom Weltkriege [Bavarian Book of the World War]*. Stuttgart: Belser Verlagsbuchhandlung.

Domarus, Max, and Patrick Romane, editors. 2007. *The Essential Hitler: Speeches and Commentary*. Wauconda, IL: Bolchazy-Carducci.

Escher, Felix. 2010. "Simon, Hugo." In *Neue Deutsche Biographie 24*. Berlin: Duncker und Humblot, [435–436].

Evans, David, and Jane Jenkins. 1999. *Years of Weimar & the Third Reich*. London: Hodder & Stoughton Educational.

Evans, Richard J. 2005. *The Third Reich in Power*. New York: Penguin.

———. 2009. *The Third Reich at War*. New York: Penguin.

———. 2015a. *Rereading German History: From Unification to Reunification 1800–1996*. Abingdon: Routledge.

———. 2015b. *The Third Reich in History and Memory*. Oxford: Oxford University Press.

Fellgiebel, Walther-Peer. 2006. *Elite of the Third Reich: The Recipients of the Knight's Cross of the Iron Cross*. Solihull: Helion.

Gill, Anton. 1994. *An Honourable Defeat: A History of the German Resistance to Hitler*. London: Heinemann.

Gillette, Robert H. 2011. *The Virginia Plan: William B. Thalhimer and a Rescue from*

Bibliography

Nazi Germany. Charleston, SC: History Press.

Götzel, Hermann, and Kurt Student. 1980. *Generaloberst Kurt Student und seine Fallschirmjäger: die Erinnerungen des Generaloberst Kurt Student [Colonel-General Kurt Student and his Paratroopers: the Memoirs of Colonel-General Kurt Student]*. Eggolsheim: Podzun-Pallas-Verlag.

Gowrie, Grey, and Vince Rea. 2001. "Countess Elisabeth von der Schulenburg: German aristocrat who became a nun and a sculptor—and formed her own special relationship with the Durham miners." *The Guardian*. March 8. https://www.theguardian.com/news/2001/mar/08/guardianobituaries.religion [retrieved June 22, 2022].

Gregory, Don Allen. 2018. *After Valkyrie: Military and Civilian Consequences of the Attempt to Assassinate Hitler*. Jefferson, NC: McFarland.

Hammerstein-Equord, Kunrat Freiherr von. 1966. *Flucht: Aufzeichnungen nach dem 20. Juli. Texte und Dokumente zur Zeitgeschichte [Escape: Testimonies from the July 20 Plot: Texts and Documents in Contemporary History]*. Olten und Freiburg im Breisgau: Walter.

Haupt, Werner. 2001. *Elite German Divisions in World War II*. Atglen, PA: Schiffer.

Heinemann, Ulrich. 1994. *Ein konservativer Rebell: Fritz-Dietlof Graf von der Schulenburg und der 20. Juli [A Conservative Rebel: Fritz-Dietlof Graf von der Schulenburg and the July 20 Plot]*. Munich: Goldmann.

Hellenic Army History Directorate. 1985. *Επίτομη Ιστορία του Ελληνοϊταλικού και Ελληνογερμανικού Πολέμου 1940-1941 (Επιχειρήσεις Στρατού Ξηράς) [Abridged History of the Greco-Italian and Greco-German War 1940-1941 (Land Operations)]*. Athens: Government Publications.

Hepburn, Ainslie. 2012. "Reconciliation and the Work of Herbert Sulzbach." *Kirchliche Zeitgeschichte* 25, no. 1: Vertriebene und die Kirchen—Eine neue Debatte? [Expellees and the Church—A New Debate?] Göttingen: Vandenhoeck & Ruprecht, [180–195].

Herwarth, Johnnie von (Herwarth von Bittenfeld, Hans-Heinrich). 1981. *Against Two Evils*. New York: Rawson Wade.

Hull, Isabel V. 2004. *The Entourage of Kaiser Wilhelm II, 1888–1918*. Cambridge: Cambridge University Press.

Judt, Tony. 2005. *Postwar: A History of Europe Since 1945*. New York: Penguin.

Kershaw, Ian. 1993. "'Working Towards the Führer': Reflections on the Nature of the Hitler Dictatorship." *Contemporary European History* 2, no. 2 (July): [103–118].

———. 2008. *Hitler: A Biography*. New York: W.W. Norton.

Kimmelman, Michael. 2009. "High-Born Prussians Who Defied Their Origin." *New York Times*. July 15. https://www.nytimes.com/2009/07/16/arts/design/16abroad.html [accessed April 16, 2022].

Klee, Ernst. 2005. *Das Personenlexikon zum Dritten Reich. Wer war was vor und nach 1945 [The Encyclopedia of People in the Third Reich: Who was what before and after 1945]*. Frankfurt am Main: Fischer Taschenbuch Verlag.

Kramarz, Joachim. 1967. *Stauffenberg: The Architect of the Famous July 20th Conspiracy to Assassinate Hitler*. New York: Macmillan.

Krebs, Albert. 1964. *Fritz-Dietlof Graf von der Schulenburg: zwischen Staatsraison und Hochverrat [Fritz-Dietlof Graf von der Schulenburg: Between Reasons of State and Treason]*. Hamburg: Leibniz.

Kulish, Nicholas. 2008. "Germany Confronts Holocaust Legacy Anew." *New York Times*. January 29. https://www.nytimes.com/2008/01/29/world/europe/29nazi.html [accessed July 2, 2022].

Kurowski, Franz. 1965. *Der Kampf um Kreta [The Battle for Crete]*. Bonn: Maximilian.

———. 2010. *Jump Into Hell: German Paratroopers in World War II*. Mechanicsburg, PA: Stackpole.

Lingen, Kerstin von. 2009. *Kesselring's Last Battle: War Crimes Trials and Cold War Politics, 1945–1960*. Lawrence: University Press of Kansas.

Longerich, Peter. 2012. *Heinrich Himmler: A Life*. Oxford: Oxford University Press.

Bibliography

Mabire, Jean. 1997. *Objectif Crète [Objective Crete]*. Paris: Grancher.

Malaya Tribune. 1923. "Battles of Crown Prince: The Blame for Verdun." January 30, [2].

Malinowski, Stephan. 2020. *Nazis and Nobles*. Oxford: Oxford University Press.

Marschik, Matthias. 2020. *Bewegte Körper: Historische Populärkulturen des Sports in Österreich [Moving Bodies: History of Sport as Popular Culture in Austria]*. Vienna: Lit Verlag.

McNab, Chris. 2000. *German Paratroopers*. St. Paul: MBI.

Meding, Dorothee von. 1997. *Courageous Hearts: Women and the Anti-Hitler Plot of 1944*. Providence, RI: Berghahn.

Mengden, Guido von. 1980. *Umgang mit der Geschichte und mit Menschen: Ein Beitrag zur Geschichte die Machtübernahme im deutschen Sport durch die NSDAP [Handling History and People: A Contribution to the History of the Seizure of Power in German Sport by the Nazi Party]*. Berlin-Munich-Frankfurt am Main: Bartels und Wernitz.

Mercuri, Chiara. 2020. *Il mestiere delle armi: Guida ai sacrari e ai musei militari [The Profession of Arms: Guide to Military Memorials and Museums]*. Rome: All Around.

Minow, Martha. 1998. *Between Vengeance and Forgiveness: Facing History after Genocide and Mass Violence*. Boston: Beacon.

Mitcham, Samuel W., Jr. 1996. *Why Hitler? The Genesis of the Nazi Reich*. Westport, CT: Praeger.

Möller, Horst. 2004. *Die Weimarer Republik: Eine unvollendete Demokratie [The Weimar Republic: An Unfinished Democracy]*. Munich: DTV.

Mommsen, Hans. 1992. "The German Resistance against Hitler and the Restoration of Politics." *The Journal of Modern History* 64 (December) [Supplement: "Resistance Against the Third Reich"]. Chicago: University of Chicago Press, [S112–S127].

———. 2009. *Germans Against Hitler: The Stauffenberg Plot and Resistance Under the Third Reich*. London: I.B. Tauris.

Moskin, J. Robert. 2013. *American Statecraft: The Story of the U.S. Foreign Service*. New York: Thomas Dunne Books.

Myers, Kevin. 2004. "An Irishman's Diary." *Irish Times*. July 27. https://www.irishtimes.com/opinion/an-irishmans-diary-1.1150891 [retrieved July 8, 2022].

National Archives, London. 1944a. "Exhibit 'U'; Report of Events at Matera on the Evening of 21st September 1943" [attached to the above (WO [War Office] 310 / 102)]. November 7.

———. 1944b. WO [War Office] 310 / 102. "(SIB.67/WC/44.3) War Crimes at Matera—21st September 1943." November 7.

———. 1944c. WO 170 / 3594. War diaries of the SIB (Special Investigation Branch).

Niemann, Mario. 2000. *Mecklenburgischer Großgrundbesitz im Dritten Reich: Soziale Struktur, wirtschaftliche Stellung und politische Bedeutung (Mitteldeutsche Forschungen Serie) [Mecklenburg Landowners in the Third Reich: Social Structure, Economic Position and Political Significance (Central German Research series)]*. Köln: Böhlau.

Nohlen, Dieter, and Philip Stöver. 2010. *Elections in Europe: A Data Handbook*. Baden Baden: Nomos.

Orwell, George. 1958. *The Road to Wigan Pier*. New York: Harcourt, Brace.

Paoletti, Paolo. 1999. *L'eccidio dei Limmari di Pietransieri (Roccaraso); Un'operazione di Terrorismo [The Limmari-Pietransieri (Roccaraso) Massacre: an Act of Terrorism]*. Roccaraso: Comune di Roccaraso.

Perry, Marvin, Matthew Berg, and James Krukones, editors. 2010. *Sources of European History: Since 1900*. Boston: Wadsworth Cengage.

Prekatsounakis, Yannis. 2017. *The Battle For Heraklion. Crete 1941: The Campaign Revealed Through Allied and Axis Accounts*. Solihull: Helion.

Pross, Christian. 1998. *Paying for the Past: The Struggle Over Reparation for Surviving Victims of the Nazi Terror*. Baltimore: John Hopkins University Press.

Ruvigny, Marquis of (Massue, Melville Henry). 1914. *The Titled Nobility of*

Bibliography

Europe: An International Peerage. London: Harrison and Sons.

Sangster, Andrew. 2015. *Field-Marshal Kesselring: Great Commander or War Criminal?* Newcastle-upon-Tyne: Cambridge Scholars.

Scherzer, Veit. 2007. *Die Ritterkreuzträger 1939–1945: Die Inhaber des Ritterkreuzes des Eisernen Kreuzes 1939 von Heer, Luftwaffe, Kriegsmarine, Waffen-SS, Volkssturm sowie mit Deutschland verbündeter Streitkräfte nach den Unterlagen des Bundesarchives [The Knight's Cross Bearers 1939–1945: The Holders of the Knight's Cross of the Iron Cross 1939 by Army, Air Force, Navy, Waffen-SS, Volkssturm and Forces Allied with Germany, According to the Documents of the Federal Archives].* Jena: Scherzers.

Schreiber, Gerhard. 1996. *Deutsche Kriegsverbrechen in Italien: Täter, Opfer, Strafverfolgung.* Munich: C.H. Beck.

Schulenburg (Tisa von der) Foundation. N.d. https://tisa-von-der-schulenburg.de/leben.php [retrieved November 27, 2021].

Seymour, Miranda. 2013. *Noble Endeavours: The Life of Two Countries, England and Germany, in Many Stories.* London: Simon & Schuster.

_____. 2014. "A Rather Racy Nun." http://www.mirandaseymour.com/index2.php?e=24&w=weblog [retrieved April 8, 2022].

Shirer, William L. 1960. *The Rise and Fall of the Third Reich: A History of Nazi Germany.* New York: Simon & Schuster.

Short, Neil. 2013. *Kill Hitler: Operation Valkyrie, 1944.* Oxford: Osprey.

SIB (Special Investigation Branch) — see National Archives, London.

Singapore Free Press and Mercantile Advertiser. 1930a. "Last days at German GHQ: Ex-Kaiser's Indecision." December 3, [18].

_____. 1930b. "Pre-war Germany and England: The Kaiser Intervenes; Glimpses into Letters and Documents." May 23, [8].

_____ 1939. "German Countess Stopped At Croydon." June 16, [12].

Snyder, Louis L. 1991. *Hitler's German Enemies: Portraits of Heroes who Fought the Nazis.* London: Robert Hale.

Stacklberg, Roderick. 2007. *The Routledge Companion to Nazi Germany.* New York: Routledge.

Steinau-Steinrück, Robert von. 2020. "Memoire of Fritz-Dietlof von der Schulenburg."

Student, Kurt see Götzel, Hermann.

Taylor King, Matthew. 2019. "The Forgotten Hero of Two World Wars." *Wall Street Journal.* November 28. https://www.wsj.com/articles/the-forgotten-hero-of-two-world-wars-11574967153 [retrieved April 13, 2022].

Teichler, Hans Joachim. 1991. *Internationale Sportpolitik im Dritten Reich [International Sports Policy in the Third Reich].* Schorndorf: Hofmann.

Timpe, Julia. 2017. *Nazi-Organized Recreation and Entertainment in the Third Reich.* London: Palgrave MacMillan.

Trebbow Tea House Memorial. August 10, 2020. [http://teehaus-trebbow.de/geschichte/erinnerung-an-fritz-dietlof-von-der-schulenburg.html [retrieved April 16, 2022].

Wilhelmsmeyer, Helmut. 1995. *Der Krieg in Italien, 1943–1945 [The War in Italy, 1943–1945].* Graz and Stuttgart: Stocker.

Index

All Quiet on the Western Front see
  Remarque, Erich Maria
Anglo-German relations 13–14, 20–21,
  23–25, 62–65; *see also* Germany since
  1945
aristocracy *see* German aristocracy

Berlin 27, 34, 51, 53; decadent society 29,
  127–128; Plötzensee prison 114, 120

Crete *see* Second World War military
  campaigns

DNVP (German National People's Party)
  see Germany: political parties
Dorsten *see* Ruhr
DRL (German Reich Association for
  Physical Exercise) *see* Germany:
  sports
Durham, England 49, 72, 129–131, 135–137

Eastern front *see* Second World War
  military campaigns

Fallschirmjäger *see* Germany: parachute
  units; Second World War military
  campaigns

German aristocracy 12–13, 27–28, 143;
  aspirations after First World War
  12–14, 142–144; naming customs 19–20,
  55; responses to Hitler and Nazism
  12–16, 109, 142–145; values and self-
  understanding 55–56, 109, 139, 145
German foreign relations *see* Anglo-
  German relations; German-Soviet
  relations
German philosophical traditions 16–17,
  19, 83, 108, 118–119, 145
German Resistance 75–76, 84, 105–
  106, 109–110, 111, 119; aristocratic

involvement 109, 144; communist
  Resistance 115, 119; Roman Catholic
  Resistance 133–134; *see also* July plot
German-Soviet relations 57–59, 62–70,
  115
Germany: civil service 21, 31–33, 45, 108;
  military's relations with Nazism 32–33,
  46, 139–140; parachute units 76–78;
  political parties 29–31, 33, 36–39, 43;
  sport and Third Reich 39–41, 48–49, 52,
  73–74; *see also* Germany since 1945
Germany since 1945 121; Anglo-German
  reconciliation 146–150; democracy
  153–154; memorials and remembrance
  153–155; reparations and restitution
  10–11, 150–152

Hitler, Adolf 10–11, 52, 54, 139–140;
  attitude to aristocracy 74, 107–108, 143,
  145; and divisions in Nazi party 43–46,
  140; rise of 30–33, 36–37; strategic
  decisions 82, 98–99; *see also* German-
  Soviet relations; July plot; National
  Socialism; Second World War military
  campaigns
Holland *see* Second World War military
  campaigns

July plot 105–114; backgrounds of the
  plotters 107–110; and communism 115;
  consequences of 114–115, 121; desired
  outcomes 114–115, 118–120; motivations
  116–117, 118–120

Kaiser Wilhelm II 24, 27, 34
King George I *see* Anglo-German
  relations
KPD (Communist Party) *see* Germany:
  political parties
KVP (Conservative People's Party) *see*
  Germany: political parties

Index

Limmari massacre *see* War crimes investigations

Matera massacre *see* war crimes investigations

Molotov-Ribbentrop pact *see* German-Soviet relations

National Socialism 10, 13, 140; and aristocracy 42, 74–75; development and factions 10, 30, 32, 42–46; Nazi party 30–31, 33, 42–44, 74; Night of the Long Knives 36, 46–47; popularity post–1933 50–51, 52–53; Reichstag fire and consequences 37–39; *see also* Germany: military's relations with Nazism; Germany: political parties

Nazi party *see* National Socialism

Nazi-Soviet pact *see* German-Soviet relations

Netherlands *see* Second World War military campaigns

nobility *see* German aristocracy

NSDAP *see* National Socialism; Germany: political parties

NSRL (National-Socialist Reich Association for Physical Exercise) *see* Germany: sport and Third Reich

Olympics *see* Germany: sport and Third Reich

Operation Valkyrie *see* July plot

Potsdam 24, 45, 54, 75, 85

Recklinghausen *see* Ruhr

Remarque, Erich Maria 9–10, 12, 16–17, 29, 138

reparations *see* Germany since 1945

Ruhr 11, 31, 132–135

Russian front *see* Second World War military campaigns

SA (Sturmabteilung) 33–34, 36–37, 40–41, 140; *see also* National Socialism: development and factions; National Socialism: Night of the Long Knives

Schulenburg, Adolf-Heinrich Graf von der 23, 29, 33, 72–73, 126

Schulenburg, Elisabeth Gräfin von der 15, 47–48, 54, 70–72, 173–177; childhood and student years 15, 23, 27–29, 126–127; in exile 48, 49–50, 129–131; opposition to Nazism 34, 86–87, 110, 127–129; and Roman Catholic Church 11–12, 27, 133–135; Second World War and after 120, 121, 124; 131–132, 135–137

Schulenburg, Freda Gräfin von der 22–24, 26–29, 52, 54, 73

Schulenburg, Friedrich Graf von der 21–29, 51–52, 128, 138–139, 159–162; death and funerals 53, 54–55; political activity 34–35; in the SS 48, 53

Schulenburg, Friedrich-Werner Graf von der 55–57, 162–165; arrival in Moscow 57–59; helping Jews and other actions 60–62; and Resistance 110–111, 114; working for peace 62–68, 69–70; *see also* German Resistance; German-Soviet relations; July plot

Schulenburg, Fritz-Dietlof Graf von der 23, 25, 170–173; career 31–32, 48, 51, 72; family 44, 141–142; military service 75–76; Nazi membership 42–45, 71–72, 108, 117–118, 140–141; and Resistance 71, 83–86, 106–114, 124–125; views 115–116, 117–121, 140–141; *see also* July plot

Schulenburg, Johann-Albrecht Graf von der 22, 26, 33, 45, 125–126

Schulenburg, Melusine (Princess) 13–14, 20–21

Schulenburg, Tisa *see* Schulenburg, Elisabeth Gräfin von der

Schulenburg, Wilhelm Graf von der 24–25, 34, 49–50, 128, 129

Schulenburg, Wolf-Werner Graf von der 22–23, 26, 28, 29–31, 33, 166–170; at the NSRL 40–41, 48–49, 73–74; Second World War 76, 78–83, 88–104, 122–125; *see also* Germany: sport and Third Reich; Second World War military campaigns; war crimes investigations

Schulenburg family life 12–17, 126–127, 141–142; children's upbringing and education 23, 24; family tree (chart) 157; and First World War 24–28; genealogy 13–14, 19–22; internal relationships 16, 47, 49–50, 71–73; political disagreements 15, 41–42, 47–48, 71–73, 138–139, 144; Tressow Castle 20, 34, 54, 126, 132

Schutzstaffel *see* SS

SDP (Social Democratic Party) *see* Germany: political parties

Soviet-German pact *see* German-Soviet relations

188

Index

sport *see* Germany: sport and Third Reich
SS (Schutzstaffel) 33–34, 36, 40–41, 46, 82, 109
Stauffenberg, Claus von 76, 82, 86–87, 106, 109–114, 118–119; *see also* German Resistance; July plot
Sturmabteilung *see* SA

USSR-German pact *see* German-Soviet relations

Valkyrie *see* July plot

war crimes investigations 93–94, 97–98; Limmari massacre 98–101; Matera massacre 91–98
Weizäcker, Richard von 75, 85, 107, 110, 127, 138, 153
World War II military campaigns 76, 78; Crete 78–82; Italy 90–104; Netherlands 78; Normandy 122–125; Russia 68–70, 83, 85, 88–89; *see also* war crimes investigations

www.ingramcontent.com/pod-product-compliance
Ingram Content Group UK Ltd.
Pitfield, Milton Keynes, MK11 3LW, UK
UKHW042012140426